Focus on Reading

Focus on Reading

Esther Geva and Gloria Ramírez

OXFORD
UNIVERSITY PRESS

OXFORD
UNIVERSITY PRESS

ACKNOWLEDGMENTS

*The authors and publisher are grateful to those who have given permission to reproduce the following extracts and adaptations of copyright
material:* p.7 Figure from *Psychological Assessment of Culturally and Linguistically Diverse Children* by Esther Geva and Judith Wiener
(Authors) Copyright 2014. Reproduced with the permission of Springer Publishing Company, LLC. ISBN: 978-0-8261-2348-0.
p.10 Extract from "The Ice Returns... the Hunt Begins", http://www.athropolis.com/arctic-facts/fact-sealhunt-inuit.htm, accessed
March 2015. p.20 Extract from "The Middle East Today", update to *Pathways: Civilizations Through Time* by Michael Cranny, Pearson
Canada, 1998. Reproduced by permission of Michael Cranny. p.35 Abridged extract from "Investigating graphemes in Grade 1"
by Word Works Kingston, www.readworks.org, uploaded 17 May 2011. Reproduced by permission of Peter Bowers and Skot
Caldwell. p.81 "Reaching for the Sky: A History of Great Buildings", www.readworks.org, 2013. Reproduced by permission of
ReadWorks, Inc. p.93 Extract from "Designing for Diversity: The Role of Reading Strategies and Interactive Vocabulary in a
Digital Reading Environment for Fifth-Grade Monolingual English and Bilingual Students" by Bridget Dalton, C. Patrick Proctor,
Paola Uccelli, Elaine Mo and Catherine E. Snow, *Journal of Literacy Research*, Volume 43 (1), 2011. Reproduced by permission
of SAGE Publications Inc. pp.98–99 Extract from Manitoba Education and Training. *Grades 5 to 8 Science: A Foundation for
Implementation.* Winnipeg, MB: Manitoba Education and Training, 2000. Available online at www.edu.gov.mb.ca/k12/cur/science/
found/5to8/. Adapted by permission. All rights reserved. pp.100–101 Extract from "Enhancing Social Studies Vocabulary and
Comprehension for 7th Grade English Language Learners: Findings from Two Experimental Studies" by Sharon Vaughn, Leticia
R. Martinez, Colleen K. Reutebuch, Coleen D. Carlson, Sylvia L. Thompson and David J. Franci, *Society for Research on Educational
Effectiveness*, Volume 2 (4), 2010. Reprinted by permission of the publisher (Taylor & Francis Ltd, http://tandfonline.com). pp.106,
111 Extracts from "Connectives: Fitting Another Piece of the Vocabulary Instruction Puzzle" by Amy C. Crosson and Nonie K.
Lesaux, Volume 67 (3), 2013. Reproduced by permission of John Wiley and Sons. p.109 Extract from "Practical Guidelines for
the Education of English Language Learners: Research-Based Recommendations for Instruction and Academic Interventions",
www.centeroninstruction.org, 12 November 2007. © Center on Instruction 2007. Reproduced by permission. p.112 Adapted
extract from "Putting Two and Two Together: Middle School Students' Morphological Problem-Solving Strategies For Unknown
Words" by Mark B. Pacheco and Amanda p. Goodwin, *Journal of Adolescent & Adult Literacy*, Volume 56 (7), 2013. Reproduced
by permission of John Wiley and Sons. p.115 Extract from "Using Cognates to Scaffold Context Clue Strategies for Latino
ELs" by José A. Montelongo, Anita C. Hernández, Roberta J. Herter and Jaime Cuello, *The Reading Teacher*, Volume 64 (6), 2011.
Reproduced by permission of John Wiley and Sons. p.132 Extract from "Decision Map for the Use of AT" by Dr. Todd Cunningham,
http://learndifferent.org/. Reproduced by permission of Dr. Todd Cunningham.

Sources: p.19 Percy Jackson & the Olympians: *The Lightning Thief* by Rick Riordan (Puffin Books, 2005). p.25 Screenshot from
www.mheducation.ca/school/applets/bcscience7/bioaccumulation/index.htm.

This book is dedicated to my parents, for whom reading in multiple languages was simply a way of life; and to Benny, my lifelong partner, who is continuously expanding his L2 reading repertoire, one language at a time.

Esther Geva

To my late father, who instilled in me a curiosity for learning, exploring the unknown, and a love for reading.

Gloria Ramírez

To L2 teachers, wherever they are.

Esther Geva & Gloria Ramírez

Contents

Acknowledgments

Writing this book forced us to distill our knowledge of L2 reading to its essence. But synthesizing the implications of current L2 research for teachers is not an easy task. To achieve this we needed to be mindful of a vast body of research and consider implications of research for practice. We strived to integrate various models and approaches, and to offer a coherent, accessible, and reliable guide to L2 teachers in the trenches.

This book would not have been possible without the support of funding agencies such as the Social Sciences and Humanities Research Council of Canada (SSHRC), the Ontario government, the (late) Canadian Language and Literacy Research Network, and the University of Toronto, enabling us to carry out research on L2 reading with various collaborators and with an excellent cadre of brilliant and dedicated graduate students.

Needless to say, we did not rely only on our own research. We also relied on excellent research conducted by numerous L2 reading researchers in various countries. The list of countries is long, and the list of colleagues we wanted to cite but could not because of space constraints is even longer. Nevertheless, we thank each and every one of these (hidden) researchers for their insights.

Funding is essential for carrying out research, but it is not sufficient. One has to gain access to L2 learners in real classrooms and to their teachers. We want to thank the thousands of children and adolescents, and the hundreds of teachers who enabled our studies on L2 reading over the years. These include ESL students from all corners of the world—students in immersion programs and in bilingual programs, students whose schooling was interrupted, poor students in rural areas and privileged, mainstream and aboriginal students. We thank all these students who tried their best and demonstrated the immense diversity of L2 learning contexts. We also thank the school administrators and teachers who tolerated us. Without the research base, without the experience we gained in conducting research with different kinds of L2 learners, and without interacting with their teachers, we would not have had the insights about the development and teaching of L2 reading that we are trying to share with others in this book.

We also want to thank our respective universities—OISE/ University of Toronto and Thompson Rivers University—that provided the conditions for writing this book.

A special thank you is extended to Dr Todd Cunningham, whose deep insights about how technology can be used in the classroom continue to amaze us, and who graciously made major contributions to the section on assistive technology.

We would be remiss not to acknowledge how privileged we were to have had a fantastic, highly professional, and intelligent editorial team at OUP. Simply put, we could not have asked for a better team.

Working on a book stretches over long periods of time, with lots of ups and downs, and pressure to meet deadlines. This book would not have seen the light of day without the vision, encouragement, patience, persistence, and critical yet supportive nudging of the series editors, Patsy and Nina. You are the best!

Series Editors' Preface

The Oxford Key Concepts for the Language Classroom series is designed to provide accessible information about research on topics that are important to second language teachers. Each volume focuses on a particular area of second/foreign-language learning and teaching, covering both background research and classroom-based studies. The emphasis is on how knowing about this research can guide teachers in their instructional planning, pedagogical activities, and assessment of learners' progress.

The idea for the series was inspired by the book *How Languages are Learned*. Many colleagues have told us that they appreciate the way that book can be used either as part of a university teacher education program or in a professional development course for experienced teachers. They have commented on the value of publications that show teachers and future teachers how knowing about research on language learning and teaching can help them think about their own teaching principles and practices.

This series is oriented to the educational needs and abilities of school-aged children (5–18 years old) with distinct chapters focusing on research that is specific to primary- and secondary-level learners. The volumes are written for second language teachers, whether their students are minority-language speakers learning the majority language or students learning a foreign language in a classroom far from the communities where the language is spoken. Some of the volumes will be useful to 'mainstream' teachers who have second language learners among their students, but have limited training in second/foreign language teaching. Some of the volumes will also be primarily for teachers of English, whereas others will be of interest to teachers of other languages as well.

The series includes volumes on topics that are key for second language teachers of school-age children and each volume is written by authors whose research and teaching experience have focused on learners and teachers in this age group. While much has been written about some of these topics, most publications are either 'how to' methodology texts with no explicit link to research, or academic works that are designed for researchers and postgraduate students who require a thorough scholarly treatment of the research, rather than an overview and interpretation for classroom practice. Instructors in programs for teachers often find that the methodology texts lack the academic background appropriate for a university course and that the scholarly works are too long, too difficult, or not sufficiently classroom-oriented for the needs of teachers and future teachers. The volumes in this series are intended to bridge that gap.

The books are enriched by the inclusion of *Spotlight Studies* that represent important research and *Classroom Snapshots* that provide concrete examples of teaching/learning events in the second language classroom. In addition, through a variety of activities, readers will be able to integrate this information with their own experiences of learning and teaching.

Introduction

The aim of this book is to help current and aspiring teachers of English as a second language (EL2) become effective teachers of EL2 reading. We draw on a range of theoretical frameworks to examine the multiple dimensions of reading comprehension. We also examine classroom research in EL2 reading development and discuss how it can inform effective assessment and teaching practices with child and adolescent EL2 learners.

In today's Information Age, we are flooded with unprecedented amounts of written information, which needs to be processed quickly and effectively. A substantial number of people are reading this information in a second or foreign language. Language teachers face the challenge of helping their EL2 students develop sophisticated reading skills. It is our hope that this book will help EL2 teachers rise to this challenge.

Reading comprehension is a central skill in developing overall proficiency in a second language (L2). Once basic skills (decoding and sight word reading) are acquired, reading is the primary vehicle for learning new vocabulary and expanding knowledge across a variety of subjects (Nagy, Herman, & Anderson, 1985). Therefore, a sound EL2 program should have a solid reading instruction component that is adapted to the needs of the learner. A solid EL2 reading instruction program is grounded in empirical evidence that can help us answer questions of what, why, and how for successful teachers of EL2 in contexts where English is the dominant language of the society, as well as in those where it is a foreign language. For these reasons, we will consistently make links between research and teaching throughout the book.

In Chapter 1, we first invite you to reflect on your current beliefs about reading comprehension in both first language (L1) and L2. Then a preliminary examination of its complexity is provided, and the main factors intervening in EL2 reading comprehension are considered. The different skills required to be able to extract meaning from a passage are discussed.

Finally, we examine the challenges that different EL2 readers may experience depending on their age, the nature of their L1, their prior experience with reading in their L1 and L2, and the type of text they are reading.

In Chapter 2, theory and background research that inform effective teaching of EL2 reading are presented and discussed. Psycholinguistic, developmental, cognitive, and crosslinguistic perspectives are considered. This chapter provides the lenses through which research related to EL2 reading with young learners and adolescents will be discussed in Chapters 3 and 4. Based on the background established in Chapter 2, Chapter 3 focuses on the teaching of reading to children in preschool through Grade 6. We will present research that has investigated the teaching and learning of EL2 reading abilities in elementary grades in specific settings. Here, careful consideration will be given to the transition from 'learning to read' to 'reading to learn', which typically occurs at around Grade 4. In Chapter 4, we focus on classroom research related to teaching and learning EL2 reading for children beyond Grade 6. We examine the demands of academic texts and of teaching EL2 reading to adolescents with little or no prior reading instruction or experience in their L1. Chapter 5, the concluding chapter, provides a summary of key points addressed in detail in earlier chapters and also reinforces how research findings with younger and older learners may support different teaching practices for each age group.

Detailed summaries of seminal studies, many of them classroom-based, will appear as *Spotlight Studies* in Chapters 2, 3, and 4. In each chapter, we will provide *Classroom Snapshots* and *Activities*. *Classroom Snapshots* illustrate, in a concrete way, the different concepts as applied to the variety of learners and teaching situations we have to consider when teaching EL2 reading. The activities offer readers opportunities to gain a better understanding of issues and topics that are addressed in each corresponding chapter. Some of these activities invite you to reflect on key concepts through different tasks. Others suggest ways you can put some of the ideas and concepts into practice with your own students. Some may lead you to read more of the research literature on EL2 reading and encourage you to relate what you read to information you have acquired from other reading or from your experience as a teacher or learner. Some activities will help you deepen your understanding of hypotheses, assumptions, or research findings by doing some research of your own—with language students, with friends or family members, or perhaps through observing your own reading processes.

The Suggestions for Further Reading section on page 145 will highlight some of the many excellent sources that have been consulted in the writing of this book. The Glossary on page 153 provides definitions of terms that may either be unfamiliar to many readers or have a special meaning in the context of EL2 reading. These terms will be shown in bold the first time they appear in the text. The References section provides all the bibliographic information that will allow you to follow up on information summarized in this book. Every publication that is mentioned in the text will be included there, and we recommend that you pursue further reading of them to deepen your knowledge of EL2 reading acquisition and instruction. A guide to the phonetic symbols we use throughout the book will be provided in the Appendix on page 151. Finally, please note that we have used the terms 'learning disabilities' and 'reading disabilities' in this book. In other contexts, these may be known as 'difficulties' or 'differences'.

49 different languages in Springdale
Schools 1/19

✓ English / Spanish
   - initial ⎫
   - medial ⎬ sounds
   - final ⎭

+ freight train metaphor

1

The Multifaceted Nature of English L2 Reading Comprehension

Preview

Before we examine the multiple facets of **EL2** reading comprehension, we would like you to take a few minutes to reflect on your current beliefs about reading by completing Activity 1.1 on page 6.

What Is Reading Comprehension?

Reading comprehension is a complex and multifaceted process whose nature changes with development and experience. Whether one is reading for enjoyment, to access information, or to learn something new, the main goal of a reading task is to extract meaning from printed text. Typically, when people think of reading comprehension, they think of the **strategic knowledge** readers should use to extract meaning, for example, identifying main ideas and supporting details. In fact, reading comprehension involves the orchestration of a variety of **word-level reading skills**; **text-level reading skills**; strategic knowledge; **cognitive skills** such as memory; vocabulary knowledge; and, of course, language comprehension. All these 'bits and pieces' need to work together seamlessly in order for reading comprehension to occur. Furthermore, what we have learned from research on reading is that all these elements are important for reading comprehension in any language, whether it is one's first, second, or third language. The multiple intra-individual, developmental, family, and contextual facets of second-language (**L2**) reading comprehension are summarized in Figure 1.1 on page 7.

Activity 1.1

The following are statements that people have made about EL2 reading. Take a moment to reflect on your own views. As you read further in this book, you may want to keep these statements in mind. You will have opportunities to consider whether these statements are supported by research and whether the new knowledge that you gain helps you to confirm or revise your current beliefs. In Chapter 5, you will be asked to go through the list again.

Read each statement and check one of the columns to indicate how much you agree or disagree with it.

SA = Strongly Agree   A = Agree   D = Disagree   SD = Strongly Disagree

	SA	A	D	SD
1 Learning to read in L2 is the same as learning to read in L1.			X	
2 All L2 learners need to be taught the same set of reading skills regardless of their L1.		X		
3 Lack of language comprehension explains the difficulties that EL2 learners may have in comprehending texts.		X		
4 L2 learners have difficulties reading in the L2 because they have underdeveloped L2 language proficiency.		X		
5 To identify L2-reading-related strengths and weaknesses, it is necessary to assess skills in the L1.		X		
6 To learn to read in L2, students just need to be exposed to rich literature.			X	
7 The best strategy for figuring out word meaning is to use context clues.			X	
8 It is easier for younger children to learn to read in L2 than for adolescents.			X	
9 Learning to read and comprehend is more complex in L2 than in L1.		X		
10 Digital reading (e.g. on tablets or on the internet) poses unique reading comprehension demands for L2 readers.		X		
11 It is easier for L2 readers to understand narrative texts (stories, novels, etc.) than expository or non-fiction reading material (e.g. a passage from a social studies textbook).			X	
12 It is more beneficial for L2 learners to receive reading instruction in their L1 first.		X		
13 Cultural background and strategic knowledge are the most important factors in reading comprehension.			X	

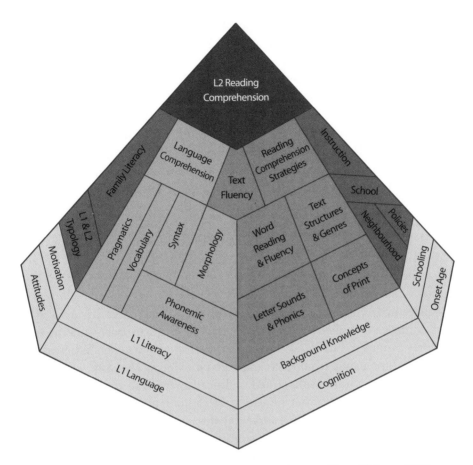

Figure 1.1 The multifaceted nature of L2 reading comprehension (Geva & Wiener, 2015)

The factors involved in reading comprehension include the reader's familiarity with the meaning of words, the role of these words in sentences, how certain words can be used to connect ideas, and how the position of words in a sentence may alter its meaning. Other essential skills include learning to match sounds to letters and how to figure out the meaning of unfamiliar words by using context or by dividing words into smaller familiar parts. Regardless of whether one reads for enjoyment or to learn something new from the text, it helps to have a good memory, familiarity with the topic, and reading comprehension strategies for working out what the text is about. Of course, to invest effort in comprehending a text, the reader needs to be interested and motivated, and receive quality teaching.

When examining L2 reading development, it is also important to consider the age at which the L2 learner is first exposed to the L2 and whether or not the learner has already developed L1 literacy skills. Think about EL2 learners who started learning to read in EL2 in the primary grades as opposed to those who were first exposed to English in secondary school. How might their learning experiences and needs differ? Now compare EL2 adolescent immigrants who have solid reading skills in their L1 with adolescent immigrants who have insufficient or no L1 reading skills. Consider, for example, the case of Mohammed, a 14-year-old Somali immigrant living in New York City. He arrived with his family over a year ago, after spending several years in a refugee camp in Africa. His L1 is Somali, but he does not know how to read or write in it. During his first year in the USA, he was placed in an ESL classroom with other students who were also recent immigrants from a variety of countries, but most of whom had gone to school in their home country. Mohammed is just learning to speak in English, and he continues to get some ESL support, but because of his age and to help him catch up quickly with his peers, he has been placed in a regular Grade 9 class.

Mohammed represents a typical case of an adolescent EL2 learner who faces numerous challenges. Not only does he need to learn how to read in a new language but he also needs to learn new concepts. Whereas his EL1 peers are using reading to expand knowledge about several topics across the curriculum, Mohammed will need to learn to read first—and as quickly as possible—so that he can start capitalizing more on reading to learn. Moreover, unlike L2 learners who already have literacy skills in their L1, Mohammed cannot count on prior literacy knowledge to accelerate the development of his L2 reading skills.

There are a number of other ways in which the contexts for teaching and learning EL2 reading can vary. For example, some EL2 readers are in bilingual schools where they receive equal amounts of instruction in L1 and EL2, whereas others are in immersion schools where they learn to read first in EL2 and receive all instruction in that language. In contrast, there are EL2 learners who receive instruction in EL2 for very limited periods of time. One such learner is Sarita, a seven-year-old student currently halfway through Grade 2. She lives in Medellín, Colombia, and since age five, she has been attending a school where she has six hours of instruction in English every week. Of this time, only a portion is dedicated to direct teaching of English reading skills. She has already learned how to read in Spanish in kindergarten and Grade 1, and now she is learning to read in English. A learner like Sarita has limited instruction in EL2 reading, which may be seen as a disadvantage. However, she has learned to read in her L1, and this may facilitate the development of her EL2 reading skills.

The story of EL2 reading development becomes even more complex when one begins to think of how characteristics of a reader's L1 may influence learning to read in EL2. Imagine that you are teaching reading to a Grade 6 class in an English-speaking country. What specific challenges might be faced by newcomers from China and from Mexico in your class? Will they be struggling with the same issues as they learn to read English? Will they be benefiting from similar aspects of their L1 reading skills? Will you need to adapt your teaching strategies to the needs of each student?

In this book, we will examine the wide range of factors that play a role in EL2 reading development. We believe that it is important to equip EL2 teachers with evidence-based strategies for teaching reading skills to school-aged EL2 learners in a manner that considers those learners' L1s and their current EL2 reading and language proficiency. The book will describe theory and research on the development of reading comprehension from a variety of perspectives, focusing on topics such as:

- instructional tools and approaches that can enhance EL2 word reading and reading comprehension
- classroom assessment methods that can inform teachers about the strengths of their EL2 students, and the weaknesses or knowledge gaps that may impede the development of EL2 reading comprehension
- instructional and remediation strategies that teachers can use in order to adapt their teaching to EL2 students' strengths and weaknesses
- strategies for adapting EL2 reading instruction for EL2 students at different grade levels
- strategies to facilitate reading of different types of text, for example, **narrative**, **expository**, and digital
- the use of digital tools to enhance EL2 reading development and support EL2 learners with learning disabilities
- methods for adapting EL2 reading instruction to the needs of adolescents with interrupted schooling or without L1 reading skills.

What Is Actually Involved in Teaching Reading Comprehension to EL2 Learners?

In this section, we examine the range of demands of teaching reading to a variety of EL2 learners. Classroom Snapshot 1.1 illustrates some of the complex factors that might influence EL2 reading comprehension with different groups of learners. It also demonstrates how teaching may be modified to support the unique needs of each learner.

Classroom Snapshot 1.1

Xu Ming lives in Xian, China, and since age five, he has been attending a school where he receives five hours of instruction in English per week. The rest of the instruction is provided in Mandarin. Xu Ming is now ten years old and is in Grade 5. Today, in his social studies class, which is taught in English, he is learning about Inuit life during the hunting season. Sitting in front of a laptop, he has been assigned to read a passage from the internet written in English, and to answer some **factual** and **inferential comprehension questions** related to it.

The Ice Returns … The Hunt Begins

October in the Arctic brings limited hours of daylight and plunging temperatures. The ice fields start to re-form quickly and as soon as they are solid enough, hunters, like the polar bears, set out after the seals. Nets are set under the ice. Experienced hunters know which locations have been best in the past, and a well-placed net may catch several seals a week. With no shortage of refrigeration, the seals can provide a supply of meat for the long winter months.

As winter sets in, the ice pack becomes too thick to be able to set seal nets, and it's much harder to find the seals' breathing holes. Hunters often have to set out on expeditions that can last over a month. Now the seals have to be stalked. To do this, Inuit hunters use a 'blind' – a screen of white cloth mounted to a slide on the ice. The rifle muzzle sticks through a hole and the hunter crawls along the ice pushing the screen ahead of him.

It is important to avoid firing before the seal can be killed in the first shot. Otherwise the wounded animal may escape through its breathing hole in the ice – not a good situation for the seal or the hunter.

('The Ice Returns … The Hunt Begins', Athropolis Productions Limited, 2005) ■

Activity 1.2

Answer the questions below to start thinking about factors that influence EL2 reading comprehension in EFL contexts.

1 What aspects of this activity may be challenging for Xu Ming?
2 What aspects of this activity might be easy for him?
3 What skills would Xu Ming need to have to be able to read words such as 'refrigeration', 'seals', 'through', 'Inuit hunters', and 'where'?
4 What skills does Xu Ming need in order to comprehend this passage?

1.   –vocab: plunging, nets, refrigeration
      –bk: w/ snow, seals, hunters
      –structure: otherwise

2.

To read and understand this passage, Xu Ming needs skills that are similar or identical to the ones required for reading in Chinese, but he also needs others that are unique to English. Each word must be read accurately and fluently so that Xu Ming's memory and cognitive resources can be allocated to making connections throughout the passage, using prior knowledge, and making inferences. To efficiently process each individual word, Xu Ming must apply a variety of strategies. He needs to know the rules that govern the correspondence between sounds and letters and apply this knowledge to accurately and fluently read regularly spelled but perhaps unfamiliar words like 'sticks' and 'thick'. He also needs to be able to read accurately and fluently highly frequent words that cannot be **decoded** letter by letter because of their irregular spelling, such as 'was', 'the', and 'through'. If Xu Ming does not know the meaning of 'daylight', he can perhaps figure it out by identifying smaller familiar units of meaning in this word: 'day' + 'light'.

Xu Ming may be overwhelmed if there are too many unfamiliar words in the text. He needs to know the meaning of at least 95 percent of the words in the text to comprehend it with ease. Having some prior knowledge of the Inuit culture and of winters in the Canadian Arctic would also facilitate understanding of this text.

Importantly, Xu Ming needs to identify what connects the different ideas and information presented in the passage. For example, he has to know that the word 'otherwise' signals how the sentence 'the wounded animal may escape through its breathing hole in the ice' is related to the previous sentence. Finally, Xu Ming needs to apply effective reading strategies, such as trying to visualize what he is reading and identifying the main idea and the supporting details, among others. If he knows about these reading strategies and uses them when reading in Chinese, he will be able to apply them to his reading in English. On the other hand, unlike EL2 readers such as Sarita, whose L1 (Spanish) shares orthographic similarities with English, Xu Ming faces the task of learning a completely new writing system.

To examine other considerations for the teaching of EL2 reading, re-read the description of Sarita presented on page 8 and then answer the questions in Activity 1.3.

Activity 1.3

1 What skills does Sarita need to become a successful reader in English?
2 Can the teacher capitalize on her already developed literacy skills in Spanish? How?
3 Considering that Sarita already knows how to read in Spanish, what aspects of learning to read in English would be easier for her and what would be more challenging?
4 What strategies would Sarita have to develop in order to be able to read words such as 'when', 'the', 'cat', 'night', 'shop', and 'caterpillar'?
5 Would Sarita need to know the meaning of these words before she learned to read them?

Some of the skills Sarita needs in order to learn to read in English are similar or identical to the ones she has already developed in the context of learning to read Spanish, but some are unique to English. For example, to be able to read in English, she must know that words can be divided into smaller parts, like **phonemes** and **syllables**. Since she can read in Spanish, she can already apply this principle when learning to read in English. Sarita also needs to know that each sound in a word has a corresponding letter or combination of letters in print. Again, as she can already read in Spanish, she can use the same principle for reading English words that have a one-to-one letter-to-sound correspondence, such as 'cat', which can be sounded out as /k/ … /æ/ … /t/. (See the Appendix for a guide to these phonetic symbols.) However, unlike in Spanish, not all English words have one-to-one letter-to-sound correspondence. This means that Sarita must also become familiar with **sight words—high-frequency words** like 'was', 'the', and 'through' that do not have a regular spelling—and memorize them as whole units. To read a word like 'shop', she needs to learn that in English, unlike in Spanish, the letters s and h together make the sound /ʃ/. To be fluent when reading longer words such as 'caterpillar', Sarita must be able to break them down into syllables and then reassemble the syllables. These basic skills would lay a firm foundation for successful reading in English.

These prerequisite skills are not, however, sufficient to successfully extract meaning from a written text. Sarita needs to gradually increase her familiarity with English vocabulary. The task of learning new vocabulary in English will be easier for Sarita if she already knows the meaning of the similar word in Spanish. Take, for example, the Spanish word 'montaña'. When Sarita reads this word in Spanish, she knows exactly what it means; she can picture a mountain in her mind because she has seen one in the city where she lives. When she encounters the English word 'mountain', the teacher can draw a

[handwritten annotation in top margin: orthographic mapping]

picture of a mountain and Sarita will immediately understand what it refers to. Furthermore, because 'montaña' and 'mountain' are **cognates**, the only remaining task for Sarita is to remember the slightly different way that this word is written in English. Sarita's teacher will be able to capitalize on a variety of vocabulary and early reading skills that Sarita has already acquired in Spanish in order to teach her to read in English. Yet she will also have to teach several new skills, such as recognizing sight words that cannot be figured out on the basis of simple decoding rules; knowing that *ña* does not exist in the spelling of English words; and identifying the pronunciation variations for the *ou* and *ai* letter combinations in different words. All these aspects related to EL2 reading instruction for young learners will be discussed in Chapter 3.

Let us now turn to the issues surrounding EL2 readers with interrupted schooling and poor L1 reading skills by revisiting the case of Mohammed.

Classroom Snapshot 1.2

Today Mohammed's class is expected to learn about bioaccumulation. After introducing the topic and defining bioaccumulation, the teacher has assigned the following task:

Remember:

- Bioaccumulation occurs when substances that are non-biodegradable become stored in organisms.
- Starting in small concentrations at the bottom of the food chain, these substances end up in large concentrations at the top of the food chain.
- If the substance is toxic, the health of animals and plants can be threatened, especially for those organisms at the top of the food chain that accumulate it in large concentrations.

Watch an online video clip on bioaccumulation. Then answer the following questions:

- What are the consequences of bioaccumulation?
- How can we help reduce bioaccumulation?
- Whose responsibility is it to reduce bioaccumulation?
- Provide other examples of bioaccumulation. ■

Activity 1.4

1 What are the reading-related skills Mohammed needs in order to understand the written instructions on the worksheet?
2 What are the main challenges Mohammed will face in completing this task?
3 How can the science teacher support Mohammed to help him complete this task successfully?

The challenges Mohammed faces in grappling with the instructions on this worksheet and in being able to complete this task are numerous. First, he needs to understand key terms such as 'bioaccumulation', 'pollution', 'biodegradable', 'non-biodegradable', 'organisms', 'substances', and 'toxic'. The knowledge gaps he has as a result of his interrupted schooling mean that his familiarity with these terms, even in his L1, will likely be very limited. Although Mohammed's science teacher is already facilitating this task for him by using visual aids such as videos, she would need to give him additional, individual support to help him understand these concepts through a variety of strategies, including using graphic organizers and reducing language barriers by lowering the level of difficulty of the text. In addition, some prerequisite concepts and terminology will have to be taught.

Mohammed might also find the task challenging if he struggles to read simple high-frequency words with ease and fluency. The video might run too quickly for him to be able to follow the spoken language, particularly if it requires him to read written captions at the same time. EL2 learners like Mohammed might also be unfamiliar with certain words that would be known by EL1 learners, like 'biology', 'waste', and 'eagle'. We elaborate more on the challenges faced by adolescents with interrupted schooling in Chapter 2 and examine effective instructional practices in Chapter 4.

As these snapshots illustrate, EL2 learners bring different types of background knowledge and experience to the task of learning to read in EL2. To teach reading skills effectively, EL2 teachers need to have a solid understanding of the various components required to successfully comprehend text, how these skills may vary depending on a reader's age or prior literacy experience in another language, on the specific demands of different reading material, and on the teaching and learning context. The aim of this book is to help EL2 teachers develop and consolidate knowledge of the skills involved in reading comprehension so that they can confidently select, modify, adapt, and create effective strategies for teaching different groups of learners.

Crosslinguistic Transfer and L2 Reading

The concept of transfer has been pivotal to education and learning in general, but it is especially ubiquitous in research on L2-related language and literacy learning. Whereas in the past much of the emphasis was on the development of spoken language, there has, in recent years, been an exponential increase in studies that examine **crosslinguistic transfer** in relation to various aspects of L2 literacy, including word reading and spelling, **fluency**, reading comprehension, and writing. The objective of this section is not to provide a reader's digest of the many studies addressing the question of transfer; rather, our intent is to provide an introduction to the issue of crosslinguistic transfer, which is discussed in Chapter 2 and illustrated with classroom research in Chapters 3 and 4.

Why is there so much interest in L1–L2 transfer? There are probably two fundamental reasons in the domain of reading development. One is the assumption that learners who have good reading skills in their L1 can be expected to transfer those skills and develop good reading skills in their L2 as well. The second is that learners should be able to utilize the resources they have crosslinguistically. So, for example, if we provide extra support in Spanish (L1) to children with a **reading disability**, we would expect that intervention also to be helpful in their English (L2) reading. When these two assumptions are not met, we look for explanations. These explanations are usually related to:

- contextual factors, such as lack of opportunity to learn
- intra-individual factors, like problems with **working memory**, lack of relevant prior knowledge, or perhaps lack of motivation
- typological differences, for example, the fact that English words are made of letters whereas Chinese uses logographs.

In Chapter 2, we discuss some of the research that reflects these basic ideas and the conditions in which they actually apply.

Inherently, L2 reading involves the interaction between two language systems: the reader's L1 and L2 (Koda & Zehler, 2007). Similarities and differences across readers' languages affect L2 reading. In some instances, the languages interfere with each other, create confusion, and mislead the reader. On the other hand, if there are similarities between the reader's first and second languages, L1 can facilitate L2 reading. A more thorough examination of crosslinguistic aspects of L2 reading development will be provided in Chapter 2, and relevant research will be presented to illustrate implications for teaching L2 reading to learners from different L1 backgrounds.

Strategies have been a central issue in research examining transfer of reading skills from L1 to L2. The transfer of higher-level reading skills, and in particular **metacognitive strategies**, has been a popular topic in the field of L2 reading comprehension. Examples of metacognitive strategies that are useful in reading include the ability to decide which strategies one should use to regulate the reading process (Schoonen, Hulstijn, & Bossers,

1998). For example, reading a text in order to find specific information involves a different strategy than reading a text for memorization of details or writing a critique. Good readers can adapt their reading strategies to their reading goals, and this adaptation reflects metacognitive skills. Depending on the context for L2 learning, metacognitive reading strategies learned in the L1 can transfer to L2 reading. In other words, the knowledge that different strategies can be used for different purposes when reading does not have to be learned separately for the L1 and L2. Obviously, one needs to possess sufficient metacognitive knowledge about reading strategies and text characteristics in the first place in order to be able to transfer this knowledge and use it in the L2 as well. In addition, the reader needs to have sufficient language and reading skills in the L1 and L2. When L1 reading and language skills are very low, drawing on L1 **higher-order reading skills** may not be feasible.

Both EL1 and EL2 students can be trained to use various metacognitive strategies such as **comprehension monitoring**. They also need to use cognitive strategies like predicting; summarizing; making inferences; re-reading; mental imagery; connecting what is read to prior knowledge; using knowledge of text structure to facilitate understanding; and using cohesion clues in the text to understand how different parts of the text are related to each other. EL1 and EL2 students who are taught how to utilize these strategies and activate them are more successful at comprehending what they read (Baker & Beall, 2009).

Accessing prior knowledge is important for reading comprehension (Afflerbach, Pearson, & Paris, 2008; Grabe, 2009). Yet having prior knowledge does not ensure comprehension (Droop & Verhoeven, 1998). Depending on prior knowledge can lead to inaccurate comprehension when readers are not attending to information in the text that contradicts their prior knowledge. L2 language proficiency may also be related to how prior knowledge is accessed. For example, less proficient learners may rely more on their prior knowledge and overlook contradictory facts in the text, whereas more proficient readers have the reading and language resources to process and comprehend the text without needing to rely on prior knowledge as a 'crutch' (see a related discussion by Goldenberg, 2008).

There is some evidence in the research to suggest that prior cultural knowledge can enhance reading comprehension (Goldenberg, Rueda, & August, 2006). However, it is important to remember that neither well-developed L2 word-level reading skills nor familiarity with the topic or cultural context will suffice alone. To comprehend text well, readers need to use both lower-level and higher-level reading skills (Stanovich, 1994).

Considering the Needs of Young and Adolescent EL2 Readers

We know from EL1 reading research that learners move through distinct stages when learning to read. During the initial stages of reading acquisition, readers learn to break the code and develop reading fluency. During this period, vocabulary, background knowledge, and comprehension strategies are important, but the focus is on mastering word-level skills. Around Grade 4, there is a gradual transition from 'learning to read' to 'reading to learn' (Chall, 1996). Once readers have reached the reading to learn stage, they are expected to read in order to acquire new knowledge, whether on paper or on digital devices. Higher-order skills—such as **academic vocabulary** and the ability to synthesize what was read, make inferences, evaluate, and draw conclusions—become more central for reading comprehension. A similar shift has been identified in EL2 reading with regard to learners who have begun their EL2 schooling in the lower grades (August & Shanahan, 2006; Geva & Farnia, 2012a). Research on issues related to EL2 reading at different points in development is discussed in Chapter 2.

A **developmental** perspective on reading suggests that the literacy 'diet' cannot and should not be identical for younger and older EL2 learners. It is important to adapt reading instruction to the developmental level of readers and to be cognizant of the fact that the foci of EL2 reading instruction in the lower and upper grades are different. Of course, it is necessary for EL2 learners to develop a range of EL2 language skills, such as vocabulary, grammar, and the ability to comprehend and communicate in the EL2, but this is not sufficient to enable them to read fluently in the EL2 and become good comprehenders. We have learned from the research that to become good comprehenders, novice EL2 learners need to develop their basic word-level reading skills, regardless of the age when they begin to learn EL2. More experienced and slightly older EL2 learners need more emphasis on higher-order thinking and problem-solving skills as they have to be able to handle the meaning of the texts they read, whether narrative or expository. Word-level **reading accuracy** and fluency will also be a challenge for EL2 learners with interrupted schooling, as well as for those who begin their exposure to the L2 orthography and language beyond primary school. Therefore, word-level reading skills need to be taught to these learners as well. As noted above, this task may be somewhat easier when the learners' L1 shares orthographic and language features with the L2, but it will be more challenging for L2 learners whose L1 does not use a similar writing system, and for L2 readers who have not had prior literacy instruction in their L1. In other words, 'one size does not fit all'.

Comprehending Narrative and Expository Texts

Narrative and expository texts differ from each other with regard to internal organizational structures and conventions of language use. Young children become familiar with the structures of narratives through exposure to stories that are either told orally or read to them. Through repeated exposure, children learn to recognize the **story grammar** of narratives—that is, they gradually come to realize that a story always has a setting, characters with traits, a theme, and the unfolding of a plot that often starts with a conflict, progresses to reach a high point of tension, and is finally resolved. A reader needs to be aware of these story elements to be able to identify them, follow them throughout the reading, generate expectations about what comes next, understand and recall the story, and express opinions about the narrative.

Comprehending Narrative Texts

Like their EL1 peers, young EL2 learners are just developing their awareness of story grammar. Exposure to storytelling in either their L1 or their L2 will contribute to the development of knowledge and understanding of story grammar. Unless they have grown up without schooling, older EL2 readers can be expected to have this knowledge. Teaching story elements is therefore particularly important in the primary grades and can be achieved through stories read aloud by the teacher, followed by discussions of story elements. For EL2 learners who have not had consistent schooling, these skills should be taught in the upper grades as well. In Chapter 3, we discuss studies that illustrate effective ways of helping young EL2 learners to develop their understanding of story grammar.

Sometimes the narration of events does not follow a chronological order. Writers often use flashbacks, narration of events from an earlier time. This storytelling technique adds complexity and may be more difficult for EL2 readers. Another characteristic of narrative texts is the use of literary devices such as similes, allegories, analogies, metaphors, hyperboles, puns, and personification. The use of such literary devices is aesthetically pleasing, but it is challenging for EL2 learners whose language skills are less developed. For these learners, the meaning of these devices is obscure and their presence can pose comprehension difficulties. Consider, for example, the reading task presented in Classroom Snapshot 1.3, which was assigned to ninth graders in a Language Arts class.

[handwritten margin note: As different cultures tell stories the same?]

Classroom Snapshot 1.3

A class of ninth graders is reading a novel. The following is a short excerpt from one of the chapters in the book.

> The bull-man wheeled toward him, pawed the ground again, and got ready to charge. I thought about how he had squeezed the life out of my mother, made her disappear in a flash of light, and rage filled me like high-octane fuel.

(Riordan, 2005, p. 55)

Imagine the difficulty an EL2 learner may have in trying to figure out what is meant by 'he had squeezed the life out of my mother, made her disappear in a flash of light'. To understand this short passage, the reader needs to go beyond literal interpretation and understand the use of metaphorical and figurative language. In Chapter 4, we will elaborate on these challenges and provide effective, research-informed ways of helping L2 readers comprehend idiomatic expressions and literary language. ▓

Comprehending Expository Texts

Expository texts, also known as non-fiction and informational texts, present some different comprehension challenges for readers. Most content-area textbooks, for example, in science or social studies, are primarily written in an expository format and the reading of such texts is inextricably tied to content-area learning goals.

The overall structure of expository texts can be classified into one of five text structure categories: descriptive, sequential, compare-and-contrast, cause-and-effect, and problem–solution. Teaching EL2 readers to be cognizant of and understand these text structures is beneficial for their reading comprehension. For example, EL2 learners can be alerted to the fact that descriptive texts usually organize paragraphs around a topic sentence, followed by sentences which expand on the central topic by providing additional details. EL2 learners can benefit from identifying linguistic devices associated with each type of text. For example, words like 'first', 'second', 'then', 'next', and 'finally' signal transition in sequential texts, such as those that outline steps of an experiment or give an account of historical events. Readers can also benefit from attending to conjunctions or connectives, such as 'but', 'by contrast', 'in comparison', 'on the other hand', 'similar to', and 'likewise'. One often finds these in compare-and-contrast text segments, where a comparison between two ideas or entities is developed, as in a comparison of vertebrates and invertebrates or of geographical regions. Students can also learn that conjunctions such as 'so', 'because', 'as a result', 'consequently', and 'this results in' provide clues for identifying cause-and-effect relationships between idea units in a given passage, for instance, a passage on global warming and pollution. Such linguistic devices provide clues that reveal how ideas in a passage are related to one another, and awareness of them facilitates comprehension. (See de Oliveira, 2007, for more on this topic.)

Additional sources of difficulty for EL2 learners include the complexity of the language structures, the information density, the presence of unfamiliar academic vocabulary, and domain-specific terminology. Social studies texts are particularly challenging to understand (Beck, McKeown, & Worthy, 1995). To appreciate the difficulty of a social studies text, consider the excerpt from a Grade 8 social studies unit presented in Classroom Snapshot 1.4.

Classroom Snapshot 1.4

The Middle East Today

You have undoubtedly heard about conflicts in the Middle East on television or in the newspaper. If you have family members living in the region, you may have heard some news first-hand.

Sometimes it is hard for people living far away from a conflict to appreciate why it started—or why it is difficult to resolve.

Conflict in the Middle East partly concerns achieving peace for two groups of people—the Israelis and the Palestinians. Both groups say they want peace, but both groups also say they have a right to occupy the same territory.

Many problems can be traced back to the time when the state of Israel was created in 1948. For over 50 years before that time, many Jews had been fleeing terrible persecution in Europe by moving to Palestine, the Jewish homeland in biblical times. They believed they were entitled to return to territory they had inherited from their ancestors. During World War II, millions of Jews were murdered by the Nazi followers of Adolf Hitler. After the war, hundreds of thousands of surviving Jews came to Palestine as refugees, hoping to create their own state. The Arab majority, who had lived there for generations, did not welcome their arrival, and warfare erupted. Hundreds of thousands of Palestinian Arabs were displaced from their homes and became refugees. As a result, there has been conflict between the two groups ever since. Despite many attempts to reach a lasting peace agreement, tensions in the area remain high.

(Cranny, 2012, p. 110)

Consider the complex language used in this excerpt:

- passive voice: 'millions of Jews *were murdered by* the Nazi followers of Adolf Hitler'
- sentences introduced by a conditional clause: '*If you have family members living in the region*, you may have heard some news first-hand.'
- sentences introduced with an adverbial phrase: '*During World War II*, millions of Jews ...'
- compound tenses such as the present perfect: 'You *have* undoubtedly *heard* about conflicts in the Middle East'
- sentences with relative clauses: 'The Arab majority, *who had lived there for generations*, did not welcome their arrival'
- relative pronouns like 'that', 'which', and 'who', which signal further information: 'The Arab majority, *who* had lived there for generations ...'
- academic vocabulary: 'conflict', 'refugees', 'territory', 'surviving', 'undoubtedly', and 'displaced'. ■

Such language structures and academic vocabulary are typical of expository texts. Not only do L2 readers need to become familiar with these devices and understand the ways in which they convey meaning but they also need to increase their command of academic vocabulary and of strategies for inferring the meaning of unfamiliar terms. Even readers with good EL2 oral language proficiency will find this passage difficult because the **syntax** is often more complex, the information density is higher in expository texts than in narrative texts (Geva, 2007), and the text also assumes relevant background knowledge. In Chapter 4, we will discuss ways to facilitate comprehension of expository passages for EL2 readers.

[handwritten margin note: An assumption we make]

EL2 Reading in a Digital Age

With the advent of the internet, an increasing amount of reading is done online. Twenty-first-century learners have grown up as 'digital natives' (Prensky, 2001), that is, they interact frequently and naturally with a wide range of digital technologies, such as electronic tablets, computers, cell phones, and MP3 players. They are active participants on social network sites such as Facebook and Twitter, on blogs, and on video-sharing websites like YouTube. This use of new modalities of written material raises several questions. Do learners navigate digital texts in the same way that they navigate printed text? Does digital reading require unique strategies and skills? Does digital reading decrease or increase the reading demands for

EL2 learners? Do children from different cultural and economic groups have similar access to these technologies?

The prevalence of digital technologies in the lives of our students means that EL2 learners enter our classrooms with new experiences, needs, and learning demands. Teaching EL2 reading has to reflect the unique nature of digital reading and use technology strategically to enhance reading comprehension.

Activity 1.5

To start thinking about characteristics of digital and non-digital reading, go to the internet and read any passage that contains hyperlinks, audio, and video.

As you read the digital material, think of the skills you are using as a reader, the devices the online platform provides, and what is different from and similar to reading the same material on paper. What demands are unique to the digital format of this reading task? What makes it more challenging than reading a passage printed on paper? What makes it easier?

You may want to use a diagram like to one below to record your thoughts and identify unique and shared features between reading on paper and online.

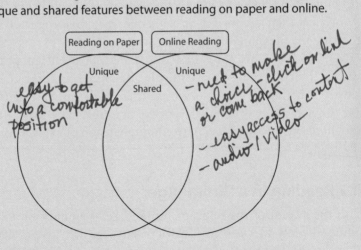

Figure 1.2 Venn diagram

Digital texts can present particular challenges for EL2 learners in several ways. For example, online materials with many hyperlinks can pose difficulties for learners with limited EL2 reading proficiency because, rather than presenting information or explanations directly in the passage at hand, they redirect readers to other passages. Inexperienced or ineffective digital readers can get sidetracked and lost in a maze of hyperlinks, which can greatly increase the amount of information to be read. This can easily overwhelm an EL2 reader whose cognitive resources and language skills are already being overtaxed as they simultaneously try to access the meaning of unfamiliar words and navigate complex, and in many instances unfamiliar, **syntactic structures** and content.

The internet is a gigantic sea of information; a search for a topic can yield thousands, if not millions, of options. To effectively navigate this sea of information, readers need a high level of what the International Society for Technology in Education (2007) calls 'research and information fluency'. Efficient internet reading requires knowing how to:

- use search terms strategically to gather optimal content and minimize the retrieval of irrelevant and unreliable information
- quickly scan results
- identify the most relevant search results for thorough reading
- synthesize information to solve problems
- store and retrieve selected sources.

Non-linear hypertext, inclusion of multiple media, and interactive design are unique characteristics of digital text and demand different types of reading and comprehension strategies (Coiro & Dobler, 2007). Lack of linearity in the information presented in many digital texts, for example, websites, can make it harder for the EL2 learner to prioritize sections to read and identify the big ideas and the supporting details. It may also require more flexibility to move from one text structure to another, as multiple pieces of information are presented in different ways on the same digital page or on different pages relating to the same topic. Finally, digital reading, particularly of material found on the internet by the readers themselves, may require higher levels of critical thinking, as what is valuable and trustworthy needs to be differentiated from what is questionable.

Digital reading presents additional challenges for readers, but it also offers unique tools that can facilitate comprehension. As you probably experienced in Activity 1.5, hyperlinks embedded in the text both allow and require you to move quickly from one part of the text to another to review previously read content, preview forthcoming content, and expand on content while reading. Moreover, the supplementary information offered by audio files and videos often aids understanding, although it also contributes to the complexity of the reading experience.

Multimedia components involving audio and video can help EL2 readers understand key concepts involving a new or challenging topic. Consider the case of Mohammed, the EL2 child depicted earlier in this chapter. In his science unit, he was learning about bioaccumulation, a topic difficult for any child but particularly so for Mohammed, who lacked academic background knowledge about it due to his history of interrupted schooling. His teacher found a YouTube video to help him understand the concept of bioaccumulation.

For an EL2 student like Mohammed, who has limited English proficiency and who also lacks academic background knowledge on this topic, a video would help but may not be sufficient. In addition to a video, interactive digital resources like the one illustrated in Figure 1.3 on page 25 may be necessary. Interactive digital material presents information in small chunks, provides visuals with animation to illustrate key points, and offers activities to monitor learning and understanding. Readers receive immediate feedback after the completion of each activity. Unlike in a video, the pace at which information is presented in interactive digital material is under the readers' control, as they decide when to advance to a new screen.

Quick access to the definition of unknown words is another facilitative feature of digital reading material. For example, e-books and some digital material found online provide readers with hyperlinks to the definitions of key and unfamiliar vocabulary. Even when the passage itself is not equipped with these hyperlinks, online readers can quickly check the meaning of unknown terminology by consulting an online dictionary, and sometimes access the meaning in their L1. An additional advantage of digital material is that it can be more current and constantly updated. Importantly, digital reading can increase reading motivation among reluctant readers. In Chapter 3, we will discuss classroom research on the use of technology to enrich and support EL2 reading, and in Chapter 4, we focus on the use of technology to assist EL2 learners experiencing reading difficulties.

Choosing the L1 or the L2 for Initial Reading Instruction

Much discussion and debate revolves around whether L2 learners benefit more from learning to read first in their L1 or in their L2. This is perhaps the issue of greatest controversy among policy makers, educators, and researchers. Part of the reason this is such a contended issue is that the arguments supporting one position or the other have traditionally been rooted more in ideology than in research evidence. Policy makers generally take a pragmatic approach, as the decision has budgetary implications; bilingual educators generally advocate for instruction in learners' L1 first,

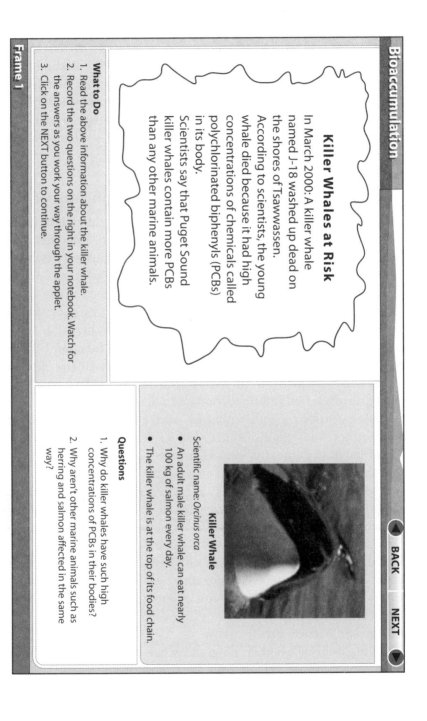

Bioaccumulation ▲ BACK NEXT ▼

Killer Whales at Risk

In March 2000: A killer whale named J-18 washed up dead on the shores of Tsawwassen. According to scientists, the young whale died because it had high concentrations of chemicals called polychlorinated biphenyls (PCBs) in its body. Scientists say that Puget Sound killer whales contain more PCBs than any other marine animals.

Killer Whale

Scientific name: *Orcinus orca*

- An adult male killer whale can eat nearly 100 kg of salmon every day.
- The killer whale is at the top of its food chain.

Questions

1. Why do killer whales have such high concentrations of PCBs in their bodies?
2. Why aren't other marine animals such as herring and salmon affected in the same way?

What to Do

1. Read the above information about the killer whale.
2. Record the two questions on the right in your notebook. Watch for the answers as you work your way through the applet.
3. Click on the NEXT button to continue.

Frame 1

Figure 1.3. Screen shot of interactive digital text on bioaccumulation (from http://www.mheducation.ca/school/applets/bcscience7/bioaccumulation/index.htm)

rooting their arguments in the importance of supporting the linguistic and cultural identity of EL2 learners; and researchers are still seeking a clear answer. A body of research supports teaching reading in L1 first (for Spanish-speaking EL2 learners, see August & Shanahan, 2006; Dixon et al., 2012), but in other contexts there is support for teaching L2 first (for English-speaking students learning L2 French, see Turnbull, Hart, & Lapkin, 2003). Although there is not a definitive answer to date, the available body of research that will be reviewed in Chapter 3 provides valuable insights that can inform your decision on this issue.

A Learning Disability or Lack of EL2 Proficiency?

One of the main challenges EL2 teachers face is differentiating between learners who are struggling with reading because of underdeveloped **EL2 proficiency** and those whose struggle is due to a **learning disability (LD)**. To be diagnosed with an LD in reading, writing, or math, one's current academic skills must be well below the average range of scores on culturally and linguistically appropriate tests of reading, writing, or mathematics. Persistent difficulties in reading, writing and mathematics can have a negative long-term impact on a person's ability to function because many daily living activities require a mastery of reading, written expression, and number facts (American Psychiatric Association, 2013). A psychologist must gather relevant information that can demonstrate that the individual's difficulties interfere significantly with academic achievement, occupational performance, and activities of daily living, and that these difficulties cannot be attributed to contextual factors such as L2 language proficiency, age of arrival, or opportunities to learn.

Of relevance to this book's focus on EL2 learners is the fact that low academic achievement may be due to 'psychosocial adversity, lack of proficiency in the language of academic instruction, or inadequate educational instruction' (American Psychiatric Association, 2013, p. 67). These are especially important considerations for EL2 children and adolescents who need to adjust to living in a new country, and who may have had inadequate or interrupted schooling, exposure to a different curriculum, or who may have suffered from trauma in the immigration process. (For further discussion, see Geva & Wiener, 2015.)

The question of whether, how, and when to identify EL2 children and adolescents with an LD has been controversial and challenging due to a number of factors. These factors are related to a history of **over-identification** of EL2 learners as having an LD (Cummins, 1984), **under-identification** of EL2 learners who actually have an LD (Limbos & Geva, 2001), and lack of clear legislation regarding the educational rights of EL2 learners who may have an LD (Geva & Wiener, 2015). Over-identification has been attributed to biased assessment assumptions and processes (Cummins, 1984), whereas under-identification has been related to injudicious attribution of EL2 children's learning difficulties to lack of EL2 proficiency or to cultural differences (Limbos & Geva, 2001). Clearly, one would want to avoid both types of errors. The challenge is how to determine whether academic learning difficulties observed in EL2 learners reflect inadequate proficiency in the societal language or whether they also reflect an LD.

[handwritten margin note: are we being the same thing in native language?]

In the past, it was believed that this kind of differentiation could not be carried out reliably and without bias until the EL2 learner had developed acceptable levels of EL2 proficiency (Cummins, 1984). This precaution has meant that some EL2 children and adolescents who actually have an LD have not received assessment, identification, and proper intervention in a timely fashion. This is a complex and sensitive problem, but in recent years, thanks to much attention from developmental research (to be discussed in Chapter 2), we understand better what aspects of literacy, language, and cognitive development are reliable markers of LDs in individuals who are also EL2 learners. We know what aspects are highly related to EL2 language proficiency, for instance, EL2 reading comprehension, text reading fluency, and writing. We also understand what components of reading are not as closely correlated with EL2 proficiency because they involve basic, lower-level cognitive processes that can be carried out by EL2 learners even when their EL2 proficiency is low, like **phonological memory**, **processing speed**, **phonological awareness**, and word decoding. There is much more awareness of how to use alternative assessment methods to overcome the challenges of inadequate tests. We also know a lot more now about crosslinguistic relationships. For example, we know that when EL2 learners have **persistent difficulties** with word decoding and phonological awareness in their L1, they are likely to experience similar difficulties in the L2 as well. Sound approaches for assessment and ongoing monitoring of EL2 reading development in young learners and adolescents will be examined in Chapters 3 and 4 respectively. (For further discussion, see Geva & Wiener, 2015.)

Summary

In this chapter, we have provided an overview of the complex set of skills that contribute to EL2 reading comprehension, while also highlighting the importance of considering the needs of diverse EL2 learners. This diversity may reflect a variety of factors, including prior reading instruction in the L1; the varying intensity of English instruction across school contexts, for example, **bilingual education, immersion,** or **foreign language** classes; features of the L1; the learners' age; everyday and academic aspects of EL2 proficiency; and individual differences in cognitive skills. We have asked you to consider component skills at the word level and at the text level, and to take into account the characteristics of the text itself: narrative, expository, and digital. Finally, we have brought to your attention the importance of assessment to provide optimal support for normally developing EL2 learners as well as for those with an LD. In Chapter 2, we will elaborate further on key considerations pertaining to word-level reading skills, reading fluency, and reading comprehension. We will also provide an overview of relevant linguistic, **psycholinguistic, cognitive,** and **developmental** theories, and research evidence pertaining to EL2 reading development.

2

Theoretical Perspectives and Research on English L2 Reading

Preview

In this chapter, we describe key theoretical frameworks that drive the research on reading development. Awareness of the key features of these frameworks should help EL2 teachers appreciate this complexity and guide them in choosing teaching strategies and adapting instruction to the strengths and weaknesses of EL2 learners. The theoretical frameworks we discuss include Jeanne Chall's reading stages, the orthographic depth hypothesis, the Simple View of Reading, the role of EL2 proficiency in reading, word and text reading fluency, and crosslinguistic transfer.

Learning to Read in EL2

Let us begin this journey by thinking of two hypothetical students: Salim, who arrived at the end of Grade 5 from Syria, and Biljana, who arrived at the end of Grade 3 from Serbia. These 13-year-old EL2 students have had very different educational experiences and different degrees of preparation for learning from text in either their L1 or their L2. Well-intentioned teachers may often have a favorite explanation of why Salim and Biljana are having difficulty in comprehending what they are reading in their Grade 7 science class. Examples of such beliefs may include:

- The parents do not speak English at home.
- Both Salim and Biljana need more time to learn the school language, the L2, so it is best to wait and see what happens.
- Both Salim and Biljana should be taught first in their L1—this will alleviate the problems.
- Salim is confused because in Arabic you read from right to left and because he cannot use cognates.
- Biljana has not been given opportunities to transfer her prior knowledge from Serbian to English.

The challenge is to adapt instruction to meet the needs of both Salim and Biljana, and to avoid a one-size-fits-all approach. It is useful to think of a range of relevant factors at both the contextual and the intra-individual levels that can guide teaching adaptations for Salim and Biljana. For example, are the parents literate? Given the political conflicts in their countries of origin, have they attended school regularly? Can Salim read well in Arabic? Does Salim show better listening than reading comprehension? How does Salim's sister do in her Grade 6 class? Has she learned to speak and read English faster than Salim or does she also have difficulty? Does Biljana read in Serbian? Is Biljana's reading comprehension better in Serbian than in English? Is her English improving? In addition to being an EL2 learner, Salim may have a **language impairment** or a reading disability, which is likely to be evident in his L1 as well. Meanwhile, there is evidence that Biljana did well at school in Serbia before the family immigrated, though she may be depressed and dealing with pressures related to **acculturation** (Geva & Wiener, 2015). These kinds of questions may lead to better informed formulations of the source of difficulties experienced by these two adolescents and point to **teaching adaptations** that address their learning needs.

Reading Development Benchmarks: Chall's Developmental Reading Stages

From a developmental perspective, it is understood that higher-level aspects of reading comprehension and language skills—such as activating relevant prior knowledge, monitoring comprehension, and drawing inferences from the text about new word meanings (Oakhill & Cain, 2012)—can take place when lower-level word reading skills have become automatized, or fluent, so that they do not require much attention and effort. In EL1 children or EL2 learners who begin to learn to read in the primary grades, reference is often made to a gradual shift in focus from 'learning to read', that typically happens in lower grades, towards 'reading to learn', that takes over in the middle elementary grades (Chall, 1996). It would be difficult to become a fluent and critical reader without being able to read words accurately and effortlessly, but it would also be difficult to extract meaning from written material without strong language skills such as knowledge of vocabulary and grammar and the ability to draw on relevant prior knowledge. To appreciate key components that develop over time, we describe Chall's developmental reading stages, discuss relevant research that illustrates what happens in each stage, and explore the implications of this broad framework for EL2 reading development.

What Happens Before Grade 1?

A lot! For one, children learn about story grammar during this period. This experience comes from being read to, and from dialogic reading activities such as listening to stories and engaging in communication about stories, either in the L1 (Snow & Dickinson, 1990; Nelson & Grundel, 1986) or in the L2 (Schwartz & Shaul, 2013). At the same time, children gradually learn to recognize the alphabet, to understand the **alphabetic principle**—that letters and letter patterns represent the sounds of spoken language—and to recognize some environmental print (Ehri, 1992). They learn to hold a pencil, handle books, recognize and write their name, follow directions and routines, and use language to communicate with others. With language development comes a gradual understanding that words can be divided into smaller parts—syllables, **onset-rimes**, and phonemes—and that by changing a phoneme, a new word can be created. They learn to pay attention to rhymes in songs and to sounds in words, a skill that prepares them to pay attention to word parts and to segment words into their smaller components. Classroom Snapshot 2.1 presents an example of an activity that can be used to raise children's awareness of **phoneme segmentation**.

Classroom Snapshot 2.1

To help children understand the phoneme segmentation concept, teachers often use the metaphor of 'stretching' words. Many preschool and kindergarten teachers use popular cheerleader chants to practice blending phonemes in a fun way.

Teacher: Give me a /p/!
Children: /p/
Teacher: Give me an /ɑ/!
Children: /ɑ/
Teacher: Give me a /t/!
Children: /t/
Teacher: What word did I say?
Children: 'Pot'!

Exposure to language contributes to an increase in **receptive** and **expressive** vocabulary (Anglin, 1993; Biemiller & Slonim, 2001), and to an emerging intuitive knowledge of the various ways that words are made and are related to meaning and grammar. For example, young EL1—and EL2—children learn very early the rules that govern inflections such as the regular past tense—'walk'/'walked'—and plurals—'dog'/'dogs'—that are systematic markers of the grammar and occur frequently in English (Berko, 1958). They combine **morphemes** to create new and sometimes non-existent **compound words**—such as 'finger-brush', offered by a child to describe a brush that cleans fingers (Clark, 1982). They are also increasingly able to give correct answers to questions like 'Does "doll" come from "dollar"?' or 'Does "run" come from "runner"?' (Derwing & Baker, 1986). This points to their emerging implicit knowledge of **derivational morphology**. Children continue to develop their knowledge of derivational morphemes over the school years (Berninger, Abbott, Nagy, & Carlisle, 2010).

These interrelated facets of language and early literacy skills that emerge before children begin formal schooling are related to reading comprehension in later years (Scarborough, 2005; Sénéchal & LeFevre, 2001). Much of the vocabulary and syntax used in the stories EL2 learners hear will already be familiar to EL1 children. For the latter, the development of foundational oral language skills precedes reading acquisition, and these skills serve as a springboard for learning to read (Chall, 1996; Nation & Snowling, 2004). EL2 learners have some catching up to do and can benefit from story-reading and exposure to narrative structures in their L1.

Whether they are EL1 or EL2 learners, children who are exposed at home to high-quality language—in their L1 or L2—benefit from parental literacy mediation activities such as discussing the pictures in a book they read, using words that relate to characters' feelings and mental states, or paying attention to words and letters in the story (Aram, Fine, & Ziv, 2013). This helps to broaden their vocabulary and enables them to comprehend and produce well-formed narratives in their L1 or L2 (Schwartz & Shaul, 2013). Children coming from backgrounds with a low **socio-economic status** (SES) typically have fewer opportunities to benefit from parental literacy mediation and to experience oral interactions like storytelling, reading street signs, or playing rhyming games that contribute to their language and story comprehension. Their language and narrative skills will need a boost once they begin to attend school (Orçan, 2013). This underscores the importance of developing and implementing school and community programs that enhance the language skills of children who, because of contextual and home factors, do not have the language and pre-literacy skills needed to become good readers in either their L1 or their L2 (Pelletier, 2011).

It is important to find out what the children can actually do in each language. When young L2 learners have very rich storytelling skills in their L1, it can be expected that they will be able to use their L1 as a resource for learning the L2 (Cummins, 2012). However, minority children who come from low-SES families often have poorly developed L1 skills in addition to a less developed command of the societal language, i.e. the L2. This makes it harder for L1-to-L2 skills transfer to occur (Shany, Geva, & Melech-Feder, 2010). This is an important issue to consider because language and literacy skills that emerge before the onset of formal schooling set the stage for later reading performance. Some children may be developing these skills in their L1 and can therefore transfer them to their L2, even when their L2 proficiency is minimal. Others, however, may not.

What Typically Happens in Grades 1 and 2?

In Grades 1 and 2, children develop **word recognition** skills by learning to decode systematically and to read sight words with accuracy and speed. They learn to associate letters and letter sequences with corresponding parts of spoken words and to quickly and accurately read high-frequency words that cannot be decoded (see Chapter 3 for examples). Most of these skills are learned through systematic instruction of letter–sound relationships and visual rehearsal of high-frequency words. They are then reinforced through extensive reading and writing. The words children learn to read— and spell—are often of high familiarity and share certain spelling patterns, forming **rhyming word families**. The stories and language they are exposed to when learning to read are usually simple in terms of vocabulary and content. Typically, the vocabulary and language structures that L1 children encounter in the texts they read are familiar to them. This is not, of course, the case for L2 learners. Despite the language proficiency disparities between L1 and L2 learners, research suggests that typically developing L2 readers who begin to learn to read in the primary grades can develop accurate and fluent word recognition skills—of both decodable and sight words—at the same rate as their L1 peers (Lesaux & Geva, 2006).

What Typically Happens in Grades 2 and 3?

In Grades 2 and 3, children gradually learn to 'unglue from print'. They begin to be more at ease with reading recreational and content-area texts. One notices an increase in their ability to read isolated words—both decodable and sight words—accurately and at a good pace, and also in their ability to read connected text with fluency, especially when the texts they read include high-frequency words and the syntax is not too complex (Nakamoto, Lindsey, & Manis, 2007). Children may stumble when decoding new and unfamiliar words, but they are able to apply their word recognition, **morphological awareness**, and syntactic skills to tackle the reading of unfamiliar words, and capitalize on learning the meaning of new words through reading. They begin to read with expression, using appropriate patterns of **stress** and **intonation**.

Classroom Snapshot 2.2

Skot is a primary school teacher who systematically integrates spelling, reading, and vocabulary instruction to help students master English writing by focusing on reading fluency and understanding. To make word study meaningful, he selects short passages from reading material he is currently using in his class. In the lesson we are depicting here, he has selected text from a story his class has been reading and has given a copy of the excerpt to each student. Skot asks his students to look for **grapheme**–phoneme correspondences and morphemes they have been studying. He has also posted these on the **Word Wall**, and draws students' attention to new vocabulary. The following transcript of part of the lesson illustrates how Skot guides his students to analyze the graphemic and morphemic structure of words.

Skot: Look carefully at the words on the page … read the text … and I want you to … try this word with me.

Student: 'Highlight'.

Skot: 'Highlight'. Good for you! Highlight letter teams (letters often seen together) that you find. And so …

Student: What does 'highlight' mean?

Skot: I'm just going to show you. These markers that you got … are called highlighters. When I use them on text, they show through. So, what letter team could I highlight in this word here [pointing to the word 'read'] … in the word 'read'? Adriana?

Student: ea

Skot: ea is a letter team. What sound is it making, Adriana?

Student: /i/

Skot: It says /i/ and so what I'm doing … [highlighting the letters ea] I'm highlighting that. I've gone over it with some color to show that I found a letter team. Can someone tell me another letter team that they spot up here?

Student: Hmm … th!

Skot: *th* … Can you tell me what the word is? Is it this one here? [pointing at the word 'the'] Is that what you were thinking?

Student: 'The'!

Skot: 'The', OK. So, yeah, you can take your highlighter [highlighting the letters *th*] and highlight it.

[…]

XX just noticed that 'highlight' is two words put together. Does anyone remember what those are called? … Right, compound words. What are the two words?

Student: 'High' and 'light'.

[…]

Skot: Yes, 'high' plus 'light'. Good for you.

(WordWorksKingston, 2011)

Note: The teacher in the video, Skot Caldwell, wishes to highlight an important change in his instructional language since the video was made. At the time, he used the phrase 'letters or letter teams' rather than the actual linguistic terms 'grapheme', 'digraph', and 'trigraph'. In contrast to his original fear that the linguistic terminology might be too advanced for Grade 1 students, he found that the specificity of the terms added clarity to their understanding. ▨

What Typically Happens in Grade 4 and Beyond?

Chall suggested that a gradual qualitative shift occurs around Grade 4 from 'learning to read' to 'reading to learn'. Beyond Grade 4, there is much more emphasis on learning new facts and understanding points of view in the texts children read. They begin to read from a variety of textbooks and reference works, newspapers, narratives, and digital texts on the internet. They encounter unfamiliar academic vocabulary, including novel academic words coming from Greek—like, 'bibliography', 'diagonal', and 'idiosyncrasy'—and from Latin—like 'benefactor', 'circular', and 'proximity'. They are also exposed to novel morphemic structures, words that have multiple meanings and different grammatical functions—such as 'cause' as a verb or noun—and more complex syntactic structures. Children are now expected to read texts in order to learn, answer questions, write, and express their opinions (Beck & McKeown, 1991).

Chall (1989) noted that whereas in the early school years many children are able to comprehend the simple texts used, children who come from low-SES backgrounds begin to struggle and fall behind in Grade 4. She attributed this 'grade four slump' to the changing demands of texts, as the vocabulary becomes more demanding and the words become longer and more complex (RAND Reading Study Group, 2002). Differences in exposure to print and the learning that is associated with it also begin to show their effect (Cunningham & Stanovich, 1991).

In earlier years, listening comprehension may be easier than reading comprehension because decoding is effortful and not fluent. Around Grade 4, however, typically developing children will do equally well when they listen to or read texts. Indeed, some may actually comprehend better when they read texts on their own than when they listen to them. Some children may be able to read single words with fluency but have difficulty with reading fluency and comprehension of the linguistically demanding texts that are common beyond Grade 4. Comprehension at this stage requires children to make logical connections between different bits of information and infer these connections when they are not explicitly made in the text. It involves an increase in the need to infer the meaning of new words and access comprehension monitoring strategies (Afflerbach et al., 2008). It also entails working through texts that are denser in terms of the information conveyed, with fewer repetitions and new ideas that are closely compacted together (Oakhill & Cain, 2012).

Activity 2.1

1   Can you read the word 'pholeme'? What kind of knowledge helped you to read it? If you think that 'pholeme' is not a word in English, is its spelling typical of some English words? On what basis can you tell that the spelling is typical?
2   Present the word 'pholeme' and the questions above to two beginner EL2 learners: one learner whose L1 uses a writing system that is different from English (Chinese, Japanese, Greek, Urdu, Arabic, etc.) and another whose L1 uses the Roman alphabet (Spanish, French, German, etc.). Note differences in their attempts to read the word and answer the questions.
3   Try the same activity with more advanced EL2 learners. Are the results different? How?

In the upper elementary years, learners will continue to encounter new root words, novel spelling patterns of words coming from Greek or Latin, and more complex syntax. The increase in demands on cognitive and linguistic resources means that EL2 learners are unable to catch up with their EL1 peers in terms of their language skills and will lag behind in reading comprehension. For example, Canadian longitudinal research following children's language and reading skills from Grade 1 to Grade 6 has shown that the gap in reading comprehension between EL1 and EL2 children does not close, even when these children have been going to school in Canada since Grade 1 (Farnia & Geva, 2013). At this stage, as we explain in Chapter 4, difficulties that are not related to decoding but to unexpected problems with reading comprehension can sometimes be noticed and identified.

In high school, students are exposed to a variety of genres. They read in order to learn content in various school subjects and under increasing time pressure. It may be assumed that adolescents do not need help with decoding. However, as we discuss in more detail below and in Chapter 4, this assumption is not justified in the case of EL2 learners who have not been exposed to EL2 reading from an early age. Inadequate reading comprehension and language skills that are not on a par with those of their EL1 peers can prevent EL2 adolescent learners from completing high school requirements and lead to higher rates of school dropout (Ornstein, 2000). Students who immigrate in adolescence experience even greater difficulties. They face the challenge of learning the school language—often their L2—while completing the demanding academic curriculum of their new country (Garnett, 2010; see also Spotlight Study 2.2).

Beyond high school, individuals read for a variety of purposes. They engage in reading to integrate their prior knowledge with that of others, to synthesize knowledge based on reading multiple sources, and to discover new knowledge. Decoding is not usually a major issue if students have had many years of education in the new country. However, decoding skills and fluent word recognition can be stumbling blocks that slow down older EL2 learners and can impede reading comprehension even for advanced students. For example, Nassaji and Geva (1999) found that English word recognition skills were positively correlated with English reading comprehension and with reading rate in a group of advanced Iranian students who passed the English proficiency exam (TOEFL) and attended graduate school in a Canadian university. In other words, having accurate and fluent word recognition skills is an aspect of reading that cannot be ignored, even when one teaches English to highly educated adults who read in EL2 mainly for academic purposes. It appears that those decoding skills learned in elementary school—coupled with morphological and syntactic skills—come in handy when unfamiliar words are encountered in print. This observation is true for EL1 readers and also relevant when EL2 adolescent or adult learners need to learn from text.

Activity 2.2

Imagine that you see the words 'univorous' and 'hypermnesia' in a text you are trying to understand.

1   Have you ever seen the words 'univorous' and 'hypermnesia' before? (Be honest—we have not seen them either.)
2   Did you first sound them out, that is, decode them? Did you notice familiar word parts, such as *hyper* or *uni*?
3   Can you figure out what each word might mean? What skills did you use to help you?
4   Did it take you a bit longer to read 'univorous' and 'hypermnesia' than it would take you to read other academic words such as 'argument' or 'trajectory'? Why do you think that is?
5   What would happen to your reading fluency and comprehension if numerous words like 'univorous' and 'hypermnesia' appeared in a text you were trying to comprehend?

Implications for Teaching

It is important to realize that Chall's stages of literacy development are not cast in stone, especially when we are concerned with learners coming from diverse linguistic and educational backgrounds, and should be considered as **developmental benchmarks**. First, just as with EL1 speakers, there are individual differences among EL2 learners. Some EL1 and EL2 students may struggle with reading comprehension because they have a language impairment and find it difficult to process and comprehend complex grammatical structures when they listen or read (Catts, Adlof, & Weismer, 2006; Geva & Massey-Garrison, 2013). Other EL1 and EL2 students may do relatively well when they listen to texts read to them but find it difficult to comprehend what they read because they struggle with word decoding (Geva & Herbert, 2012; Geva & Wiener, 2015). Some learners may not have had the opportunity to develop essential pre-literacy skills in either EL1 or EL2. This is seen, for example, in work with First Nations people in Canada and Australia (Walton & Ramírez, 2012), Roma children in Europe (Biro, Smederevac, & Tovilović, 2009; Orçan, 2013), and with children who immigrate with their families from a predominantly oral society (Shany et al., 2010). Some adolescent refugees may have missed out on school altogether. In this case, learning to read and comprehend in the EL2 is extremely difficult. They will face many language, social, acculturation, employment, and adjustment challenges, but to learn to read, they also need support with the basic skills that make word reading possible.

This range of scenarios underscores the argument that the stages described by Chall and others should not be thought of as rigid and tied to specific ages and grade levels. Rather, they should be considered as developmental benchmarks, or perhaps part of a checklist, that can guide teachers in understanding the kinds of skills that EL2 learners need to develop in order to be able to comprehend what they read, notwithstanding their age or grade level. These benchmarks draw attention to specific skills that teachers may take for granted when teaching adolescent or adult EL2 students but that should be addressed systematically when there are educational gaps. They are essential prerequisite skills that need to be established so that learning and EL2 development through reading can take place.

Another useful application of Chall's developmental benchmarks is that they help both researchers and EL2 teachers to think of two pivotal reading skills clusters that need to work in tandem:

1   skills related to word reading that typically—but do not always—develop in the early years of schooling, such as decoding unfamiliar words, reading high-frequency words with fluency, spelling, and recognizing letter sequences that are typical of English orthography
2   skills related to text processing that typically develop beyond the primary years, such as **vocabulary depth**, text reading fluency, considering text structure, accessing prior knowledge, processing **cohesion markers**, and recognizing points of view.

This more complex and nuanced approach reflects our aim to offer EL2 teachers the tools for developing a deep understanding of the multiple lower-level and higher-level skills involved in EL2 reading, and the practical instructional skills that can make the most of this understanding.

The Orthographic Depth Hypothesis

Until not too long ago, predominant theories about reading were based on reading in English. However, since the 1990s, there has been an explosion of studies that examine the relevance of various theoretical frameworks to reading processes in different languages, writing systems, and language combinations. As Katz and Frost (1992) pointed out, alphabetic writing systems differ in orthographic depth, and these reflect differences in the **phonology** and **morphology** of different languages. Katz and Frost indicate that these differences can lead to variation in how quickly words are read or how quickly lexical decisions are made—that is, the speed with which participants can decide whether stimuli such as 'bame' are real words. Readers whose L1 is an alphabetic language will respond more quickly and more accurately to whether this is a real or fake English word than EL2 learners whose L1 is Chinese. This is because the former group can more easily match the letters to the phonemes, assemble the phonemes into a word—/b/+/eɪ/+/m/—and then quickly search their memory to see if they have heard the /b/+/eɪ/+/m/ sequence in English. Chinese EL2 learners are more likely to struggle with this task because they will be using their well-rehearsed whole-word visual strategy that serves them well for automatic Chinese word reading and when they learn to recognize real words in English, but not for decoding unfamiliar letter strings (Ziegler & Goswami, 2005).

When thinking of the factors that influence reading comprehension among EL2 learners, it is important to think of differences between writing systems, or orthographies, because this influences how easy or hard it may be to develop word reading skills. Some languages can be characterized as having **transparent** or **shallow orthographies**. In such orthographies, there is consistent one-to-one correspondence between letters and phonemes. English is considered as having a **deep** or **opaque orthography** because the correspondence between letters and phonemes is far less consistent. This makes learning to read words and decode unknown words in English especially challenging (Katz & Frost, 1992; Ziegler & Goswami, 2005) and it means that teachers need to spend some time teaching and practicing the pronunciation and spelling of such confusing elements in words.

To illustrate, consider the cluster of letters *ough* that appears in English in words such as 'thought', 'though', 'through', and 'tough'. Not only is there no simple correspondence between the graphemes, or letters, in this sequence and the phonemes, or how they are pronounced, but the *ough* sequence is also pronounced differently in different words. Alternatively, consider the two related words 'heal' and 'health'. They are related in terms of meaning, and this relationship is evident from the spelling, but it is not so obvious from hearing them. The meaning connection may be obvious to proficient English speakers, but it may be elusive to EL2 learners unless it is explicitly pointed out. In the 'heal'/'health' example, what remains stable is the spelling of the root 'heal', even though this component is pronounced differently in 'health'. The various ways that the *ea* vowel sequence is pronounced in different words provides another example of the opaque relationship between letters and sounds in English. Sometimes *ea* is pronounced /i/, as in the word 'meat', but sometimes it is pronounced /ɛ/, as in 'dead'), and in the case of 'great', the *ea* is pronounced /eɪ/. The challenge for both EL1 and EL2 learners is to read both regularly and irregularly spelled words with accuracy and fluency. The additional challenge for EL2 learners is that when they apply letter–sound correspondences to words, they may not know whether their pronunciation is correct and whether it matches a real word in English. They will have had fewer opportunities than their EL1 peers to hear these irregularly spelled words, and they may not be aware that the pronunciation cannot always be figured out simply from assembling the phonemes in the word in a linear fashion as it can in shallow orthographies (Share, 2008). We return to this point in the next section in relation to the Simple View of Reading framework.

[handwritten margin note: the case for ELD]

Spotlight Study 2.1

Seymour, Aro, and Erskine (2003) investigated differences in the orthographic depth of several European writing systems and how these affected the acquisition of various components of reading skills, such as letter knowledge, reading highly familiar words, and nonword decoding in monolingual children who spoke English or one of 12 other languages. The 13 writing systems were classified according to their orthographic depth on a continuum of shallow to deep. English, French, Portuguese, Dutch, Swedish, and Danish were considered deep orthographies, whereas Finnish, Spanish, Italian, Greek, Norwegian, German, and Icelandic were considered shallow orthographies. Finnish was identified as the shallowest orthography and English as the deepest. It was observed that at least two years of systematic basic reading instruction are required to learn to read English and other deep orthographies, as opposed to one year for children learning to read in shallow orthographies. The patterns of results did not change, whether children began to learn to read systematically at age five, six, or seven. The researchers concluded that:

> fundamental linguistic differences in **syllabic complexity** and orthographic depth are responsible. Syllabic complexity selectively affects decoding, whereas orthographic depth affects both word reading and nonword reading.
>
> (Seymour et al., 2003, p. 143) ▪

Implications for Teaching

Spotlight Study 2.1 shows why it is important to pay attention to orthographic depth and how it can affect the ease of learning to decode in different languages. In regular or shallow writing systems with one-to-one correspondences between graphemes and phonemes, typically developing children can build their decoding accuracy very quickly, often in the first year of school. When children learn to decode in opaque orthographies such as English and French, development of accurate decoding skills takes longer (Geva & Siegel, 2000). Differences between languages regarding how opaque or transparent their orthographies are is a factor to consider when teaching reading skills to L1 and L2 learners alike. These differences explain why word reading skills continue to play an important role in reading comprehension in languages with opaque writing systems but become less important for reading comprehension in languages with more transparent writing systems (Florit & Cain, 2011). Furthermore, EL2 children who have learned to use their knowledge of grapheme–phoneme correspondences may spell regular words like 'dog' correctly but take longer to learn to spell words containing less consistent components, such as 'hear' and 'here'. To enable English reading fluency, teachers need to provide a variety of word reading strategies. We elaborate on these strategies in Chapter 3.

The Simple View of Reading

The Simple View of Reading (SVR) (Gough & Tunmer, 1986) is a conceptual framework that is useful for thinking about two important skill clusters for L1 and L2 text comprehension. According to the SVR, to comprehend texts well, readers need to have well-developed decoding skills and well-developed language comprehension (Hoover & Tunmer, 1993). Over the years, many studies have shown that the SVR is a useful framework that can guide instruction and assessment. The research that supports the SVR was conducted with different groups of EL1 readers, including elementary school children (Joshi & Aaron, 2000), and university students who were typical readers or who had reading difficulties (Savage & Wolforth, 2007). The relevance of the SVR is not limited to research involving English as the home language. For example, Joshi, Tao, Aaron, & Quiroz (2012) found support for the SVR with Chinese school children in China.

Support for the SVR also comes from a variety of studies of L2 learners. To illustrate, Geva and Farnia (2012a) conducted a longitudinal study that tracked EL2 children with various home language backgrounds from Grade 2 to Grade 5. They found that the SVR framework was highly useful in understanding what factors distinguish EL2 children who are good comprehenders from those who are not. More specifically, they found that word reading skills—accuracy and fluency—and language skills—like vocabulary and grammatical knowledge—played a major role in L2 reading comprehension. Verhoeven and van Leeuwe (2012) reported similar results in a study involving Dutch L2 children whose home language was Turkish or Arabic. Likewise, studies involving EL2 children whose home language was Spanish also found support for the SVR (for example, Gottardo &

Mueller, 2009; Mancilla-Martinez & Lesaux, 2010). Prior, Goldina, Shany, Geva, and Katzir (2014) found evidence for the relevance of the SVR to L2 learners in a study of high school students whose home language was Russian and whose L2 was Hebrew.

Across these different studies, a consistent finding is that aspects of word reading skills—including accurate and fluent word recognition and the ability to decode—make an important contribution to reading comprehension. Similarly, various components of language comprehension skills—including **vocabulary depth** and **breadth**, morphological knowledge, syntactic skills, listening comprehension, and syntactic knowledge—make substantial contributions to L2 reading comprehension.

Implications for Teaching

For L2 teachers, the important conclusion of the SVR is that there is ongoing development of various components of language comprehension as well as various components of word reading skills. Both skill sets are important for reading comprehension, and deficits in either may lead to reading comprehension difficulties.

With effective teaching involving abundant exposure and practice, EL2 learners should gain skills that enable them to read increasingly complex words with accuracy and fluency, as well as to decode unfamiliar words and figure out their meaning from context or through **metalinguistic strategies**. It is important to maintain a developmental outlook because, over time, one should expect to see a shift in the relative importance of decoding and language comprehension to the reading comprehension of EL2 learners. It makes sense that developing decoding skills is salient in beginning readers, but that as word reading fluency develops, reading comprehension skills become more closely related to language comprehension skills, and that difficulties in reading comprehension are more likely to be related to an increase in the language demands of academic texts in the higher grades (Storch & Whitehurst, 2002). In adolescence, the focus is typically on academic learning from texts, the development of higher-level reading comprehension strategies, and access to culturally relevant information. Yet, as illustrated in Spotlight Study 2.2, it is important to bear in mind that EL2 adolescents who have learned to read in another language may struggle not only with developing EL2 language proficiency and strategic knowledge but also with decoding and spelling skills in the EL2. Therefore, they may also need instruction on word recognition.

In addition to maintaining a developmental outlook, it is also important to maintain an individual differences outlook. As discussed in Chapter 4, some learners may struggle with reading comprehension because of other factors, such as decoding difficulties, language impairment, or memory problems. This means that not all EL2 learners have similar instructional needs and some may require special accommodation and adaptation of the EL2 reading program (Swanson et al., 2013).

Motivation and interest play a role as well. Over time, EL2 learners develop expertise in different domains, read more in their areas of interest, and, as a consequence, gain familiarity with the more specialized reading, language, and text genre conventions that characterize their favorite disciplines. However, some EL2 learners may become disenchanted with reading and avoid it at all costs because, for them, reading continues to be effortful and the language too difficult.

Spotlight Study 2.2

Pasquarella, Gottardo, and Grant (2012) compared the factors that contribute to reading comprehension in EL2 adolescents representing 17 different L1s and an age-matched sample of EL1 adolescents. The objective of the study was to understand what factors contribute to the reading comprehension of EL2 learners who begin EL2 reading instruction in adolescence and to examine the relevance of the SVR framework for this group. All students were in either Grade 9 or Grade 10 and were 15 to 16 years old when the study was conducted. On average, the EL2 students in the study had moved to Canada at age 13. The EL1 and EL2 students were enrolled in the same math, science, and social studies classes, but the EL2 adolescents had first learned to read in their respective L1s, had lived in Canada for about two years, and were in the early stages of EL2 literacy development. The participants were assessed on decoding, vocabulary, and reading comprehension in English. As may be expected, the EL2s performed below their EL1 peers on all three areas assessed. Interestingly, factors associated with reading comprehension were different in the two groups. In the case of EL1 adolescents, vocabulary was strongly associated with comprehension but decoding was not. In other words, the EL1s had mastered and automatized their decoding skills so that individual differences on this skill were minimal and did not explain variance in reading comprehension. However, a different picture emerged in the case of the EL2 learners, for whom both decoding and vocabulary were independently associated with reading comprehension. ■

[handwritten margin note: El¹ – vocab ; El2 – decoding ; vocabulary]

Pasquarella et al.'s (2012) study shows that both decoding and language proficiency are associated with reading comprehension for recent immigrant EL2 adolescents, even though in the case of their adolescent EL1 participants, only vocabulary predicted reading comprehension. It means that decoding should not be taken for granted or ignored when teaching adolescent EL2 learners, and that both skill sets need to be attended to instructionally. The Pasquarella et al. (2012) findings are also important to consider because these EL2 learners were struggling with the high school curriculum and their reading comprehension challenges put them at risk of dropping out of high school (Collier, 1987; Hoffman & Sable, 2006). Such learners need intensive instructional supports to enable them to quickly improve their reading and their language skills (August & Shanahan, 2006; Cumming & Geva, 2012). They can also benefit from policy adjustments that would allow them more time to complete their high school education (Garnett, 2010).

The Role of EL2 Proficiency in EL2 Reading

In this section, we address the extent to which EL2 proficiency matters for word-level and text-level reading. This is an important question because there is a strong belief among some EL2 educators that it is essential to develop EL2 language proficiency before reading is introduced. Some studies of young typically developing EL2 learners have examined two related issues: firstly, whether EL2 learners lag behind their typically developing EL1 peers on word reading and spelling skills, and secondly, whether various aspects of EL2 proficiency, such as vocabulary and grammatical skills, correlate with word reading and spelling. In other words, the question is whether it is essential to have well-developed EL2 proficiency in order to be able to learn to decode and spell in EL2.

A rather consistent conclusion has emerged from a systematic review of the research. It seems that when learners begin to learn to read in EL2 during the primary grades, there is not much difference between the performance of EL2s and EL1s on word reading accuracy and spelling. While there is some association between word reading and language comprehension, children can learn to decode words with accuracy, even though their EL2 oral language proficiency is significantly lower than that of their EL1 peers (see Geva, 2006). At the same time, language proficiency is strongly and consistently associated with reading comprehension (Farnia & Geva, 2013). This distinction between the minor role of L2 language proficiency in reading isolated words and decoding unfamiliar words and its substantial role in reading comprehension has important implications for the assessment of EL2 students who may have a learning disability. (See also Chapter 4.)

Implications for Teaching

The finding that EL2 students can learn to read words and decode unfamiliar words even while their English language proficiency is developing has important teaching implications. It means that it is not necessary to wait until children have well-developed oral language skills before introducing them to reading in the L2. It also means that when EL2 students continue to struggle consistently with word-level reading and spelling skills, even though their peers are making progress, various adaptive teaching strategies need to be used to provide extra practice. In addition, it is possible that some EL2 learners may have specific learning disorders, and that their difficulties cannot be attributed simply to lack of language proficiency in the L2. These EL2 students need extra help and accommodations to help them decode unfamiliar words and recognize sight words with ease. At the same time, well-developed L2 language skills, including vocabulary, grammar, morphological skills, and understanding metaphors, are crucial for text reading fluency, reading comprehension, and writing.

Word and Text Reading Fluency

Being able to read fluently is essential for reading comprehension in EL1 and EL2 alike. A fluent reader is one who can read accurately, effortlessly, and with comprehension. The research about reading fluency in EL1 and EL2 has clarified the distinction between word and text reading fluency, the cognitive and language factors that contribute to reading fluency, and instructional approaches designed to facilitate reading fluency.

Word Reading Fluency

Recent conceptualizations of reading fluency emphasize a dynamic, developmental, and componential approach to EL1 and EL2 reading fluency (for example, Kame'enui, Simmons, Good, & Harn, 2001; Geva & Farnia, 2012a). It has been suggested that in early stages of reading development, reading fluency involves a gradual development of accurate and automatic execution of various word reading component processes, including orthographic, phonological, lexical, morphological, and syntactic skills. For example, instead of matching single sounds to letters, as is the case in earlier stages of learning to read with increased word reading fluency, readers increase their ability to recognize with ease large orthographic units like *ough* and *tion*, and use effective strategies to figure out how *ea* is pronounced in 'head', 'meat', and 'break'. They also learn to read with ease high-frequency words with irregular spelling, such as 'the' and 'was' (Lovett et al., 2008).

A consideration of differences in orthographic depth among languages is relevant in the context of reading fluency. As discussed earlier in this chapter, in languages with transparent writing systems, there are few individual differences among children in word reading *accuracy*. Individual differences in word reading *fluency* distinguish good from poor readers, while accuracy in decoding takes a back seat (Seymour et al., 2003; Share, 2008). This observation has implications for the profiles of L2 learners we see across different languages. In languages with transparent orthographies, what matters most may not be word reading accuracy, which can be learned rather easily. It is more likely to be word reading fluency, which may be a stumbling block for some and a factor that distinguishes typically developing learners from those with a learning disability.

Text Reading Fluency

As discussed above, there is general agreement that while language proficiency has less impact on the fluent reading of isolated words, it is closely linked to the fluent reading of connected text (Puranik, Petscher, Al Otaiba, Catts, & Lonigan, 2008). This is because when reading words in isolation, readers cannot take advantage of context and grammar to help them read and anticipate subsequent words in the text. Typically developing readers who are fluent in the language can take advantage of their linguistic knowledge and of the context to anticipate what is coming next. Such contextual facilitation is less likely to take place when EL2 readers are not sufficiently proficient in EL2. These difficulties with text reading fluency may be observed when students are reading academically challenging texts that use less frequent vocabulary and more complex sentences. Such difficulties may not be as pronounced when learners read highly familiar narrative structures with highly familiar content.

Once readers have developed word-level reading fluency, there is a shift to more fluent and less effortful text reading as well. This can be noticed when readers begin to read at an appropriate speed, with good expression, and use the right patterns of stress and intonation. For example, instead of reading 'once ... upon ... a ... time', they will read the phrase as a coherent chunk with the anticipated expression, stress, and intonation. It is easy to imagine that a child who reads the two words 'once' and 'upon' will be able to predict what comes next in the phrase and that the processing of 'a' and 'time' will therefore be facilitated. Completing Activity 2.3 will help you understand the difference between word fluency and text fluency and the demands of each for language proficiency.

Activity 2.3

1 **Material selection:** Select a grade-appropriate paragraph. It could be either a narrative or an expository text. We suggest selecting one that is about 100 words long. This will be your intact text.

2 **Material preparation:** Type the words from the intact text in reverse order— that is, create a list in which the last word of the paragraph is the first word of the list, and so on. Ignore capital letters or punctuation. You should end up with a word list in which there is no grammatical relationship between any two adjoining words, for example, an article before a noun. If, by coincidence, there is a grammatical relationship, move one of the words elsewhere in the list.

3 **Selecting your sample and testing procedures:** Invite some students in your class to read the word list as fast as they can. Then ask them to read the intact text as fast as they can.

4 **Data collection:** Using a timer, keep track of how much time, in seconds, it takes the student to read the word list and the intact text. Hold a copy of the intact text and the word list, recording the errors the student makes and the time it takes to read each version. You may also want to jot down other observations. For example, is the student reading the intact text with intonation? Is the student self-correcting? Is the student asking for word meanings?

 5 **Analysis and interpretation:** Now that you have your data, you can start to put things together. For example, did the student make decoding errors? Did the student make more decoding errors on the word list or on the intact text? Did the student read the word list at the same rate as the intact text, or was one read faster than the other? Which one? Did the student take a very long time to read the word list and the intact text? (Hint: as their language proficiency improves, typically developing EL2 learners will read the intact text faster than the word list.)

6 **Intervention:** Have students repeat reading the same text a few times. With repeated reading, you should expect to see an improvement in sight word vocabulary and increased text reading fluency. To motivate students, you could give each student a chart that demonstrates their personal improvement rate over time on accuracy and speed.

7 **Interpretation:** What can these data tell you about the reading skills of different students in your classroom? How can this guide your instruction?

This cycle can be repeated with materials that vary in terms of the length of the paragraph, the proportion of high-frequency words, the proportion of academic and **morphologically complex words**, topic familiarity, and so on. Try it with student pairs testing each other. This can give them further insight into how important it is to see a text as a whole rather than as a series of individual words.

Reading Fluency in EL2 Learners

As discussed above, and as likely experienced when completing Activity 2.3, word-level reading fluency is less dependent on language proficiency than text-level reading fluency. That is why EL2 learners often have word reading fluency scores that are similar to those of their EL1 peers, in spite of the fact that they have a lower command of EL2 (Lesaux & Siegel, 2003). By contrast, language proficiency plays a pronounced role in text reading fluency. This has been shown in studies with EL2 adults (Nassaji & Geva, 1999) and L2 children (Crosson & Lesaux, 2010; Geva, Wade-Woolley, & Shany, 1997). Clearly, it is difficult to read text with fluency when EL2 proficiency is underdeveloped.

Poor Decoding and Reading Fluency

Until now, the discussion has focused on EL2 learners who may not read with fluency because they are learning to read in EL2. As noted above, to read texts with fluency, readers need to have good word-level reading skills and language proficiency. But some learners, whether they read in EL1 or EL2, may have a learning disability and face difficulties in developing fluent word-level reading skills regardless of their language proficiency. Evidence for this observation comes from studies of children reading in their L1, as well as from studies involving children learning to read in different L2s (Geva et al., 1997; Quiroga, Lemos-Britton, Mostafapour, Abbott, & Berninger, 2002). For example, Geva and Yaghoub-Zadeh (2006) described the cognitive and literacy profiles of three distinct subgroups noted in EL1 and EL2 primary-level students. The profiles of EL1 and EL2 children who were accurate and fluent readers were very similar to each other on reading and cognitive measures. The EL1 and EL2 subgroup of accurate but slow decoders did more poorly on cognitive and reading measures, and their profiles were also highly similar. Finally, the profiles of the EL1 and EL2 children with severe decoding problems were also very similar to each other. They had a very slow reading rate and were the lowest on cognitive measures as well. In fact, EL1 and EL2 children in this group were unable to complete the text fluency tasks because reading was extremely effortful for them.

Implications for Teaching

To help students gain reading fluency, teachers need to include important reading-related components. Clearly, extending vocabulary and oral language skills is essential. Other instructional components include helping students recognize with ease orthographic and morphological units like –*tion*, –*ful*, and *un*–, providing opportunities for recognizing sight words effortlessly, and teaching common word parts and spelling patterns (Lovett et al., 2008). Other methods for developing reading fluency involve teaching, modeling, and providing practice in the application of word recognition strategies, and selecting texts that can help to develop the use of reading strategies. Another involves using repeated reading procedures for struggling readers, and extending reading fluency through independent reading of materials that are neither too easy nor too difficult. More teaching strategies for fluency development are presented in Chapter 3. It is also useful to monitor reading fluency development through appropriate and motivating assessment procedures (Pikulski & Chard, 2005).

Crosslinguistic Transfer and EL2 Reading

The topic of transfer is ubiquitous in the area of L2 reading. Definitions of L1–L2 transfer vary in the extent to which they emphasize cognitive, developmental, typological/contrastive, and contextual factors, and the conditions that enable learning (**positive transfer**) or hamper learning (**negative transfer**). Two crosslinguistic transfer frameworks dominate the field: the typological/contrastive framework (Lado, 1957) and the Linguistic Interdependence framework (Cummins, 1981). It is important to appreciate that each has implications for L2 reading and that the two are complementary. In this section, we discuss the main features of each of these frameworks and provide some typical examples.

A Typological/Contrastive Perspective on L2 Reading Development

According to the original typological/contrastive perspective (Lado, 1957), learners rely heavily on their L1 when learning an L2. The argument is that through careful comparison of features crosslinguistically, it should be possible to anticipate which elements of a given L2 would be challenging to L2 learners on the basis of features of their L1—that is, give rise to negative transfer—and which would be facilitated—that is, enable positive transfer (König & Gast, 2008). In general, research conducted within the original contrastive framework did not support specific a priori predictions of the type of errors that L2 learners were expected to make due to negative transfer from the L1 to the L2 (Corder, 1967).

As researchers gave up on the idea of predicting difficulties on the basis of comparisons between languages, they shifted to explanations of specific features observed in L2 learners. One area where researchers and educators look for positive transfer concerns cognates. A number of studies have explored the ability of children whose L1 is Spanish to utilize cognates common to English and Spanish when they learn English (García & Nagy, 1993). Some recent studies examine both positive and negative transfer. For example, Ramírez, Chen, Geva, and Luo (2011) found that Spanish-L1 fourth and seventh graders learning EL2 performed quite well on a task that required them to generate derivations or to extract the root word of more complex derivations, for example: 'Magic. The performer was a good ... [magician]' (Carlisle, 2000). The same children did not perform as well on a task that focused on generating compound words, for example: 'Which is a better name for a fish that wears a dress: a "fish dress" or a "dress fish"?' (adapted from Nagy, Berninger, Abbott, Vaughan, & Vermeulen, 2003). EL2 learners from a Chinese background, on the other hand, struggled with the derivation task but excelled on the compound task. This makes sense because in Spanish, as in English, applying principles of derivations is a major tool for generating words, for instance, 'construct'/'construc*tion*'/'construc*tive*'. Meanwhile, Chinese words are generated primarily by putting together two or three morphemes to create compound words like 'football'. The Spanish-L1 EL2 learners had the advantage of being able to apply their implicit or explicit knowledge of derivations in Spanish to English; the Chinese children were able to draw on their implicit or explicit knowledge of compounding in Chinese. This study is a compelling demonstration of both positive and negative transfer in the same children. It cautions about making simplistic generalizations regarding the distance between languages. It suggests that it is important to look at specific features that may be easy or hard to learn given particular characteristics of the L1 and L2.

Another illustration of this important point is provided by studies investigating crosslinguistic transfer of visual word recognition skills. These show that Chinese and Japanese EL2 learners employ EL2 word recognition procedures that are systematically different from what is typically observed among native speakers of alphabetic languages such as English or Spanish. These differences reflect the fact that individuals who learn to read first in Chinese or Japanese rely more on visual word recognition and less on phonological information and decoding, even when they read words in English. This is presumably because they transfer well-rehearsed, automatic word recognition strategies that they use when they read words in their L1 (Akamatsu, 2002; Wang & Koda, 2005).

Implications for Teaching

EL2 teachers may wonder how this discussion is relevant to teaching EL2 learners to become good readers, but it is by no means academic. Such research findings mean that when teaching reading comprehension or explaining the meaning of new words to groups of EL2 learners from a range of typologically different language backgrounds, we will find that not all EL2 learners will struggle with the same reading-related language elements. Depending on their L1 and how much they have learned to read in their L1, some language elements may be relatively easy to acquire because learners can draw on similarities with specific familiar features in their L1. Other elements may be more challenging because they are different.

It is useful to analyze the kinds of errors that EL2 learners make because they can provide hints about the underlying rules that EL2 learners draw on as they try to read new words and texts. As stated above, errors are often attributed to negative transfer from the L1 without a careful analysis of the source of the errors. In fact, not all errors made by EL2 learners should be attributed to negative transfer. Some aspects of EL2 language and literacy development may be challenging to native speakers as well as to EL2 learners, and may be developmental in nature (Paradis, Genesee, & Crago, 2011). A longitudinal study by Wang and Geva (2003) provides examples of this. These researchers asked EL2 learners whose L1 was Cantonese to decide whether pairs of words such as 'think'/'sink', presented orally, were the same or different. In Grade 1, these EL2 learners, who did not have the /θ/ phoneme in their L1, were, as expected, unable to distinguish the /θ/ and /s/ phonemes. They therefore said that the two words in word pairs such as 'think'/'sink' were the same. However, by Grade 2, as their English language skills improved, they had developed the ability to distinguish the /θ/ and /s/ phonemes and did a much better job of indicating that 'think' and 'sink' were different words. This is an illustration of a negative transfer effect that diminishes with development and proficiency in EL2. At the same time, both the EL1 and the EL2 groups took more time to learn how to spell the /θ/ correctly in words such as 'think' but had less difficulty in correctly spelling less complex orthographic word parts such as the /s/ in 'sink'. The results of the studies reviewed above illustrate the importance of taking a developmental perspective and of considering carefully what features in the spoken or written language are challenging to all learners and what features are especially difficult for a particular group because of the transfer of specific features from the L1.

The Linguistic Interdependence Hypothesis and L2 Literacy Development

The Linguistic Interdependence Hypothesis, formulated by Cummins (1981), is another prominent theoretical framework that concerns L1–L2 transfer. This framework, which has been informed by cognitive psychology, has been highly influential in the literature and in programs designed to enhance L2 language and literacy development. The Linguistic Interdependence Hypothesis claims that:

> [t]o the extent that instruction in Lx is effective in promoting proficiency in Lx, transfer of this proficiency to Ly will occur provided there is adequate exposure to Ly (either in school or [other] environment) and adequate motivation to learn Ly.

> (Cummins, 1981, p. 29)

It follows from the Interdependence Hypothesis that learning that has taken place in a child's L1 can transfer to or facilitate L2 achievement but that this transfer is not automatic. It hinges on the extent to which the L2 learner has achieved sufficient language proficiency in the L2 to be able to recognize similarities with the L1. As Cummins (1981) emphasizes, it also depends on the quality of instruction in the L1. He argues that stronger progress can be made in acquiring literacy in the L2, i.e. through positive transfer, when learners have had opportunities to develop their L1 language and literacy adequately.

Cummins makes another important observation: L2 learning tasks vary in terms of how demanding they are and the extent to which contextual and language proficiency support is available to help the L2 learner. Cummins (2000) proposes that:

> [a]cademic proficiency transfers across languages such that students who have developed literacy in their first language will tend to make stronger progress in acquiring literacy in their second language.

> (Cummins, 2000, p.173)

Cummins explains that such transfer can occur because the academic language skills are developmentally linked to common underlying proficiencies that are shared across languages. These common underlying proficiencies involve skills and knowledge that were learned in the L1 context but can be accessed in the L2.

Here is an example that illustrates how the ability to access prior knowledge can enhance reading comprehension. EL2 high school students who have acquired relevant background knowledge in their L1—for example, about the effects of global warming on vegetation in the Arctic—should be able to access this knowledge when they read an article about the same topic in EL2. However, transfer is not automatic; for transfer to occur, appropriate EL2 proficiency must have been attained.

To continue the example about global warming, it would be hard to access prior knowledge from reading if the reader has problems with working memory or does not know how to decode EL2 academic words such as 'combustion', 'degrade', 'emissions', and 'precipitation'. The Linguistic Interdependence Hypothesis emphasizes the importance of distinguishing between Cognitive Academic Language Proficiency (CALP)—the ability to use language in cognitively demanding situations—and Basic Interpersonal Communication Skills (BICS)—the ability to use language in less demanding, more contextually supported situations, such as conversations with peers (see Cummins, 2000).

Cummins' notion that there are interdependent relationships among L1 and L2 language and literacy skills has been studied extensively, especially in the context of L1–L2 transfer of higher-level conceptual and strategic abilities (Genesee, Geva, Dressler, & Kamil, 2006). These studies often seek to demonstrate associations between aspects of L1 reading—such as comprehension monitoring strategies, prior knowledge, or familiarity with certain text genres—and their impact on EL2 reading comprehension.

The idea that familiarity with text genres can transfer across languages and is less tied to L2 proficiency comes from research on the representation of story structure in young children's story retelling. Studies examining young children's ability to tell stories that comply with universal story grammar parameters show that children can demonstrate this kind of metacognitive knowledge in their L2, even though their language skills are clearly not on a par with those of their L1 peers. For example, Paradis and Kirova (2014) investigated the relationship between home language environment and kindergarten children's grammatical, vocabulary, and story-retelling quality. As was expected, the EL2 learners said less than their EL1 peers, and their sentences were shorter, less complex, and had fewer morphemes. Yet, even though they were exposed to much less English, the EL2 learners did not differ from their EL1 peers in including essential story grammar elements such as establishing the setting, describing an initiating event, describing a response, and mentioning an outcome (Gutiérrez-Clellen, 2012). Similar findings have been reported in other recent studies involving young L2 learners (for example, Cleave, Girolametto, Chen, & Johnson, 2010; Schwartz & Shaul, 2013).

When reading strategies are considered from the perspective of L1–L2 transfer, metacognitive skills are pivotal. As discussed earlier in this chapter, metacognitive skill in reading involves the ability to decide what strategies one should use to regulate the reading process (Baker & Beall, 2009; Schoonen et al., 1998). For example, reading a text in order to find specific information involves a different strategy than reading a text to memorize details or to prepare for writing a critique. Good comprehenders can adapt their reading strategies to their reading goals, and this adaptation reflects metacognitive skills. Depending on the context for L2 learning, metacognitive reading skills can be learned in the L1 and can then be used in—that is, transferred to—L2 reading. Clearly, one needs to possess sufficient metacognitive knowledge about reading strategies and text characteristics to be able to transfer this knowledge for use in the L2. In addition, one would need to have sufficient language and reading skills in the L1 and L2. When L1 reading and language skills are very low, drawing on higher-order cognitive skills in the L1 may not be feasible or sufficient (Stanovich & Siegel, 1994). Likewise, a learner may have excellent facility in accessing metacognitive skills in the L1, but when the cognitive resources are overtaxed by poor L2 language proficiency or poor decoding skills, activating these higher-level strategies may not be sufficient to comprehend text in the weaker language.

A study conducted in the Netherlands by Droop and Verhoeven (1998) is a good example of the interplay between L2 language skills and the utility of accessing prior knowledge.

Spotlight Study 2.3

Droop and Verhoeven (1998) examined the role of cultural background on the reading comprehension of Grade 3 native speakers of Dutch as compared to immigrant children learning Dutch as an additional language. The children read three text types in Dutch: texts referring to Dutch culture, texts referring to the culture of the immigrants, such as Turkey or Morocco, and neutral texts. Within each type of text, a distinction was made between linguistically simple and linguistically complex texts. The native Dutch speakers benefited from the familiar content regardless of how complex the language was, and performed more poorly when content was unfamiliar. The immigrant children also benefited from the familiar content: they were able to read the texts with more fluency and comprehend them better when they were about the children's own culture than when they were about Dutch culture. However, the advantage for comprehension of reading about familiar content was restricted to linguistically simple texts; the immigrant children had limited ability to comprehend the linguistically more complex texts, even when the texts addressed their own culture. In other words, using texts with familiar cultural background can be helpful, but it is not a panacea for all the difficulties that L2 learners face when they try to comprehend text. ■

Transfer and the Contribution of Underlying Cognitive Processes and Capacities to L2 Reading

When we try to understand what factors play a role in the association of the L1 with L2 reading tasks, it is important not to think only about the higher-order factors that may be common to the L1 and L2, such as reading strategies, prior knowledge, and cognates. We also need to consider the basic cognitive processes that underlie the ability to read and comprehend what one reads in either language. For example, working memory has been shown to be crucial for reading comprehension in L1 and L2 (Geva & Ryan, 1993; Walter, 2004). To comprehend what one reads in either the L1 or the L2, it is essential to hold in memory and integrate ideas just read as new information continues to flow in. This means that a positive correlation between reading comprehension in the L1 and L2 can be attributed, at least to some extent, to the fact that comprehension in both languages relies on a third factor, for example, the ability to hold information in working memory. It also suggests that some learners may do well on reading comprehension tasks in both the L1 and the L2, but that others will experience difficulty in both languages—not because they are not transferring their prior knowledge or strategies, but because it is hard for them to hold a lot of information in working memory. In this case, individual differences in working memory are at least partially responsible for this L1–L2 correlation.

It is important to note that the Linguistic Interdependence Hypothesis was developed with regard to higher-level skills, such as comprehension strategies, and does not address other essential lower-level cognitive processing skills. In general, this hypothesis is useful for explaining **procedural** and metalinguistic knowledge that is important for handling cognitively demanding tasks, such as inferring word meanings and using metacognitive comprehension-monitoring strategies in the L1 and L2 (Koda, 2005). At times, L1 and L2 reading skills correlate not because of transfer of skills but because these reading skills rely on cognitive processing resources that are activated automatically whether one reads in the L1 or L2. Examples of such common underlying cognitive processing resources include working memory, **executive function**, phonological awareness, and the ability to access information in memory quickly and efficiently. Another example of an underlying cognitive ability that is activated without awareness and intention is phonological memory, which involves the ability to hold phonemic strings in short-term memory. There are differences between people in their ability to remember short strings of phonemes, and it turns out that EL2 and EL1 learners who have better ability to remember short strings of phonemes will learn more vocabulary over time than those who find it difficult to remember them (Farnia & Geva, 2011).

Another example of a cognitive process that underlies reading-related skills in the L1 and L2 is phonological awareness. Phonological awareness involves the understanding that spoken words consist of sounds—phonemes, syllables, and onset-rimes—and that these units can be manipulated in various ways, for example, by omitting the first or last phoneme, or by adding or replacing a syllable with another (Yopp, 1992). This is illustrated in the game described in Classroom Snapshot 2.3 below. As discussed at the beginning of this chapter, phonological awareness is essential for learning to read in alphabetic languages and predicts word reading and spelling skills. Moreover, phonological awareness assessed in the L1 often predicts word reading skills in the L2 when typologically similar language pairs such as English/French (Jared, Cormier, Levy, & Wade-Woolley, 2011) or English/Spanish (Durgunoğlu, Nagy, & Hancin-Blatt, 1993) are examined. This kind of correlation has also been noted in the study of typologically dissimilar languages such as English/Hebrew (Wade-Woolley & Geva, 2000), Persian/English (Gholamain & Geva, 1999), or English/Chinese (Marinova-Todd, Zhao, & Bernhardt, 2010). Classroom Snapshot 2.3 is an example of a playful and spontaneous way of manipulating language that demonstrates phonological awareness.

Classroom Snapshot 2.3

In this game, speakers alter words according to a simple set of arbitrary rules. The objective of the game is to use a 'secret' language so that the meaning of communication is hidden from others who are not familiar with the rules. The rule in this case is to add the syllable *fu* at the end of each word. This kind of game is played spontaneously across different cultures and languages, but it is difficult for children with poor phonological awareness. The following interaction happened between two fourth graders in the playground during recess.

Child 1: Dofu youfu wantfu tofu playfu withfu mefu?

Child 2: Yesfu, butfu youfu needfu tofu waitfu forfu mefu tofu finishfu myfu snackfu.

Child 1: Okayfu! ▪

Aptitude and Transfer

We have emphasized in this chapter that individuals differ in their ability to achieve well-developed reading skills and to succeed in L2 learning. Numerous studies explore the fundamental question of why there are individual differences in L2 learning. Before leaving the topic of transfer, it is important to briefly describe an interpretation of transfer that emphasizes an underlying common aptitude to learn language (Sparks, Patton, Ganschow, & Humbach, 2009) or even a more general capacity to learn (Frost, Siegelman, Narkiss, & Afek, 2013) as the explanatory mechanism.

In their Linguistic Coding Hypothesis, researchers such as Sparks and Ganschow (1993) argue that aptitude to learn language is the mechanism that explains why poor language and literacy skills in one language can predict performance in the L2, even when the languages are typologically unrelated (Kahn-Horwitz, Sparks, & Goldstein, 2012). The view that L2 acquisition is a subset of general language ability assumes that L2 learning is mediated by the same underlying cognitive factors that propel L1 language development. Support for this approach comes from research showing that L1 linguistic capacities, such as phonological awareness, syntactic abilities, orthographic knowledge, and vocabulary, tend to predict success in L2 (Ganschow, Sparks, & Javorsky, 1998; Geva & Ryan, 1993). These frameworks highlight the notion that people vary in their capacity to learn language, and that differences in this capacity can, to some extent, explain observed relationships between L1 and L2 competencies. It is not therefore surprising that some studies show that L1-literacy-related skills predict the ability to acquire literacy in the L2 (Geva et al., 1997; Koda, 2007).

As suggested by Figure 1.1 on page 7, a variety of factors contribute to L2 reading comprehension; basic cognitive processing skills and language aptitude cannot be ignored. They may help in understanding why some EL2 learners continue to struggle and may suggest instructional adaptations that address the strengths and weaknesses of these learners. These adaptations are addressed in Chapters 3 and 4.

Summary

In this chapter, we have presented several frameworks for understanding the development of reading in a second language. Interwoven throughout the sections was the notion that reading comprehension requires the orchestration of a wide range of cognitive, metacognitive, linguistic, and metalinguistic skills. With regard to instruction, we also underscored the idea that 'one size does not fit all': the skills needed for reading comprehension and the learning sequence may vary as a function of several factors. For example, EL2 reading development of a kindergartner or Grade 1 child in a bilingual school would nicely fit the developmental stages presented in Chall's model. In contrast, the EL2 reading development of a kindergartner or Grade 1 child who is receiving only a couple of hours of EL2 instruction per week would progress through the stages of reading at a slower pace. The developmental progression of EL2 reading for a learner who is exposed to English for the first time in adolescence might be very different from that of a child who started the EL2 reading process at a young age, even though the necessary skills are the same. The section on the Simple View of Reading highlighted the importance of developing not only text-level EL2-proficiency-related skills—as EL2 teachers often do—but also a myriad of word-level reading skills. We then examined how orthographic differences across different L1s play an important role in the development of EL2 reading, also noting that EL2 proficiency plays a more substantial role in text reading fluency and reading comprehension than in word reading skills. The theoretical foundations and baseline research reviewed in this chapter will facilitate an understanding of the classroom research and content covered in Chapters 3 and 4.

3

Reading Skills for Young Readers: Research and Implications for Pedagogy

Preview

In Chapter 2, we examined several theoretical frameworks and background research that help us understand how L2 reading comprehension is influenced by cognitive and linguistic skills, orthographic characteristics of learners' L1 and L2, reading experience in the L1, and developmental factors. These theoretical frameworks provide the lenses through which research related to L2 reading in young learners will be explored in this chapter. We have seen that just like a child learning to read in L1, an L2 emergent reader moves through predictable stages (for example, Chall, 1996), but L2 readers move through these stages faster than L1 readers if they can apply prerequisite skills that were acquired when learning to read in their L1. We have observed that decoding and word recognition skills, fluency, vocabulary knowledge, and comprehension strategies are all critical components for successful L2 reading comprehension. We have also seen how the demands and challenges of L2 reading depend on a variety of factors, such as text complexity, as well as prior literacy experience, whether the L1 and L2 are typologically similar, sociocultural characteristics, and L2 language proficiency.

In this chapter, we will discuss classroom research to illustrate the skills that EL2 learners need in order to become successful readers in the primary (K–3) and upper elementary grades (4–6). We focus on studies with young learners from preschool through Grade 6, giving careful consideration to the teaching implications of the transition from 'learning to read' to 'reading to learn'. We will examine questions such as:

- What is the relationship between EL2 word reading, EL2 language comprehension, and EL2 reading comprehension at the primary and upper elementary grades?
- What skills need to be taught, and how?
- How much teaching time should be dedicated to the teaching of each skill?

- How can technology support EL2 reading at the primary and upper elementary grades?
- What are effective EL2 reading assessment tools at the primary and upper elementary grades?

Teaching Children to Read: Preschool to Grade 3

Effective English reading instruction in the primary grades is critical for the prevention of later reading difficulties. If young learners have a positive experience learning to read, they are more likely to enjoy reading; if they find reading pleasurable, they are more likely to read extensively; and if they are avid readers, they will continue strengthening their reading and language skills and expanding their background knowledge. The five pillars of effective EL1 reading instruction identified by the 2000 National Reading Panel are also critical for effective EL2 reading instruction: phonological awareness, **phonics**, fluency, vocabulary, and comprehension. A study of English-French bilingual children by Jared et al. (2011) illustrates this. Jared and her colleagues followed children in French immersion from kindergarten to Grade 3. They found that:

> the variables that predicted English reading development were consistent with studies of EL1 children, even though participants were concurrently learning to read in French.
>
> (Jared et al., 2011, p. 119)

From preschool to Grade 3, reading development is usually characterized as the development of phonological awareness, phonics, word recognition, and fluency. However, teaching vocabulary and comprehension strategies is just as important. We will examine each of these skills.

Activity 3.1

Try to read the following passage and then answer the discussion questions.

Em prus mweinvojdjr, sep soierioight nagt depbim sep kosadejflak es nar pukmonret. Wie es bek? Neos nar sirghow tok! Jowmivter, deir ure klope brosiminities: shodwe, chepla, ore brofpetik.

1 How successful were you at reading the passage?
2 Were you at least able to sound it out?
3 Were you able to extract any meaning from it?

If you were able to sound out this short passage, it is because you have decoding skills. In simpler terms, you know the sound that corresponds to a letter such as *s* or a letter string such as *ight*. However, even if you were able to decode this nonsense text perfectly, you were unable to extract any meaning from it because you do not know what each word means; you lack knowledge of the meaning of the words in this made-up language. Now let us put ourselves in the situation of five-year-old children in Mexico, Brazil, or China who have not yet learned to read in their L1. These children would not even be able to sound out the text. If these children have good familiarity with some of the conventions of written text, the most they will be able to get out of this passage is that there is a question and an exclamation. We will start our discussion of EL2 reading instruction with non-readers in mind. The first step we need to take is to prepare these learners for reading.

Preparing Learners for Reading

When preparing learners for reading, teachers need to help them develop the following critical skills: **letter–sound recognition**, oral vocabulary, and phonological awareness—with particular emphasis on **phonemic awareness**. Phonemic awareness is 'the ability to notice, think about, and work with individual sounds in spoken words' (National Institute of Child Health and Human Development, 2000, p. 2). By implementing phonemic awareness activities and games, EL2 teachers teach both language and critical pre-reading skills. Phonemic awareness is a prerequisite for learning to read in English and any alphabetically written language (National Early Literacy Panel, 2008), including non-Roman alphabetic languages such as Korean (Cho & McBride-Chang, 2005). Phonemic awareness instruction should be intentional and part of the daily routine in preschool and kindergarten (National Early Literacy Panel, 2008). However, under normal circumstances, it should not take up more than 20 hours of instruction per academic year (National Institute of Child Health and Human Development, 2000).

An important finding from the National Early Literacy Panel (2008) is that phonological awareness skills follow a predictable order of development, starting with awareness of larger sound units—onset-rimes—and followed by a progressive awareness of smaller and smaller units of sound—syllables and then phonemes. Therefore:

[r]ather than trying to teach any particular skill (such as phonological memory), it may be of greater value to ensure that progress is occurring and that children are becoming progressively more able to deal with smaller and smaller units of sound (e.g., words, syllables, onset-rimes, phonemes).

(National Early Literacy Panel, 2008, p. 79)

To some extent, phonological awareness is also important for the development of reading skills in non-alphabetic languages such as Chinese. However, the aspects of phonological awareness that are most critical to reading in alphabetic languages are different from the most critical aspects in non-alphabetic languages (Ziegler & Goswami, 2005, 2006). In English, the ability to segment and blend phonemes is the aspect of phonological awareness that plays the most important role in reading; in Chinese, it is tone and syllable awareness (Shu, Peng, & McBride-Chang, 2008). Given that phonological awareness is important for reading across typologically different writing systems, it is not surprising that it is one of several skills that learners transfer across languages, as demonstrated in Spotlight Study 3.1.

Spotlight Study 3.1

Bialystok, Luk, and Kwan (2005) examined the literacy skills in the two languages of bilingual children who were halfway through first grade and who were learning to read in two languages, and compared them to those of children learning to read in EL1. The children in the bilingual sample came from three different language backgrounds—Cantonese, Hebrew, and Spanish—and for all of them English was the L2. The bilingual children completed decoding and phoneme segmentation tasks in their two languages, and the EL1 students in English only. One of the questions the researchers wanted to answer with this study was whether the bilingual children transferred literacy skills across their two languages. To this end, the researchers examined the relationship between the scores on a given skill across the two languages. They found that the better the Hebrew- and Spanish-English bilingual children were at segmenting sounds and decoding in their L1, the better they were at this task in EL2. Because the phonemic segmentation task is not relevant to the Cantonese writing system, this task was not administered in Cantonese, and an orthographically suitable decoding task was adapted to test this skill in that language. The performance on the Cantonese decoding task was unrelated to the performance in the equivalent English task. The researchers concluded that the transfer of skills from one language to another depends on the degree of orthographic and phonological similarity between the two languages. ■

Several important pedagogical implications can be drawn from these findings and those of studies discussed in Chapter 2. The specific phonological awareness skills that children develop in their L1 and that are available to transfer to their L2 are closely related to the orthographic characteristics of their L1. Thus, where possible, it would be useful for EL2 teachers to be aware of and pay attention to phonological differences between learners'

L1 and EL2 and tailor instruction accordingly. For example, one feature of Chinese is that syllables are prominent and noticeable. Because of this, a Chinese emergent reader of English may have good syllable awareness but poor ability to discriminate and manipulate individual phonemes. In such cases, more instruction should be allocated to the development of phonemic awareness—changing words by substituting, deleting, or adding one sound—than to other aspects of phonological awareness. In addition, EL2 teachers can incorporate regular activities aimed at developing phonemic awareness by playing with sounds common to their students' L1 and EL2, as well as those unique to EL2.

There are several aspects of phonological awareness that teachers can address in their EL2 pre-reading instruction. The most basic one is **rhyme awareness**. Preschoolers who are good at identifying words that rhyme are also good word readers (Goswami & Bryant, 1990). Children with good rhyme awareness are able to use analogies to facilitate reading words from the same rhyming family, for example, 'fight', 'sight', and 'might'. Teachers can facilitate the development of this skill among young children through teaching nursery rhymes and playing puppet and flash card games. Sometimes these games and activities involve giving pairs of words and having children identify whether they rhyme or not. In a slightly more challenging version, teachers say a word and children are asked to provide one that rhymes with it. You may be wondering what rhyme awareness has to do with reading. One way of explaining this connection is that English orthography, among several other orthographies, frequently represents one or two final word sounds with a string of letters that do not follow a one-to-one letter–sound correspondence, such as *–ight*, *–ick*, or *– ure*. When children are learning to read and spell, they can decode and spell new words more efficiently by associating them with rhyming words that share the same spelling and that they have in their oral vocabulary.

Phoneme identification—identification of individual sounds in a word— is another important component of phonemic awareness and a strong predictor of early reading (Hulme et al., 2002). Children who cannot identify initial and final sounds in words they hear are at risk of developing a reading difficulty. Initial and final sound identification are taught through simple yet engaging games for young learners, as demonstrated in Classroom Snapshot 3.1.

Classroom Snapshot 3.1

The following exchange illustrates one way of playing 'I Spy' to teach initial sound identification:

Teacher: I spy something with my little eye.
Children: What do you spy?
Teacher: I spy something that begins with the /t/ sound. ▪

The same game can be varied to focus on final sounds ('I spy something that ends with …') or on words that rhyme with each other ('I spy something that rhymes with …'). Even children who are just developing their EL2 oral fluency can play this game easily because it follows a repetitive pattern. Moreover, variations of this game are popular across different cultures and languages, so the children may already know the game, which will facilitate understanding when playing it in EL2.

Sound segmentation and **sound blending** are two sides of the same coin and the most important aspects of phonemic awareness for English reading (National Institute of Child Health and Human Development, 2000). Segmentation involves saying each of the sounds heard in a word; blending involves saying the word that is made up of several sounds heard separately. Elkonin boxes (Elkonin, 1971) provide effective practice of sound segmentation (Clay, 1993; National Institute of Child Health and Human Development, 2000). Children hear a word and for each sound heard, they put a placeholder—buttons, beans, chips, etc.—on a box. For example, for the word 'tight', they would put markers on three boxes because only three sounds are heard in this word. This activity can also be used to help children hear initial, middle, and final sounds. For this, you would give children grids with three boxes and ask them to put the placeholder in the beginning, middle, or final box according to where they hear a given sound. For example, for the sound /k/ in 'cat', the children would mark or place a button on the first box. Numerous ideas and worksheets for using Elkonin boxes are found online.

The final components of phonemic awareness that we will examine are **sound deletion** and **sound substitution**. Through sound deletion and substitution activities, children learn to attend to the internal sound structure of words and to notice how just one sound can change the meaning of a word. In their later reading development, this sound sensitivity will translate into word reading accuracy. Yopp and Yopp (2009) propose a phonemic awareness activity in which the last word of a nursery rhyme is substituted for a rhyming word. An adaptation of this idea for practicing basic sound substitution would be to change the initial sound of known nursery rhyme. For example, the initial sounds in *Hickory, Dickory, Dock* could be replaced with the /s/ sound:

Sickory, sickory, sock
The mouse ran up the clock
The clock struck one
The mouse ran down
Sickory, sickory, sock

Another important precursor of reading is letter sound knowledge (National Early Literacy Panel, 2008; Piasta & Wagner, 2010). Teaching the sound of the letter along with the name of the letter is more effective than teaching just the name of the letter (Ehri, 2014). Most children easily learn the distinction between the name of the letter and the sound it represents. Whether it is more effective to teach the letter name first and then the sound or in the reverse order is not clear and seems to be a matter of cultural preference (Stahl, 2014). Sometimes a letter sound, for instance, a long vowel sound, is the same as the letter name. To clarify, it suffices to tell children that sometimes these letters 'say their name'.

Vocabulary is another critical area of teaching to prepare young learners for reading. Vocabulary facilitates initial reading development through its contribution to phonemic awareness and through its role in facilitating reading accuracy and speed (Metsala & Walley, 1998), and comprehension. Vocabulary knowledge assists the reading of words by offering a beginner reader a way to determine whether the word makes sense in the context.

Classroom Snapshot 3.2

Sam, who is a Grade 1 emergent EL1 reader, lives in the USA. Today, he is reading a picture book. Some of the words in the book are easy to read, but others are more challenging. He stumbles trying to read the word 'audience'; he first reads /'aʊdɪns/. He pauses and, with a puzzled face, says 'It doesn't make sense'. Then his face lights up as if he remembered something and he quickly self-corrects: /'ɔdiəns/!

Sam knew the meaning of the word 'audience'. His teacher had used it recently when preparing him and his classmates for a school presentation. During rehearsals, Sam's teacher frequently said 'Look at the audience' or 'Smile at the audience'. ▪

Sam was able to read this challenging word because it was part of his oral vocabulary. His first attempt did not make sense, but it sounded similar to a word he knew, so he was quickly able to correct himself. EL2 children in non-English-speaking countries do not have the same opportunities as Sam to hear English words used spontaneously and in meaningful contexts on a regular basis. They typically have a more limited vocabulary and find it harder to use the self-correction strategies that Sam used to read words accurately.

Whereas phonemic awareness can be taught in a similar way whether children are learning English as an L1 or L2, teaching oral vocabulary to EL2 emergent readers requires unique considerations. Basic and everyday words for EL1 speakers are new words for EL2 learners. Unlike their EL1 peers, EL2 learners are not exposed to these basic words in their day-to-day life, so the classroom is the place to learn them.

One of the most effective ways of increasing young learners' oral vocabulary is by reading aloud to them. Researchers have explored different approaches to teaching vocabulary through **read-alouds**, and have found that repeated reading—at least three times—of the same story is required for vocabulary learning (Justice, Meier, & Walpole, 2005; Leung, 2008). Repeated reading is particularly important for EL2 learners because they may not have the opportunity to listen to the target words outside of the classroom. We have also learned that although many words can be learned incidentally just by listening to stories read aloud, even more words are learned when the meanings of new words are explicitly taught (Biemiller & Boote, 2006).

Teaching vocabulary explicitly can be challenging because a proficient reader needs to know thousands of words. As indicated in Chapter 2, EL2 readers need to know at least 95 percent of the words in a passage to be able to comprehend the text without any help. To address this challenge, researchers are currently looking at ways of accelerating vocabulary learning by teaching children how to become better word learners. Some have turned to technology, which we will examine later in this chapter. Others have turned to metalinguistic strategies, such as drawing attention to morphological components in words. One way of developing morphological awareness is by bringing children's attention to the morphological structure of words, for example, by helping them notice the two words that make a compound word like 'campfire' and to identify what we are talking about ('fire') and the descriptor ('camp'). Young learners can also learn the difference the *s* makes when we add it to some words to indicate more than one thing ('car', 'cars'), that *–ed* indicates that an action already took place ('walk', 'walked'), that *–ing* means an action is currently being done ('walking'), and that *–er* at the end of some words indicates the doer of something ('teach', 'teacher'). In a recent study, Ramírez, Walton, and Roberts (2014) found that EL1 kindergartners became more effective at learning new words after they were taught to pay attention to words within words, for example, the words in 'campfire', and derived words such as 'smelly'. In this study, kindergarten teachers extracted words like 'minivan' and 'football' from picture books read aloud to their class, and used games and other educational activities to help kindergartners develop awareness of compounds. The effectiveness of teaching vocabulary through story-reading to young EL2 children has also been observed.

Spotlight Study 3.2

Collins (2005) reports on a study that examined the effects of abundant and rich explanations of vocabulary to 70 four- and five-year-old EL2 children through repeated storybook reading. The home language of all the participating children was Portuguese. The researcher read the stories to the children three times per week and provided rich vocabulary explanations by pointing to illustrations, providing brief definitions, using the new word in a different sentence from the one in the book, using a gesture or, when applicable, providing a synonym. The same stories were read to an age-matched comparison group of children without the rich vocabulary instruction. It was observed that the children receiving the rich vocabulary instruction made gains in vocabulary and comprehension that were significantly larger than those of the children in the comparison group. Moreover, even children with low initial levels of vocabulary knowledge greatly benefited from the intervention. The researcher concluded that 'explanations [of vocabulary] are helpful regardless of how little L2 is known' (Collins, 2005, p. 408). ■

Initial Reading

It typically takes three years to develop basic reading skills in EL1. Along with the continued development of oral language skills, children develop decoding skills and word recognition from kindergarten to Grade 3. Effective teachers of reading understand the complex nature of English orthography and teach a variety of reading strategies to enable children to read words with different orthographic characteristics.

Some words in English, like 'pet', 'cow', or 'map', have a transparent letter-to-sound correspondence; they are read efficiently and effectively by simply decoding them, i.e. applying letter-to-sound correspondence. Children learn these decoding skills through phonics instruction. We have learned from research that effective phonics instruction is systematic and explicit (National Institute of Child Health and Human Development, 2000). It is best to teach letter–sound correspondences in a clearly defined sequence that includes both consonants and vowels, and that provides children with substantial opportunities to put them into practice by reading short but interesting decodable books. The exact sequence of letter sound instruction is still debated. However, there is consensus on the following basic principles:

1   Teach easier letter sounds first, for example, /s/, /t/, /f/, /n/, /p/, and /m/.
2   Introduce letter sounds that can be associated with something meaningful in the child's life—for instance, /m/ because it is the first letter of 'mother', /f/ for 'father', and the sound of the first letter of the child's name.
3   Teach the short vowel sounds along with a few consonants so that children can start blending these sounds and making words by substituting one letter at a time: 'sat'/'mat'/'cat'; 'pet'/'set'/'met'; 'mop'/'top'/'cot', etc.
4   Introduce consonant diagraphs—combinations of consonants that represent one sound, for example, *sh* in the word 'shop'.
5   Introduce vowel diagraphs in groups, such as the vowel combinations that make the long sound /i/ *ee* in 'sheep', *ea* in 'seat', etc.

Some decodable English words belong to rhyming word families, like 'mate'/'gate'/'date' or 'pick'/'sick'/'thick'. When this is the case, it is more effective to introduce these words together. Some longer English words, like 'lollipop' or 'important', have transparent letter-to-sound correspondences, and reading these words syllable by syllable is more efficient than reading them letter by letter. However, for longer words which also have prefixes or suffixes, such as 'nationality', a more efficient strategy is to break the word down into its meaningful chunks: 'nation', then 'national', then 'nationality'. English also has a group of words called sight words, which appear frequently in written material and do not follow regular sound-to-letter correspondences. Sight words include 'the', 'where', 'two', 'to', 'when', 'how', 'the', and 'are'. These words cannot be decoded; instead, they need to be visually memorized and read 'by sight'. In summary, an effective reader of English has a toolbox with a variety of strategies to be used according to the varied orthographic characteristics of English words. Effective teachers instruct their students in the use of these strategies.

When teaching English phonics to EL2 children, it is helpful for teachers to be aware of contrasting L1 and L2 phonetic features so that extra practice is provided for sounds that exist in English but not in the children's L1. For example, a Japanese-speaking child may find it difficult to pronounce and read English words that contain the letter *r*; a Spanish-speaking child may find it difficult to read English words that contain short vowel sounds, such as 'pit', 'cut', and 'ship', or to differentiate between long and short vowel sounds in minimal pairs such as 'sheep' and 'ship'. One way of helping children hear these differences is to explicitly indicate the point and mode of articulation of the sounds. To teach the point of articulation, bring the child's attention to the movement and position of the mouth, teeth, and tongue. For example, notice that the tongue is floating in the mouth and slightly curled when we produce an /r/ sound. To teach the mode of articulation, ask the children to notice whether their vocal cords vibrate or not by putting their index finger and thumb on their neck. They can also observe how air is expelled when producing a sound, by putting their hand in front of their mouth.

Consolidation and Fluency

Once children have acquired the basic reading skills, their next main job is to be able to read connected text fluently—that is, quickly, accurately, and with good expression and intonation. It is important that teachers help EL2 readers to consolidate fluency at both word and text levels because, as discussed in Chapter 2, reading fluency facilitates reading comprehension.

The skills considered in the previous sections—phonological awareness, decoding, and **sight word reading**—are prerequisites to fluency development. Additionally, children need to understand punctuation, which in written text functions as a signal for the reader, indicating when to pause and for how long, when to raise the intonation, when to drop the intonation, etc. Punctuation also plays an important role in disambiguating text meaning, and interpreting punctuation marks correctly when reading is critical for fluent reading and comprehension. Luckily for EL2 readers, punctuation rules are common to many languages. For example, numerous European languages, including German, Spanish, French, Dutch, and Italian, use the same basic punctuation marks as English: period, comma, semicolon, colon, and exclamation and interrogation marks. Asian languages such as Japanese, Chinese, and Korean also use punctuation marks that have the same functions as in English. When punctuation marks have the same functions across readers' L1 and L2, it does not matter in what language they first learn how to use them.

Research to date has provided practical insights into how teachers can effectively promote the development of fluency. From this body of research, we have learned that children need mastery of the prerequisite skills—decoding and sight word reading—and extensive practice reading passages that are at their reading level. Such reading practice needs to be provided in a safe and engaging environment. Readers Theatre is an effective strategy that provides children with the opportunity to practice reading to develop fluency in an enjoyable way (Young & Rasinski, 2009). In Readers Theatre, parts of a script, or character lines, are assigned to different groups of readers. Each group rehearses what was assigned to them and, when ready, the whole class performs together. The dramatic effect is obtained through the effective use of voice tone, intonation, expression, and gestures. Classroom time is invested in practicing reading, rather than in creating props or costumes. There is abundant Readers Theatre material for teachers in print and online.

Reading material from content areas, for example, science or social studies, can also be adapted into scripts for Readers Theatre. One of the values of Readers Theatre is that it provides a meaningful and purposeful context for reading practice. Students have to rehearse reading the script several times before the final performance; because there is a clear purpose, they re-read more willingly. Another great advantage of this strategy is that weaker readers also get practice, but without being singled out. By reading along with their more able peers, weaker readers receive reading support from the group. Another way to provide additional support for EL2 emergent readers is to use books with audio. The audio provides an excellent model for fluent reading while the children read along silently.

There are many other ways to provide opportunities for young children to develop reading fluency. Whatever you do, keep in mind that repetition alone will not be helpful if children do not have the phonics, sight word reading skills, and understanding of punctuation that allow them to read accurately, at a good rate, and with proper intonation and expression. During fluency practice, readers should also be paying attention to the content and applying comprehension strategies (more on this in Chapter 4) in order to understand what they are reading.

Effective Assessment of EL2 Emergent Reading Skills and Early Intervention

Assessment of reading progress is an integral part of good EL1 and EL2 reading instruction. The main purpose of classroom assessment is to improve students' learning. To this end, the EL2 reading teacher is advised to gather information on the students' progress at least three times per year to identify their areas of weakness and strength, and to modify instruction accordingly. Another important purpose of assessment is to identify children who have a reading disability so that special programming is put in place to meet their learning needs.

Response to intervention (RTI) is an evidence-based model that can be effective for early identification and support for students who are having reading difficulties, even if no formal assessment has been done. This model, discussed further in Chapter 4, provides for different levels, or tiers, of intervention according to how much students are likely to benefit from instruction tailored to their individual needs. Tiers of intervention therefore range from whole-class teaching to intensive one-on-one support. A growing body of research supports the effectiveness of RTI in the early assessment of reading difficulties and intervention for EL1 and EL2 children (Fuchs & Vaughn, 2012). For example, Bollman, Silberglitt, and Gibbons (2007) found that after a full year's implementation of an RTI model in a school district, the reading performance of K–8 EL1 and EL2 students increased dramatically: 70 percent of the students met the reading performance expectations, as opposed to only 35 percent in previous years when the RTI model was not in place.

EL2 Learners Who Have Persistent Poor Decoding Skills

Good indicators of an underlying learning disorder in EL2 children, as in their EL1 peers, are weaknesses in decoding, phonological awareness, processing speed, and working memory. Moreover, performance on such indicators is similar whether assessed in the child's L1 or L2 (Lesaux & Geva, 2006). Measures such as phoneme detection, phoneme deletion, and pseudoword repetition can be good early screening tools for EL2 learners who are at risk for having decoding problems (Gottardo, Collins, Baciu, & Gebotys, 2008). Young EL2 and EL1 children who may be at risk for having a reading disability involving various aspects of decoding and spelling perform poorly on such phonological processing skills and have similar learning profiles on many reading-related skills (Geva, Yaghoub-Zadeh, & Schuster, 2000). Poor decoders are often limited in their ability to read text with accuracy and fluency and this, in turn, limits their ability to comprehend what they read (Geva & Farnia, 2012a). Students whose stumbling blocks are related to 'reading the words on the page' with accuracy and fluency may show better listening comprehension than reading comprehension.

A sound assessment battery of early literacy skills in English includes measurements of fluency in letter naming, familiarity with letter–sound correspondences, phoneme segmentation and phoneme blending, sight word reading, and nonsense word decoding (Gersten et al., 2007). Typically, these skills are assessed in kindergarten, first grade, and second grade. To get a sense of the strengths and weaknesses of EL2 children in these skills, teachers can use informal assessment tools available online, for example, at www.readingrockets.org and www.colorincolorado.org

As we reviewed in Chapter 2 and will discuss further in Chapter 4, current research indicates that we can reliably assess and diagnose reading disability even before EL2 learners have acquired advanced language skills in English. You may wonder how this is possible. It is because the same cognitive skills that signal the existence of a reading difficulty in EL1 learners—such as phonological awareness, processing speed, and working memory—also signal reading difficulties in EL2 learners. These skills are less dependent on language proficiency than on other skills, such as vocabulary, and this makes it possible to elicit reliable information on an EL2 learner's predisposition to develop a reading difficulty regardless of EL2 language proficiency. Therefore, tests developed to assess word-level reading skills and related cognitive skills such as phonological awareness, processing speed, and phonological memory in EL1 learners can be used to diagnose reading disability in EL2 learners as well (Gersten et al., 2007; Geva & Farnia, 2012a).

The earlier a child's difficulties can be identified, the earlier adaptations can be put in place, and the greater the chance that the struggling reader can overcome these challenges. In a study by Leafstedt, Richards, and Gerber (2004), EL2 kindergartners struggling with English reading were provided with intensive (300 minutes over a period of 10 weeks) and explicit training on phonological awareness. Teachers used picture cards and letter tiles to give children practice in blending onset and rime components like *r–at*, *m–at*, and *c–at*. By the end of kindergarten, there were no differences in word reading ability between the EL2 children and their EL1 peers. In a more recent study, O'Connor, Bocian, Beebe-Frankenberger, and Linklater (2010) examined the impact of an intervention that included phonemic awareness, alphabetic understanding, that is, letter–sound correspondences, and oral language to kindergartners struggling with reading, of whom about 50 percent were EL2 students. The range of activities included tasks such as syllable clapping; saying words slowly to hear individual sounds in one-syllable words; onset and rime segmenting and blending; manipulating letters on cards to identify where in a word a sound occurred; and creation of one-sentence messages for skill integration and in-context practice. Picture cards and objects were always used to provide a concrete visual. Half of these children received the intervention at the beginning of kindergarten and the other half received it midway through kindergarten. The researchers found that offering the intervention earlier in kindergarten was more effective than later in kindergarten, and that all students benefited from the intervention, regardless of whether they were EL1 or EL2 learners. Spotlight Study 3.3 illustrates that providing early intervention for EL2 children struggling with reading is more critical than the language—L1 or L2—in which the intervention is provided.

Spotlight Study 3.3

Vaughn et al. (2006) investigated the effectiveness of two reading interventions—one in Spanish and one in English—for Grade 1 Spanish-English bilingual children who were considered at risk for reading difficulties. The children who were schooled in Spanish received the intervention in Spanish and those schooled in English received the English intervention. The children's performance was compared to that of bilingual first graders who were receiving Spanish or English instruction but did not receive the intervention.

In both Spanish and English intervention groups, children received explicit training in phonemic awareness and phonics, word decoding and text reading fluency, and reading for meaning during 120 daily lessons of approximately 40 minutes each, delivered individually or in small groups. Each lesson plan comprised six to ten short activities aimed at developing:

- phonemic awareness, including phoneme discrimination, segmenting, and blending
- letter sound knowledge
- word recognition—moving from reading by syllables to entire words
- connected text fluency—using decodable text first and gradually moving into more complex reading material
- reading comprehension.

The teaching sequence was carefully planned. For example, for phonemic awareness, students first practiced identification and isolation of initial sounds, followed by medial and final sounds, and concluded with isolation of sounds in **consonant clusters**—the *fl* in 'flat', for example. Also taught in the initial lessons were higher-frequency letter–sound correspondences, like *s*–/s/ and *m*–/m/; high-frequency sight words like 'to' and 'am'; and closed-syllable words such as 'sat' and 'mat'. New letter–sound elements were introduced every two to three days, and potentially confusing letter–sound correspondences such as /b/ and /d/ were presented several weeks apart to avoid confusion. The ultimate goal of this intervention was to get children to read fluently—accurately and quickly—and with good understanding of the passage. Children were also taught reading comprehension strategies, such as making predictions, establishing a purpose for reading, activating background knowledge, sequencing, and summarizing. Both expository and narrative passages were used. Visuals, gestures, and explicit vocabulary teaching were also abundantly used throughout each lesson. Ten additional minutes were dedicated solely to supplementing vocabulary, listening comprehension, and oral language development through read-alouds. Before the read-alouds, three to four words were explicitly taught to the students. Then, during reading, the children were engaged in discussions about the material through questions and encouraged to use full sentences incorporating the new vocabulary.

The results showed that children in both intervention programs—English and Spanish—made statistically significant progress in their language and literacy development and greater progress than their Grade 1 peers who did not receive the instruction. Moreover, those receiving the Spanish intervention transferred letter knowledge and phonological awareness from Spanish to English. ■

After an examination of approximately 500 empirical studies of early literacy development, the National Early Literacy Panel (2008) concluded that one-on-one or small-group interventions on basic skills, such as phonological awareness—in particular, deleting or blending sounds to make words—combined with phonics instruction is the most effective remedial instruction for struggling emergent readers. Another characteristic of the most effective interventions is that they include intentional, explicit, and systematic teaching of these skills.

Should Children Be Taught to Read First in Their L1 or L2?

This is one of the most frequent questions asked by parents, teachers, and administrators in bilingual environments. The answer is that it depends. Two factors need to be considered when deciding in which language it would make more sense to begin reading instruction: the orthographic distance between the children's L1 and L2, and the dominant language of the society where the children are being schooled. As suggested by the crosslinguistic research examined in Chapter 2, there are both common and unique skills in learning to read in different languages.

Research examining bilingual education programs that start reading instruction in the learners' L2—French in French immersion programs in Canada—have shown that children transfer the reading skills acquired in their L2 to reading in English—their L1—and make quick progress in English reading (Genesee & Jared, 2008; Obadia, 1996). It is important to note that English is the main language of the society where these studies were conducted, and this may have facilitated crosslinguistic skill transfer. Outside of school, these children were regularly exposed to English, which made it possible for them to continue developing their English language skills, even though this was not the language of instruction. This situation may have enabled them to learn through their L2 and successfully demonstrate that knowledge through their L1. Moreover, English is a language with prestige and power in their society, so being instructed in their L2 would not undermine their L1 or pose a threat to their identity.

The situation can be quite different for children who live in a country where English is the dominant language of the society but not the learners' L1. These children's L1 is a **minority language**, usually lacking prestige in English-dominant societies. For these learners, issues of identity and cultural capital are at the center of discussion when deciding on the language of instruction and need to be considered carefully. Two contrasting perspectives have dominated the debate. On one side are those who argue that EL2 learners should be schooled in English only to give them a competitive edge in an English-dominant society (Porter, 1990; Rossell & Baker, 1996). On the other side are those who argue that empowering EL2 students means offering them bilingual education with initial instruction through the L1 (Cummins, 1983, 2000; Lee & Oxelson, 2006). Supporters of bilingual education disagree, however, on the issue of whether to begin reading instruction for EL2 students in English first, in their L1 first, or in both at the same time. This disparity in perspectives is reflected in the varied models of bilingual education currently offered in several English-speaking countries and in the amount of L1 and L2 instruction provided across different bilingual programs.

The most common bilingual programs in the United States are transitional bilingual education (TBE) programs. These comprise early-exit or late-exit, also called developmental, bilingual programs, and two-way, also called dual language, immersion programs. (See Lightbown, 2014, for more details.) In TBE programs with early exit, children are instructed mainly in their L1 for about three years and start transitioning into English at Grade 2 or 3. Usually, by Grade 4, students transition to English-only instruction. In late-exit TBE programs, instruction only or mainly in the children's L1 is sustained for a longer period of time and supplemented with some English instruction. One of the philosophical underpinnings of this model is that empowerment of children's cultural and linguistic identity is critical for their well-being. This model has been heavily influenced by crosslinguistic research, as it is expected that knowledge and skills acquired and developed in the learners' L1 will be transferred to English. In both TBE models, children learn to read in their L1 first. Some research has found better English reading outcomes for children in the early-exit model (see Ramírez, Pasta, Yuen, Billings, & Ramey, 1991), but it has shown that they gradually lose L1 reading skills (Proctor, August, Carlo, & Barr, 2010). Proctor et al. (2010) argue that transitioning minority children from L1 reading instruction to L2-only instruction too early—for example, at Grade 2—deprives them of the opportunity to develop higher-order L1 literacy proficiency, such as strong oral language proficiency and strategic reading skills. This is one of the strongest arguments in favor of maintaining L1 instruction beyond the primary grades. Duursma et al. (2007) also make the case for extending L1 instruction for minority learners. These researchers found that Spanish-English bilingual fifth graders living in the USA made progress in English vocabulary whether or not they received English language support at home. By contrast, their progress in Spanish vocabulary was dependent on the Spanish language support they got at home. They conclude that 'Spanish and not English is the at-risk language for children of Hispanic heritage living in the United States' (Duursma et al., 2007, p. 186). Given that many minority learners do not have rich L1 exposure at home, the authors argue that providing strong L1 instruction is critical for the maintenance of their heritage language.

Research on the literacy development of children in TBE programs reports successful development of reading skills in both languages (Kieffer & Lesaux, 2008, 2012). Slavin, Madden, Calderón, Chamberlain, and Hennessy (2011) compared the reading performance of Spanish-speaking EL2 learners who were randomly assigned for up to five years to either TBE or **Structured English Immersion** (**SEI**). The results showed an initial advantage—in Grade 1—for students in TBE over the students in SEI. However, after Grade 1, this difference decreased gradually, and by Grade 4, the reading skills of children in both programs were equivalent. One disadvantage of SEI programs is that EL2 students are taken away from the classroom and separated from their peers for periods of time. During these periods, EL2 students miss content instruction and the opportunity to learn with and from their EL1 peers.

In a two-way or dual language program, both native and non-native speakers of English receive instruction in English and another language—for example, Spanish and English in the USA. These programs seek to have a balanced number of native speakers in each of the two languages of instruction so that the students support each other's development of their respective L2s (Valdés, 1997). Within two-way programs, there are two models for language of instruction. In one model, 90 percent of the instruction is provided in the minority language and ten percent in English during the first two years of school, kindergarten and Grade 1, and reading instruction is first provided in the minority language (Lindholm-Leary, 2012). English instruction is gradually increased until a balance is achieved, and by Grade 5, there is an equal amount of instructional time in each language. In the second model, instructional time is equally divided between the two languages from kindergarten, and reading instruction is provided in both the minority language and English, with students receiving reading instruction in each language every day or on different days throughout the week. The main expectation of two-way or dual language programs is that students will develop a high level of bilingual, biliterate, and bicultural competences (Genesee & Lindholm-Leary, 2010). An important benefit of this model of bilingual education is that EL2 children schooled in this way seem to achieve better English proficiency than EL2 children schooled in English only, and they also develop strong L1 literacy skills (Genesee & Jared, 2008).

Research examining the literacy development of children in two-way or dual language programs highlights the effectiveness and advantages of biliteracy instruction (Lindholm-Leary, 2011; Oller & Jarmulowicz, 2007). Learners in these programs make significant English language proficiency gains by the time they reach upper elementary grades (Howard, Sugarman, & Christian, 2003). This research has also shown that by Grade 3, English—their L2—is the dominant language of minority-language children, for example, Spanish-speaking EL2 learners, who attend two-way or dual language programs (Lindholm-Leary & Howard, 2008). Lindholm-Leary and Block (2010) followed the literacy development of children in a Spanish-English dual immersion program from kindergarten to Grade 6. The children were first taught to read in Spanish, and started to receive literacy instruction in English in Grade 3. By Grade 6, the English literacy skills of EL1 and EL2 children in the dual immersion program were better than those of EL1 and EL2 children in English mainstream programs.

Turnbull et al. (2003) conducted a study of early French immersion programs in Canada where learners were first taught to read in French, the minority language, up to Grade 3, and then their academic performance was examined in English, their L1. The researchers found that at Grade 3, children in French immersion performed below their peers who were in English mainstream instruction, but that by Grade 6, there were no major differences between the two groups. In contrast to the research reported above on two-way and transitional bilingual programs in the USA, the minority language in this case was the learners' L2, yet the results are comparable. In both contexts, instructional priority was given to the minority language during the primary years to counterbalance the children's limited exposure to it outside the school realm. In both scenarios, children seemed to successfully transfer reading skills learned first either in the L1 or the L2 to the other language. It is important to keep in mind that the two language pairs, Spanish-English and English-French, share an alphabet, as well as cognates and other morphological features related to derivation and the use of suffixes. Such commonalities may have facilitated crosslinguistic transfer of reading skills, resulting in similar outcomes regardless of the language in which children were first taught to read. Further research is needed to determine whether similar outcomes are obtained with language pairs that have different writing systems and unrelated vocabulary, such as English-Chinese.

The studies of bilingual instruction reviewed in this section show that in most cases, students successfully transferred their reading skills to the other language, regardless of whether reading instruction began in the L1 or the L2. The data also suggest that concurrent literacy instruction in L1 and L2 is beneficial academically and socioculturally. In light of this, it is not surprising that in the USA alone, dual language or two-way bilingual programs have gained popularity and growth over the past decade. Dual language programs have increased from fewer than ten in 1971 to more than 445 in 2012 (Center for Applied Linguistics, 2012). Research also suggests that rather than focusing on the language to use first in providing reading instruction, more energy should be devoted to quality of instruction (Slavin et al., 2011). Explicit, systematic, intentional, comprehensive, and differentiated instruction is what determines the successful development of reading skills for EL2 learners (August & Shanahan, 2006).

Teaching Children to Learn Through Reading: Grades 4 to 6

Typically, starting from about Grade 4, there is a switch from learning to read to reading to learn, and **higher-level language** and cognitive skills—academic vocabulary, morphological awareness, syntactic awareness, metaphorical and figurative language, inference-making, and synthesizing—gain prevalence. A wide variety of factors need to be considered when teaching reading to EL2 learners beyond the primary grades. One important factor is whether they started EL2 reading instruction in the primary grades. The needs of upper elementary EL2 readers who have attended bilingual or immersion programs since kindergarten or Grade 1 are more similar to the needs of age-matched EL1 peers than are the needs of EL2 learners whose first introduction to English occurs in the upper elementary grades. The following activity will help you appreciate the difference.

Activity 3.2

Read the following social studies passage that a Grade 4 child, who has been attending a bilingual school since kindergarten, has been asked to read.

Reaching for the Sky: A History of Great Buildings

People have made buildings throughout human history. By studying the architecture of a society, you can better understand that society's values and beliefs. Every society has developed its own style of architecture. Many societies found ways to construct enormous buildings that were used for religious and social purposes.

Some of the most impressive early architects were the ancient Egyptians. They lived thousands of years ago in Egypt, a country in the northern part of Africa. The Egyptian pharaohs constructed huge buildings in the shape of pyramids to house their bodies after they died. Pharaohs ruled Egyptian society. They were like kings, but the Egyptians also believed that pharaohs had powers from the gods. The pharaohs thought that the pyramids would be their home after they died and filled them with furniture, gold jewelry and even pets. Now the ancient Egyptian society has vanished but the pyramids are still found in Egypt.

Today, pyramids all over Egypt stand as a reminder of the vanished ancient Egyptian culture. Over 130 pyramids have been discovered in Egypt. Egyptian pyramids have a square base with four triangular sides that rise up to a single point. Some of the pyramids are more than 4,500 years old. For thousands of years, the Egyptian pyramids were the tallest manmade structures in the world. The Great Pyramid of Giza is 480 feet above the ground. That's as tall as many of the skyscrapers in New York City. Historians believe that it took between 20,000 and 30,000 people to help build the Great Pyramid. The pyramid was built out of giant blocks of limestone, a type of rock found in Egypt. The rocks had to be brought from far away on boats on the Nile River.

One thousand years later, on the other side of the globe, the ancient Mayan civilization also decided to build pyramids. The Maya Empire was a vast empire that stretched from the area of what is now known as Mexico to Central America. They understood astronomy and had very complex calendars that they used to mark the date and time. The Mayan pyramids looked different from the pyramids built by the ancient Egyptians. Instead of rising to a point, they had flat tops. Along the sides were tiers of steps.

The Maya built two types of pyramids. One type was for their religious ceremonies. Priests would climb to the top of the pyramids to conduct important ceremonies where the entire city could see. The other pyramids the Maya built were sacred structures. These pyramids were built to honor the gods and were not supposed to be used by anyone. Humans weren't supposed to climb these pyramids, or even touch them. Though there were still steps that went up the sides of these pyramids, they were too steep to climb easily. The Maya also built tunnels and secret doors to trap people who might try to climb the sacred pyramids.

In medieval Europe, architects also wanted to build tall buildings for their religious ceremonies. In medieval times, religion was an important part of daily life, and churches were often a central gathering place for the community. Cathedrals were the biggest churches in Europe and often took hundreds of years to build. Most cathedrals were built in the shape of a cross, the symbol of the Christian religion.

Around the year 1100 A.D., Europeans began using a new design called the Gothic style in their building of churches. Gothic churches had pointed arches and many more windows than older churches. The people of the time thought that light was a symbol of God and wanted buildings that were full of windows and light.

Medieval architects had to find a way to build walls that were strong enough to support the heavy stone roof of the cathedrals but still had enough windows for light to enter the church. These architects invented flying buttresses to help the walls carry the heavy roof. Flying buttresses were a type of support beam shaped like a stone arch that started at the top of the walls and reached the ground. Because the buttresses were helping support some of the weight, the walls didn't have to be able to support as much. Now there could be many windows in the walls and the cathedrals could be filled with light.

One example of a Gothic church with flying buttresses is the Notre-Dame Cathedral in Paris. 'Notre-Dame' means 'our lady' in French and the cathedral was devoted to Mary, an important figure in the Catholic religion. Notre-Dame was built in 1160 A.D. It was the first building in northern Europe where the roof was more than one hundred feet high. Notre-Dame's windows were made with beautiful stained glass that looked like jewels when the light shone through. It took more than one hundred years to build the entire cathedral. That means the people who began building the cathedral were never able to see the finished building.

The cathedral became famous when the novelist Victor Hugo wrote a novel called *The Hunchback of Notre-Dame* about Quasimodo, a fictional cripple who was a bell-ringer in the cathedral. Years later Walt Disney made a cartoon movie based on the book and the church was brought to life in drawings.

(ReadWorks, 2013)

Keep in mind that this text is read by an EL2 fourth grader who has been attending bilingual school since kindergarten. Answer the following questions:

1 What language and reading skills are needed to successfully understand this passage?
2 What are the main reading challenges that the passage would pose for this EL2 child?
3 How would you, as an EL2 teacher, scaffold understanding for this EL2 student?

Now answer the same questions but this time thinking of an EL2 child who has just recently been introduced to English, for example, a child who immigrated to an English-speaking country at the beginning of Grade 4. Is there anything you would do differently to support reading comprehension for this student? Why?

The amount of English instruction that children have received prior to Grade 4 will greatly affect how successful they will be at understanding the passage in Activity 3.2. This passage would clearly be frustrating for fourth graders who have just started learning English. These novice EL2 learners will not have the well-developed English word recognition skills or the vocabulary knowledge to be able to make sense of the passage. Along with a rich oral-language teaching program, such learners will need to be provided with basic reading instruction. They will need instruction in phonics to learn how to decode words with regular spelling; in sight word reading for words with irregular spelling, as discussed in the previous section; and in cohesive markers, which we will discuss in Chapter 4. This passage would be more appropriate for an EL2 fourth grader who has been learning English on a regular and intensive basis from kindergarten, for example, in a bilingual or immersion program. In the following section, we will continue the discussion of the factors, issues, and skills involved in successful comprehension of upper elementary reading material, keeping in mind EL2 learners who have been learning English since kindergarten. The needs of EL2 learners who begin English instruction later will be considered in Chapter 4.

An important consideration in reading instruction is the selection of reading material that is interesting, age-appropriate, and at the learners' reading level. Commonly, reading level is classified into three major categories: independent, instructional, and frustration. Reading material that a reader can read fluently and with comprehension without someone else's help is material at the independent level. A text is considered to be at the independent level if a reader can read it with more than 90 percent accuracy and knows at least 95 percent of the words. This type of reading material is ideal for independent reading practice, such as homework. **Extensive reading** is critical for reading growth and for the development of vocabulary and general knowledge (Cunningham & Stanovich, 2003), so it is important that EL2 teachers provide abundant reading material that EL2 learners can read independently. At least ten to 15 minutes a day of independent reading has been recommended for EL1 readers (Fielding, Wilson, & Anderson, 1986). To our knowledge, there is no evidence-based recommendation of the optimal amount of independent reading for EL2 children. However, considering that EL2 learners have limited opportunities to expand their language proficiency outside of school because they do not hear English on a regular basis, we recommend that at least 20 to 30 minutes should be set aside each school day for independent reading in EL2 classes.

Material that a reader can read with 90 percent accuracy and with understanding but with help is considered to be at the instructional level. This type of reading material is ideal for classroom time because either the teacher or a more able peer can provide support. This **scaffolded reading** gives EL2 learners the opportunity to develop their reading skills. Guided reading (Fountas & Pinnell, 1996), a small-group reading activity that teachers use to scaffold students' reading, is an appropriate strategy for reading texts at the students' instructional level. During guided reading, the teacher works for about 20 minutes with a group of four or five students at a time. They are all reading the same book or passage, either silently or taking turns, while the rest of the class is engaged in other activities. The teacher provides support for sight word reading, decoding, and comprehension. Several modifications are required in guided reading to suit the needs of EL2 learners; for example, there is a need to incorporate more explicit vocabulary teaching before and during reading. EL2 teachers may also need to explain the meaning relationships embedded in different sentence structures and encoded in English syntax, such as the use of conjunctions to join two ideas—'a small but comfortable car'—or word order in embedded questions—'She asked me what she should do'. The reading material selected should give EL2 learners the opportunity to develop their understanding of English grammar—for example, subject–verb agreement, word order, tense, or subject-verb-object patterns—at an appropriate instructional level.

Finally, reading material with fewer than approximately 75 percent of words known to the reader is considered to be at the frustration level. Such material should be avoided because it could ultimately lead to lack of motivation to read. One way to address this issue is to use simplified reading material that is designed to be of interest to students of different ages. (See Chapter 4 for a discussion on **authentic** versus **graded**, or **modified**, **reading materials** for EL2 learners.) These materials, sometimes referred to as 'high-interest-low-vocabulary' books, are designed to enable poor readers to access interesting and age-appropriate content that uses simpler vocabulary. Currently, there are numerous commercial resources available, offering adaptations of fiction and non-fiction reading material for students with different reading ability levels. Adaptations typically involve reducing the difficulty of the text in terms of vocabulary, sentence structure, content density, and length, as well as providing abundant visual illustrations, captions, and marginal notes summarizing key points. The series *Ladders* from the National Geographic is one example of adapted reading materials. Other excellent examples are *Oxford Bookworms* and the new *Oxford Read and Discover* series from Oxford University Press. Many other similar resources can be found on the internet.

Teaching Vocabulary to Facilitate Reading Comprehension

Once mastery of basic reading skills has been attained, lack of vocabulary knowledge becomes the greatest obstacle to reading comprehension (Snow, Porche, Tabors, & Harris, 2007). Therefore, vocabulary teaching should also be an integral part of reading instruction in Grades 4 through 6. The vocabulary challenge for EL2 learners at times seems overwhelming, particularly when we consider that a proficient reader needs to know the meaning of most of the words in a passage to make sense of a written text when reading independently—without the help of a teacher. On the bright side, it has been observed that EL2 learners are more efficient vocabulary learners than their EL1 peers (Marinova-Todd, 2012). One reason for this is that EL2 learners with prior L1 schooling are simply attaching a new label to a concept they already have. Another reason is that EL2 learners are 'more practiced vocabulary learners' (Marinova-Todd, 2012, p. 124) because of their learning experiences in two languages. Classroom Snapshot 3.3 shows how an EL2 teacher offers rich academic vocabulary instruction to her students in the context of social studies.

Classroom Snapshot 3.3

Mrs Libeiro is a Grade 6 teacher in a Portuguese-English bilingual school in Brazil. For an English reading and vocabulary lesson, she selected the passage *Reaching for the Sky: A History of Great Buildings* (see the passage in Activity 3.2), to be used in a shared reading activity. Each student had a copy of the passage. Before the lesson, Mrs Libeiro read the passage and identified vocabulary she anticipated would be unfamiliar to her students. Some of the words she identified were 'beliefs', 'believed', 'purposes', 'ancient', 'northern', 'ruled', 'furniture', 'vanished', 'cathedral', 'civilization', 'tiers', 'religious', 'ceremonies', 'churches', 'gathering', 'flying buttresses', and 'beam'. Of these words, she selected the following as target words for explicit instruction: 'ancient', 'vanished', 'cathedral', 'civilization', 'beliefs', 'ceremonies', and 'northern'.

These are the steps she followed in her lesson:

1 First, she showed pictures of great historic buildings, such as the Egyptian pyramids, the Mayan pyramids, and Notre-Dame cathedral, asking the students to share with each other anything they knew about these buildings.
2 She briefly discussed the words selected for direct instruction by using child-friendly definitions. When appropriate, she also drew students' attention to English–Portuguese cognates—'ceremonies'/'cerimônias'—or to the structural elements within morphologically complex words—'northern' = *north* + *ern*.
3 Then she read the text aloud and had the students follow along silently.
4 Next, she asked students to underline new words they were learning in this passage and to discuss their possible meaning with a peer.
5 She asked students to volunteer the new words they were adding to their vocabulary. She wrote them on the board, directing all students' attention to where they were found in the passage, and expanded on students' understanding of the word by providing further examples and asking follow-up questions.
6 Finally, Mrs Libeiro asked students several comprehension questions, such as: What did Egyptians and Mayans use the pyramids for? What are the similarities in the ways Egyptians and Mayans used the pyramids? How is a cathedral similar to a pyramid? What are the architectural differences between pyramids and cathedrals? What did these three types of historic buildings represent for the communities that used them? ▪

Among the many words that could be unfamiliar to her students, Mrs Libeiro selected for direct instruction only key words that were important to understanding the text. To determine this, she paid attention to words that appeared repeatedly throughout the text. She also asked herself which words would be useful for the students in other content areas—social studies, science, math, Language Arts, etc.—and that students would find difficult to learn on their own. Although the list of words she predicted to be challenging for her students was quite long, she selected only seven of them for explicit instruction because, according to research findings, this is about the right number of words to target for explicit instruction in a given lesson (Baker et al., 2014). Words such as 'flying buttresses' and 'beam', although unfamiliar to the students, were not included because they were not part of the central ideas in the text, and their meaning could be demonstrated by showing pictures. Other words were not selected for direct instruction because they were adequately defined in the text through context or visuals, for example, 'churches'. Rather than teaching these words directly before reading, Mrs Libeiro made the wise decision to expand on these words after reading. She had already taught students the meaning of the suffix *–ous*, so her students already knew that it means 'the property or quality of' and that it is a suffix that attaches to nouns and converts them into adjectives. Because Mrs Libeiro's students knew the root word 'religion' and had already been taught word analysis strategies, they were able to apply morphological analyses to the word 'religious' and successfully deduce its meaning. Showing students visuals prior to the lesson and asking questions about them provided an opportunity for background knowledge to be activated and, at the same time, for some of the words to be discussed.

In sum, Mrs Libeiro's selection of words for direct instruction was based on evidence-based criteria identified in research synthesis (for example, August and Shanahan, 2006; Baker et al., 2014). Thus, she chose words that would be:

- frequently encountered in other texts and content areas
- critical to understanding the main ideas
- too hard for students to learn independently through the use of context and illustrations—for example, abstract terms such as 'beliefs'
- morphologically complex, i.e. with prefixes or suffixes

Interactive post-reading activities have also been found to be valuable in supporting vocabulary development. For example, in a study of sixth graders in Turkey learning EL2, Atay and Kurt (2006) examined the effectiveness of post-reading activities to enhance students' vocabulary knowledge.

Two classes with comparable English language proficiency were randomly assigned to either an experimental or a comparison condition. All students had been studying English since Grade 4—for two hours per week in Grades 4 and 5, and for four hours per week in Grade 6. At the time of the study, the students were completing the second half of Grade 6. Students in the comparison group continued with their regular instruction. This consisted of reading a text and completing vocabulary tasks individually, for example, copying the definition of new words into their notebooks and transcribing the sentence from the dialogue that contained the word. Students in the experimental group, on the other hand, worked in small groups, completing jigsaw post-reading activities. In these activities, students read paragraphs to each other, studied key words from each paragraph, organized the paragraphs in the correct order, and provided oral summaries of the complete paragraph, always making an effort to include the key words learned. The results were clear. Children who participated in the interactive post-reading vocabulary activities performed significantly better than the students who continued their regular instruction. The researchers concluded that using interactive tasks, such as the jigsaw activity, after reading a passage enhanced EL2 vocabulary learning.

EL2 Reading Across the Content Areas

In addition to reading for pleasure, learners beyond the primary grades use reading as one of the main vehicles for learning new knowledge across the content areas, such as science, social studies, and math. As discussed in Chapter 2, this shift in reading purpose brings new challenges for reading comprehension. In this section, we will review classroom research on ways to help upper elementary learners overcome these challenges.

Graphic organizers are effective in helping readers develop text structure awareness by visually representing the structure of academic material and processing content-area readings (Blachowicz & Ogle, 2001). They can be used before, during, and after reading. Although research on the impact of using graphic organizers to aid comprehension has been conducted primarily with EL1 learners, the teaching and learning implications are also relevant for EL2 situations. The pedagogical value of graphic organizers is that they help readers identify and represent the way key ideas and the supporting details are organized in a text, connect them to their background knowledge, and visualize how ideas and concepts are connected throughout the text. Dymock and Nicholson (2007) identified six text structures that elementary students encounter regularly: three descriptive structures—

list, web, and matrix—and three sequential structures—string, cause-and-effect, and problem–solution. Each of these structures can be matched with a graphic organizer to facilitate the identification of how the ideas in each type of text are organized. Witherell and McMackin (2009) provide excellent examples of these graphic organizers and lesson plans using them to scaffold reading for learners with different levels of ability.

In a study by Griffin, Case, and Siegler (1995), Grade 5 EL1 students improved their reading comprehension after receiving explicit instruction in the use of graphic organizers over ten days in daily 45-minute sessions. The researchers created 11 different graphic organizers to help learners understand social studies readings. The graphic organizers helped students differentiate between main ideas and related supporting details. The students were gradually coached in how to create the graphic organizers until they were able to construct them on their own. One of the most powerful results from this study is that students were able to apply the strategies learned during the graphic organizer intervention to the reading of new material. After the intervention, the students in the study and a comparison group from another Grade 5 class, who had not been coached in the use of graphic organizers, were asked to read a new passage from social studies content. The ability to recall the passage was significantly better among the students who learned how to use graphic organizers to comprehend text than among those who received traditional instruction.

As discussed in Chapter 2, good knowledge of academic vocabulary is critical for comprehension of reading material across the content areas. To substantially increase the academic vocabulary of elementary and middle school EL2 students, academic vocabulary should be taught intensively across several days, using a variety of instructional activities and integrating oral and written English language instruction into content-area teaching (Baker et al., 2014).

A number of studies have demonstrated the importance of teaching a set of academic vocabulary intensively, systematically, and through a variety of strategies. For example, August, Branum-Martin, Cardenas-Hagan, and Francis (2009) examined the effectiveness of teaching science vocabulary to EL2 students in Grade 6. Ten sixth grade science teachers were trained in how to teach academic vocabulary for science in a systematic, explicit, and intentional way. For each teacher, two lessons were randomly assigned to be taught following structured, high-quality teaching of English and science, and two lessons to be taught following the district curriculum guidelines, which did not include specific guidelines for explicit and systematic vocabulary instruction. The sixth graders' science and vocabulary knowledge were assessed before and after the implementation of the project. The results showed that students learned significantly more science concepts and science vocabulary in the lessons that were carefully planned to teach science vocabulary explicitly throughout the lesson. Academic vocabulary plays an increasingly important role in reading comprehension as children progress through the school grades. It is for this reason that we will continue the discussion about effective instruction in academic vocabulary for adolescent EL2 learners in Chapter 4.

Effective Assessment of L2 Reading Comprehension in Grades 4 to 6

Unless a learning disability is present, children have already mastered basic reading skills and fluency by Grade 4. Therefore, beyond Grade 3, reading assessment focuses on comprehension skills. Teachers seek to determine whether students are able to:

- identify main ideas and establish associations between them
- differentiate between main ideas and supporting details
- synthesize a passage
- identify and understand both explicit and implicit information
- make inferences
- establish meaningful connections with the reading material.

Under normal conditions, children who develop strong basic reading skills are also good comprehenders. However, there are learners who, despite being good decoders and fluent word readers, are poor comprehenders. These learners have recently been referred to as 'unexpected' poor comprehenders. The characteristics of these learners and their instructional needs are examined and discussed in Chapter 4.

Using Technology to Enhance the Development of Basic Reading Skills and Reading Comprehension

While researchers, educators, parents, and policy makers debate the place of digital technology in the classroom, students are already integrating it into their daily lives for social and academic purposes. Mobile technology, in particular, is making an aggressive entrance into the classroom, and whether or not teachers intentionally incorporate technology into lessons, learners use it regularly for academic and non-academic purposes.

There are thousands of websites, applications, and online resources that can be used to enhance the teaching of EL2 reading. The challenge is to identify the digital resources that offer the most pedagogical value. In this section, we review research that informs us about effective digital resources and introduce some of those whose effectiveness has been supported directly or indirectly by research. First, we will focus on research and digital resources that can be used to facilitate initial reading development of EL1 or EL2 for young children in Grades K–3. We will then examine research and digital resources that facilitate and promote EL2 reading development in upper elementary and middle school, Grades 4–6.

Activity 3.3

Review three to four technological resources or tools, for example, software, websites, or apps, that could be used to enrich L2 reading development or to help learners experiencing reading difficulties. As you review them, complete the chart below.

Name of Resource/ Tool	Target Skills (e.g., decoding, fluency, vocabulary, comprehension)	Features That Scaffold Learning	Level/Age	For Enrichment or for LD Learners?

Photocopiable © Oxford University Press

The objective of this activity is to help you to reflect on how various features of technology can be used for different learning needs. See Figure 4.2 on page 132 for examples of appropriate technology tools that can be used to support the development of different aspects of reading.

Websites with interactive activities and reading-related skill-building games, voice recognition software, audiobooks or audio assistance for online reading, online dictionaries with audio, educational TV programs, and graphic-organizing software are all good examples of the wide range of technological tools available to assist L1 and L2 reading development. Some of these tools address lower-level reading skills and others target higher-order skills. Most are beneficial to all learners, but others are specifically developed to assist students with an LD. Their effectiveness, however, depends on strong instructional support. *Between the Lions*, a learn-to-read series offered through Public Broadcasting, is one technological resource available to support early reading development. Linebarger, Kosanic, Greenwood, and Doku (2004) examined the effects of viewing this television series on the literacy and vocabulary development of kindergartners and first graders who viewed episodes at school. The researchers found that after viewing 17 episodes, the children in the study had better phonemic awareness, word recognition, and overall reading skills than children of the same age who did not view the episodes. However, the impact on vocabulary learning was not statistically significant. Uchikoshi (2006) obtained similar results in a study with EL2 kindergartners. Neither program included scaffolding for learning—that is, the children were merely exposed to the TV series, but there were no lessons planned around them. The researchers concluded that lack of instructional support may have been the main reason that children's vocabulary did not benefit from viewing the series.

The digital resources we have described so far are designed to promote basic reading skills. We turn now to research on digital resources that promote the development of higher-order reading-related skills, such as vocabulary. Silverman and Hines (2009) conducted a study of EL1 and EL2 children in pre-kindergarten through second grade. They compared the effects of two types of academic vocabulary instruction through read-alouds. In the first condition, the read-aloud was multimedia-enhanced, that is, the content was presented through a combination of visuals and sounds, for example, through video clips. In the second condition, there was no multimedia support for either vocabulary or the general content of the story. In both teaching conditions, 'teachers implemented a scripted intervention lesson, 45 minutes per day, for three days a week over the course of 12 weeks' (Silverman & Hines, 2009, p. 307). In both groups, the read-alouds included the same narrative and expository passages on animal habitats such as rainforests, savannahs, coral reefs, and deserts, taught in four three-week cycles. The topics were introduced in the same order in both conditions, and the same words were selected for direct instruction: eight words per book, plus four core thematic words—'discover', 'habitat', 'community', and 'explore'—that were essential for the habitat theme. The only difference between the groups was that multimedia enhancement was used in one condition only. In this condition, five-minute segments of four videos, each illustrating one of the four habitats of the unit, were presented to the students after several readings of the book on that topic to reinforce concept understanding and vocabulary learning. The results showed that the use of the videos did not make any difference for EL1 children, but that it enhanced learning for EL2 children. Silverman and Hines concluded that the use of multimedia, such as videos, within well-scaffolded lessons supports the development of EL2 children's vocabulary and content knowledge in general.

In a study by Dalton, Proctor, Uccelli, Mo, and Snow (2011), Spanish-English bilingual students and English monolinguals in Grade 5 read eight multimedia folktales and informational texts online. These provided scaffolding both for vocabulary learning and for reading comprehension strategies before and during reading. The online platform contained embedded audio that read stories aloud, translation tools, and other features, such as:

> pedagogical agents that function as coaches, providing models, think-alouds, and hints, including a Spanish-English bilingual coach; an electronic work log that collected student responses and was revisable; a multimedia glossary; anaphoric reference highlighting; and graphics illustrating the narrative and informational text content.
>
> (Dalton et al., 2011, p. 78)

The researchers examined how reading comprehension strategies and **interactive vocabulary** improved reading comprehension online. Classrooms were assigned to one of three conditions: reading comprehension strategies, vocabulary, or a combined version of comprehension strategies and vocabulary. Students in the three conditions read the same digital texts, but the embedded supports differed across conditions:

1 **Comprehension strategy**: Students were prompted to apply a particular reading strategy [predict, question, clarify, summarize, visualize, etc.] at the end of each 'screen' of digital text, typing or audio-recording their response to an electronic work log.

2 **Vocabulary**: Students completed prereading and within-reading vocabulary activities designed to promote depth and breadth of word knowledge relative to 40 'power words' (five per text). They also added words to their personal digital glossaries and listened to language alerts to heighten awareness of words and strategies for using first-language knowledge, such as Spanish–English cognates.

3 **Combination**: Features from (1) and (2) above were combined into what [the researchers] hypothesized would be an optimal learning environment.

(Dalton et al., 2011, p. 76)

Results indicated that all students benefited from the support provided by the scaffolded digital text, but students in the vocabulary and combination conditions outperformed the students in the comprehension strategy condition. Of particular interest is the observation that for the EL2 children in the comprehension strategy condition, vocabulary, which was not explicitly taught in this condition, did not improve. This suggests that teaching comprehension strategies alone is not sufficient to advance the reading comprehension of either EL1 or EL2 children; explicit teaching of vocabulary must be an integral part of any teaching—online or offline—aimed at accelerating EL2 vocabulary and reading comprehension.

The effective use of digital technology to teach reading has also been reported in EL2 education environments where English is not the societal language, as illustrated by Spotlight Study 3.4.

Spotlight Study 3.4

For 10 weeks, Lan, Sung, and Chang (2009) followed 52 fourth graders at an elementary school in Taipei, Taiwan, using technology in small collaborative groups. Students were assigned to one of three reading ability groups—high, medium, and at-risk—based on their performance on the Oral Reading Fluency and Retell Fluency subtest of the Dynamic Indicators of Basic Early Literacy Skills 6th edition (DIBELS) (Good & Kaminski, 2002). EL2 teachers were given five teaching packages, each of which contained two activities to be completed during two scheduled 40-minute sessions over two weeks. Three video cameras were used in each class to record all the activities: two cameras were dedicated to recording small-group work and one to capturing the dynamic of the whole class. Students were first instructed on basic reading skills, such as sight and phonetic word reading, and practiced reading sets of words aloud. They were asked to teach subsets of words to each other, and were then randomly chosen to represent their group in an oral reading contest, which consisted of reading aloud 16 words (sight words or phonetic words). Following this, students each received a paragraph containing many of the words learned, practiced reading the paragraph aloud to each other, and collaborated in putting the paragraphs in the right order to complete a story. Once these tasks were completed, the students read the whole story and answered comprehension questions. They also assessed each other's reading performance on the assigned paragraphs. Students in the technology condition completed these reading activities using a tablet and a headset. A computer software called CAREER was used for the activities. Students worked together in the collaborative activities by logging into the CAREER system and contributing to the completion activities assigned to their group through interacting and sharing. For individual activities, the readings were tailored to the different reading needs of the EL2 students. Students in the comparison group used the same reading materials and completed the same activities, except that everything was done with paper and pencil.

At the end of the intervention, all students were assessed again on oral reading fluency and retell fluency. Lan et al. (2009) found that children using the mobile technology made greater improvements in their reading comprehension than students using paper and pencil only. Moreover, the technology was beneficial for children across the three different ability levels. All groups, however, had difficulty retelling the whole story in English. Information gathered through the videos showed that the use of digital technology was particularly beneficial for the collaborative work. ▪

The studies reviewed in this section suggest that digital technology—including videos, interactive websites, computer software, and digital devices like tablets—can enhance different aspects of EL2 reading development in young learners. In Chapter 4, we will discuss how digital technology can be effectively used to assist EL2 children and adolescents experiencing learning difficulties.

Summary

Once children master basic reading skills, reading becomes one of the main vehicles for learning new vocabulary and academic content, and for expanding background knowledge in general. To capitalize on the power of reading, however, EL2 reading needs to be well taught. There is need for intentional, explicit, and systematic instruction of basic skills, vocabulary, text structure, and comprehension strategies. In bilingual learning contexts, children benefit from reading instruction in both L1 and L2, as the skills developed in one language support the development of reading in the other. Early and ongoing reading assessment should always be an integral aspect of EL2 reading instruction. Learning disabilities can be seen in both languages of bilingual children and should be identified as early as possible because remediation that is put in place early is more effective. Technology can be used to support normal L2 reading development and assist children with learning disabilities related to language and literacy.

4

Reading Skills Beyond Grade 6: Research and Implications for Pedagogy

Preview

In Chapter 3, we discussed the importance of developing strong word-level reading skills and highlighted the finding that while lower-level word reading skills are important, they are not sufficient to achieve deep comprehension. Once these basic skills have been developed, higher-order reading skills take a central role. In this chapter, we center the discussion on these higher-order skills.

Congruent with Chall's (1996) stages of literacy development and the demands of reading to learn across the curriculum, this chapter focuses on how EL2 readers can tackle unfamiliar academic vocabulary, consolidate reading fluency, develop their ability to notice multiple viewpoints, analyze texts critically, make inferences while reading, and construct deep understanding based on analysis and synthesis. In secondary school, EL2 teachers have the responsibility of preparing their pupils for post-secondary levels of schooling and for the workplace in today's information economy. Therefore, we will expand on the discussion begun in Chapter 3 about how to enhance reading comprehension of non-fiction academic texts. We will discuss classroom research that illustrates effective ways to help EL2 adolescent readers develop academic vocabulary, an understanding of cohesion markers that link ideas in a passage, and cognitive, metacognitive, and metalinguistic awareness. We will also examine instructional considerations in the use of authentic texts versus modified reading material, and the challenges of literary language such as the interpretation of poetic and idiomatic expressions commonly used in secondary schools.

An important feature of this chapter is the discussion of effective EL2 reading instruction for adolescents with interrupted schooling or for those without literacy skills in their L1—for example, refugees—as well as for those who have had schooling in their L1. To illustrate the challenges of EL2 reading in the upper school years, we provide illustrations from research in a range of EL2 learning contexts.

This chapter closes with three interrelated topics: considerations for the assessment of reading comprehension in EL2 adolescents; considerations for the assessment of reading difficulties in EL2 adolescents; and the use of **assistive technology (AT)** to facilitate reading for adolescents who struggle with it.

Language Comprehension Demands in Secondary School Reading Materials

As discussed in Chapter 2, language comprehension takes center stage in reading comprehension in high school (Catts et al., 2006). In secondary school, the demands of reading comprehension increase significantly, along with the complexity of written materials, which use more complex grammar and syntax, more sophisticated and discipline-specific vocabulary, and increasing amounts of metaphorical and figurative language—'the pearls in your mouth when you smile', 'the labyrinths in your heart', etc. These materials are extensive and content-dense, require higher levels of abstraction, involve multiple viewpoints, and widen the spectrum of text genres. Secondary school readers are expected to be able to 'read between the lines', identifying ideas that are implicit in the passages they read and drawing inferences. For these reasons, an emphasis on effective reading instruction in high school also includes a focus on language components such as cohesive devices that convey meaning. Classroom Snapshot 4.1 provides an example of a task typical of a secondary school science curriculum. Connecting ideas presented in the passage and successfully completing the task requires effective interpretation of cohesive devices, such as pronouns, and the activation of prior knowledge.

Classroom Snapshot 4.1

A group of seventh graders are studying the particle theory of matter in their science class. Today, they have been asked to complete the following worksheet:

Bars of Gold?
A chest is located at the bottom of the Gulf of Mexico and some metal bars are found inside. It is believed that ships that travelled in the area carried gold bars and jewels. Often captains of the ships would substitute fake bars in the chests so that if the ships were boarded by pirates, the real gold would not be stolen as it would be hidden elsewhere on the ships.

A lab heats up the bars to 955°C before they begin to melt. The scientist working in the lab consults the chart below to determine whether the bars are gold.

Substance	Melting Point (°C)	Boiling Point (°C)
Gold	1063°	2600°

Are the bars gold? How do you know?

(Grade 7: Cluster 2: Particle Theory of Matter, Manitoba Education and Advanced Learning) ▄

To understand the ideas and concepts that are presented throughout a text, readers need to establish both local and global coherence (Geva, 1992; Cain, 2009). Local coherence markers establish relations of meaning between successive clauses. In the passage presented in Classroom Snapshot 4.1, the pronoun 'it' in the second sentence of the text refers to the clause that follows: 'ships that travelled in the area carried gold bars and jewels'. Toward the end of the first paragraph, the pronoun 'it' is used again, but this time to refer to information provided earlier, namely, 'the real gold'. For the seventh graders presented with the task in Classroom Snapshot 4.1, the final and most critical task is to determine whether the metal bars found in the chest are real gold. To infer the answer, the readers need to integrate the information provided in the second paragraph with the information provided in the chart.

Successful completion of the reading task depicted in Classroom Snapshot 4.1 demands that the reader makes inferences by establishing connections between pieces of information presented in the text; in other words, it only involves establishing local coherence. However, to understand the passage at a deeper level, a reader would need to establish global coherence—notice text elements that make the text hang together as a whole, go beyond the information presented explicitly in the passage, and integrate the information presented in the text with prior knowledge. For example, the passage does not explain why a chest was found at the bottom of the Gulf of Mexico, but by drawing on prior knowledge, the learner would infer that a ship sank there.

Classroom Snapshot 4.1 above and Spotlight Study 4.1 on page 101 underscore the importance of engaging in reading instruction for EL2 learners in secondary school across content areas such as math, science, and social studies (August & Shanahan, 2006). This should include direct, explicit, and systematic instruction of vocabulary across all content areas and of reading comprehension strategies.

Academic Vocabulary in Secondary School Reading

As discussed in the preceding chapters, rich vocabulary knowledge is critical for understanding written material. While it is true that EL2 readers can infer the meaning of new words if the text is not too difficult, there is strong evidence that explicit instruction of vocabulary is also crucial. This is because the demands on academic vocabulary knowledge increase substantially in secondary school. The academic vocabulary encountered in secondary school reading material is increasingly less familiar and more abstract (Scarcella, 2003). Therefore, secondary school readers need to become familiar with a large number of words—vocabulary breadth—and develop deep knowledge of their multiple layers of meanings—vocabulary depth. EL2 learners lack both breadth and depth of vocabulary (Baker et al., 2014; Lin, Ramírez, Shade Wilson, & Geva, 2012). Lin et al. (2012) conducted a study that focused on the development of language and reading skills in high school students, many of whom were EL2 learners living in a highly vulnerable urban neighborhood. Results indicated that many of these EL2 adolescents had English vocabulary knowledge similar to that of EL1 children in Grades 2 and 3. Importantly, they were not familiar with most of the academic vocabulary found in reading material in various school subjects. Given the crucial role that vocabulary plays in reading comprehension, it is not surprising that these EL2 adolescents struggled to understand many of the texts they were asked to read.

Vaughn et al. (2009) demonstrated the effectiveness of teaching academic vocabulary to EL2 seventh graders in a meaningful context. In this intervention study, academic vocabulary was taught explicitly, systematically, and comprehensively through social studies lessons. During the 12-week treatment, students worked collaboratively with peers to discuss the use of target vocabulary, watched videos to expand on concepts and to promote discussion, and used graphic organizers. Teachers followed a daily instructional routine that included:

- a brief overview of the 'big idea'
- explicit vocabulary instruction that integrated paired students' discussion of the [target] word
- discussion built around a short video clip (2–4 min) that complemented the day's reading
- a teacher-led or paired student reading assignment followed by generating and answering questions

- a wrap-up activity in the form of a graphic organizer or other writing exercise.

(Vaughn et al., 2009, p. 306)

In the vocabulary component of the lessons, teachers taught four topic-related words lifted from the readings, the video clips, and the teachers' repertoire. Teachers provided student-friendly definitions, cognates in the students' language when relevant, visual representations, and two sentences for each new word. One sentence used the word in the context of social studies and another used it in a context relevant to the students' experience. Students in the comparison classes received 'business as usual' teaching. After 12 weeks' implementation of this program, students in the treatment classes—including the EL2 students in those classes—performed significantly better than students in the comparison classes on curriculum-based vocabulary and on comprehension measures.

Explicit vocabulary instruction can improve oral language skills, listening and reading comprehension, and writing (Baker et al., 2014). It is important to remember that EL2s continue to develop oral language and vocabulary skills while building core literacy skills (Kieffer & Lesaux, 2012; Lovett et al., 2008). Effective vocabulary instruction involves multiple exposures to new words in a variety of contexts (Proctor et al., 2011), as well as opportunities for students to use the words orally, and in reading and writing (Baker et al., 2014). Spotlight Study 4.1 provides another example of how adolescent learners, many of whom were EL2s, benefited from explicit, systematic, and comprehensive vocabulary instruction.

Spotlight Study 4.1

Lawrence, Capotosto, Branum-Martin, White, and Snow (2011) examined the impact of a comprehensive academic vocabulary intervention program on the learning and long-term retention of academic vocabulary by EL2 learners in Grades 6 to 8. Students were taught five academic words per week over 24 weeks. The types of words selected were those identified by Beck, McKeown, and Kucan (2013) as Tier Two words, that is, words that appear in a variety of content areas and are moderately uncommon. Examples of the words used during the intervention program are 'perspective', 'amend', 'attribute', 'assume', and 'relevant'. Every Monday, students read a passage on a controversial topic—such as pet rental, stem cell research, or multi-million-dollar salaries for athletes—that contained the five target words for the week. They then read the definition of each target word and answered comprehension questions. On Tuesdays and Wednesdays, students participated in 15-minute lessons expanding on the controversial topic of the week through engaging tasks in social studies, science, math, or English. Activities included a debate in social studies, a problem in math, and a cloze reading in science. These lessons offered students opportunities to experience using the target words in a variety of contexts. The week-long word work culminated in a writing assignment, in which students wrote a persuasive essay taking a specific position on the controversial issue that had been used to engage the students in academic vocabulary learning throughout the week.

One of the main findings was that the increase in academic vocabulary knowledge was significantly larger for students in the intervention group than for the comparison group of peers who did not take part in the intervention. Moreover, students retained the vocabulary knowledge for at least one year after the intervention. The researchers also compared the gains of learners from three different language profiles: students from English-speaking homes, proficient English speakers from language-minority homes, and students with limited English proficiency. These comparisons revealed that English-proficient students from language-minority homes made larger gains than students from English-speaking homes and students with limited English proficiency. ■

This study demonstrates the importance of explicitly teaching academic vocabulary. However, it is important to note that the EL2 learners with limited English proficiency did not improve their academic vocabulary as much as EL2 learners with high English proficiency. This is a reminder that explicitly teaching a particular set of academic vocabulary in the classroom may not have the same effect with all EL2 learners; it may depend on the learners' level of English proficiency and the kind of academic vocabulary selected for instruction. It is possible that 15 minutes per day is not sufficient to make a significant impact on the vocabulary learning of EL2 learners with limited English proficiency. It appears that to close the gap between these learners, the intensity of academic vocabulary instruction needs to be increased for students with low proficiency levels. In addition, as shown in the Lin et al. (2012) study, when EL2 learners are not familiar with academic vocabulary that is typically learned in the lower grades, it may be hard for them to learn the more advanced academic vocabulary required in later grades. This means that with less proficient EL2 learners, it may be important to take time also to target academic vocabulary that EL1 learners typically learn in earlier grades. For example, an explanation of the meaning of the word 'perspective' could be 'an opinion on a topic that may be different from the opinion of another person'. Knowledge of the word 'opinion' would be critical to understanding this explanation. Most EL1 adolescents would be familiar with the word 'opinion', but this is not necessarily the case for EL2 adolescents.

Lawrence et al. (2011) offer some suggestions on how best to meet the needs of secondary school students with limited English proficiency:

- Provide complementary reading material at students' reading level so that they have additional exposure to the words outside of school.
- Adapt the reading material used in lessons to the reading levels of students with limited English proficiency.
- Provide individual support on phonological, grammatical, and pragmatic features of the target words and language structures used in the reading materials.

To these important recommendations, we would add:

- Remember that one size does not fit all; take the time to introduce less proficient EL2 learners to simpler academic vocabulary found in the reading materials that may already be known to the more proficient EL2 learners.

Key features of effective academic vocabulary intervention for EL2 adolescents are the comprehensiveness, systematicity, consistency, and cohesiveness of the approach across the curriculum. Students need abundant opportunities to learn and use the words through different modalities, such as reading, speaking, and writing, and across a variety of subjects. This requires cooperation between content-area teachers so that their lessons can be adapted to intentionally incorporate target words throughout the week (August & Shanahan, 2006).

Cohesion Markers

Adolescent EL2 readers benefit from instruction that facilitates the development of language awareness at the word, sentence, and connected discourse levels. One aspect of language awareness is understanding the function of language devices such as conjunctions, pronouns, and suffixes, which help to create cohesion in texts and facilitate reading comprehension. The ability to understand and attend to cohesion markers develops gradually over the school years (Geva, 2007) and is critical for understanding complex written materials. In this chapter, we focus on lexical familiarity with conjunctions. We highlight the importance of developing a deep understanding of how conjunctions signal meaning across clauses, sentences, and text segments, and how this understanding is mirrored in reading comprehension.

Conjunctions like 'because' and 'although' are important linguistic devices that facilitate reading comprehension by making explicit the logical relationships between ideas in a text (Halliday & Hasan, 1976; Geva, 2007). We begin this section by noting that while conjunctions such as 'but', 'because', 'so', and 'although' may appear quite early in children's language, it in fact takes time to develop a deep understanding of how these words can be used to indicate the relations between ideas.

Consider, for example, the frequently used conjunctions 'but' and 'although'. Both are used to express the idea that something is different from what has been stated. This is why they are referred to as **adversative conjunctions**. Examples 1(a) and 2(a) below demonstrate how we can use either 'but' or 'although' to connect the clauses 'Sam studied hard' and 'he failed the exam'. However, this does not mean that 'but' and 'although' are interchangeable or that they mean exactly the same thing.

1 (a) Sam studied hard, *but* he failed the exam.
1 (b) So he decided to drop the course.
2 (a) Sam failed the exam, *although* he studied hard.
2 (b) So he decided to drop the course.
2 (c) He barely slept the whole week.

These two conjunctions are different because 'but' is a **coordinating conjunction**. This means that the order of mention of the two events ('Sam studied hard' and 'Sam failed the test') fits the order in which the events occurred. From a cohesion perspective, highly fluent EL2 learners will therefore expect the next sentence to elaborate on what was stated last— namely, that he failed the exam. For example, a reasonable continuation to the first sentence may be 1(b), which elaborates on the outcome of having failed the course.

'Although' is a **subordinating conjunction**; in other words, it states the relationship between the dependent or subordinate clause and the rest of the sentence. The clause that follows the conjunction 'although' always signals the **subordinate clause**, whether it appears at the beginning of the sentence or later on. In Example 2(a), the main clause—'Sam failed the exam'—is stated first, and the subordinate, or dependent, clause—'he studied hard'— is stated second, even though the event, studying hard, actually occurred prior to failing the exam. This takes us to another, often unstated, cohesion rule that readers gradually acquire: that to maintain cohesion among ideas, one is expected to elaborate on the main clause, even if the main clause actually occurs before the subordinate clause. Thus, 2(c) is a reasonable continuation of 2(a) because it elaborates on the main clause.

Poor comprehenders have problems with conjunctions (Ge & Xuehong, 2002; McColgan & Cormack, 2008). To illustrate, Geva and Ryan (1985) explored the relationships between reading comprehension and the knowledge and use of conjunctions by EL1 students in Grades 5 and 7. The students were divided into two groups according to whether they had been classified as poor or good comprehenders. In one condition, the children read passages in which the conjunctions had been printed in boldface. This was intended to direct explicit attention to the conjunctions and their text-connecting function. In the other, implicit, condition, the children read texts from which conjunctions had been omitted. Both groups were able to establish more meaningful connections between sentences and comprehend texts better in the explicit condition. Meanwhile, in the implicit condition, the poor readers had more serious difficulties in comprehending the text and making inferences. In other words, unlike the good comprehenders, the poor comprehenders were unable to infer the logical relationships between ideas when these were not explicitly indicated in the texts.

Just like younger EL1 readers, EL2 learners struggle to make sense of ideas that have been connected using conjunctions in a passage. It is easier to infer the logical relationships of ideas in narratives than in expository texts (Geva, 2007). This may be because the information in narratives is typically less dense than in expository texts. With narratives, readers may also have more relevant prior knowledge to help them to infer meaning. Conjunctions are a special kind of vocabulary related to L2 proficiency and reading comprehension in EL2 (Crosson & Lesaux, 2013a).

With increased oral proficiency, EL2 learners become more familiar with the meaning of various conjunctions. For example, they become acquainted with the meaning of a variety of additive conjunctions ('in addition', 'as well as', 'furthermore', 'moreover'); adversative conjunctions ('although', 'in spite of', 'nevertheless', 'albeit'); and causal conjunctions ('consequently', 'as a result of', 'therefore'). They also increase their repertoire of conjunctions that express temporal relations ('since', 'whenever', 'by the time') and conditions ('provided that', 'assuming that', 'unless'). With this increased L2 proficiency, learners are better able to pay attention to these connecting words, understand the logical relations expressed by them, and allocate mental resources to synthesizing and integrating larger text segments.

Familiarity with conjunctions supports the reading comprehension ability of EL2 school children with poor reading comprehension and poor background knowledge (Crosson & Lesaux, 2013a). To help EL2 learners with reading comprehension, it is important to explicitly teach the meaning of conjunctions and their functions in signaling logical relationships between clauses or sentences. It is also helpful to foster the habit of systematically paying attention to conjunctions in order to understand the meaning nuances they carry (Crosson & Lesaux, 2013b). However, direct teaching of conjunctions needs to take place in meaningful and engaging contexts, and should be embedded in a comprehensive vocabulary program (Crosson & Lesaux, 2013b). The following activity demonstrates ways in which conjunctions affect the meaning relationship between two propositions.

Activity 4.1

1 Read the following statements and underline the conjunction in each.
   - Global temperatures continued to increase, even though Congress passed a bill to reduce carbon emissions.
   - Global temperatures continued to increase until Congress passed a bill to reduce carbon emissions.
   - Global temperatures continued to increase, even as Congress passed a bill to reduce carbon emissions.
   - Global temperatures continued to increase; however, Congress passed a bill to reduce carbon emissions.

(Crosson & Lesaux, 2013b, p. 195)

2 Explain how the conjunction in each statement changes the meaning.
3 For each statement, write a follow-up sentence that fits the argument.

In each of these examples, the first clause ('global temperatures continued to increase') and the second clause ('Congress passed a bill to reduce carbon emissions') are the same. Yet the specific conjunction that connects the two clauses changes the meaning of the whole statement. The reason for such a change is that each conjunction indicates a different relationship between the two clauses. In the first statement, the conjunction 'even though' is adversative or contrastive. 'Even though' tells us that what will follow is, in some way, a contradiction of the first clause. The first statement tells us that the legislation intended to stop global warming but that it was not successful. The third example emphasizes the temporal relationships between the two events. It tells the reader that the two events—passing a bill to reduce carbon emissions and global temperatures continuing to increase—occurred at the same time. When students are unaware of the need to attend to conjunctions, they may not appreciate the fact that these sentences have different meanings and that this change in meaning is signaled by the specific conjunction used. As a result, they may misunderstand the message conveyed in the text (Crosson & Lesaux, 2013b).

The following are useful guidelines for the effective instruction of conjunctions to both EL1 and EL2 students. (See Crosson & Lesaux, 2013b.)

- Teach common conjunctions like 'but' and 'because' before more academic conjunctions like 'notwithstanding' and 'nevertheless'.
- Never teach conjunctions as isolated vocabulary lists; rather, select the target conjunctions embedded in texts students are reading.
- Select conjunctions from both narrative and informational texts, as the typical conjunctions that appear in each genre tend to be different.
- Teach conjunctions as part of a robust integrated vocabulary-literacy instruction program that provides multiple opportunities for practice in reading and writing across the content areas.
- Engage students regularly in active thinking about the changes in meaning that result from the use of different conjunctions.
- Use graphic organizers to show the logical relationships between ideas connected by conjunctions—causal, adversative, temporal, etc.

Metacognitive and Cognitive Reading Strategies

Metacognitive and cognitive strategies concern the extent to which the reader monitors comprehension, can select steps to gain feedback, and undertakes various measures to enable comprehension. Metacognitive strategies include thinking about what one knows and does not know, and about what kinds of steps are needed to comprehend text or complete an assignment. A variety of strategies are available to readers to monitor and improve their reading comprehension. These can be stated as a set of questions and actions taken in response to these questions as illustrated by Table 4.1 on page 108.

Increasingly demanding reading materials in high school require increased emphasis on explicit teaching of metacognitive and cognitive reading strategies. EL2 readers need to be shown how to be active readers who monitor their comprehension during reading; make predictions about the information in the texts they read; monitor whether their predictions were correct; modify their predictions; summarize key points during and after reading; and use their knowledge of text structure to create an overall picture of how different text segments relate to each other and to the whole. Active use of these reading strategies helps EL2 readers navigate written material successfully (Francis, Rivera, Lesaux, Kieffer, & Rivera, 2006a).

Metacognitive Strategies	Cognitive Strategies
Do I know something about this topic that can help me figure out this text?	activate prior knowledge
What is new about this text that I did not know before?	
Do I understand the text?	identify the main idea and summarize the main points
Can I summarize what I read?	
What steps can I take to figure this text out?	re-read from the place where I lost track
	use assistive technology to help me clarify the ideas
Do I know what the central argument is?	identify the central argument
Do I agree with the argument?	state agreement or disagreement
What else do I know that makes me agree or disagree?	retrieve prior knowledge and decide whether it supports agreement or disagreement
Do I see how ideas and arguments are structured and organized throughout the text?	identify text structure and use it to figure out where new information, supporting details, explanations, and examples are located
	represent the idea organization graphically
Can I anticipate what will happen next in the text? Was I right?	comprehension monitoring
	self-assessment of understanding

Table 4.1 Examples of Metacognitive and Corresponding Cognitive Strategies

Metacognitive strategies also involve the ability to decide what strategies one should use to regulate the reading process (Baker & Beall, 2009). Effective EL1 and EL2 readers apply a variety of reading strategies to make sense of text. They are aware of the need to monitor their comprehension 'online'—that is, as they read—by asking themselves questions such as: 'Does this make sense?', 'Where can I get help?', and 'What else do I need to do to comprehend what I am reading?'

Other strategies that facilitate reading comprehension are summarization, elaboration, and explaining. Text summarization, which is a challenging task, involves the ability to focus on the most important concepts in the text and then to express those ideas in one's own words (Dole, Duffy, Roehler, & Pearson, 1991). Good comprehenders elaborate on what they have read by making connections between new information in the text and old information they may already have (Gagné, Weidemann, Bell, & Anders, 1984). Explaining is demonstrated when students ask themselves 'why' questions and then attempt to answer these questions.

Metacognitive and cognitive strategy instruction can enhance reading comprehension for EL1 and EL2 readers (Edmonds et al., 2009). It is important to remember, however, that when EL2 proficiency is insufficient for tackling texts, EL2 learners may find it cognitively challenging to engage in strategy use in the L2, even when they can use these strategies in their L1 (García, 1998). Therefore, teachers of EL2 reading need to be aware that while teaching the use of reading strategies is an important aspect of EL2 reading instruction for adolescents, it is critical to ensure learners have the necessary knowledge and skills. Without word and text fluency, relevant vocabulary knowledge, understanding of cohesive markers, and knowledge of text structures, it may be too challenging to learn metacognitive reading strategies. We emphasize this point because we have found, through our classroom observations and research, that teachers of adolescents tend to focus too much on metacognitive and cognitive strategies. Too often, secondary school teachers do not consider that for some adolescents, the struggle is due to poor basic reading skills and that these are important prerequisites for comprehension. If these basic skills are not also addressed, adolescents with poor reading comprehension will continue to fall behind.

There is general agreement that strategy instruction is most effective when taught within a framework that begins with high levels of scaffolding and support from the teacher, emphasizing a gradual transfer of responsibility for the activation of strategies to the EL2 readers (Francis et al., 2006a). Francis et al. explain that:

> [t]eachers typically begin by explaining the purpose and characteristics of a given strategy, and by extensively modeling their own strategy use, often through thinking aloud while reading a text, and provide many opportunities for structured practice, whether oral or written. Teachers must push students to use these strategies critically and purposefully when reading independently. This final step can sometimes be the most difficult. When the task requires students to transfer strategies to new contexts or apply strategies to new texts, many students have difficulty transferring and/or adapting the strategies to the new text or context.
>
> (Francis et al., 2006a, p. 24)

Knowledge of Text Structure

As noted earlier in this chapter, one of the main challenges for EL2 learners in comprehending reading material in high school is that they need to successfully navigate both unfamiliar language and unfamiliar content. This new language and content is encountered in texts in a variety of content areas, including Language Arts, business studies, social studies, science, and math, among others. Francis et al. (2006) propose that for effective comprehension:

> [s]tudents must also understand how this process [the comprehension process] has to be adjusted for the type of text (e.g., expository or narrative) being read, the purposes for the reading (e.g., to learn about a science concept or to solve a math problem), and the format of the content (e.g., the format of instructions for a science lab or a primary document in social studies). When students are actively engaged, effective instruction promotes meta-cognition—students' ability to reflect on, monitor, and control their own thinking processes.
>
> (Francis et al., 2006a, p. 23)

Analyzing text structure is one of the metacognitive reading strategies whose benefits are consistently supported by research (Dymock & Nicholson, 2010). Readers need to be explicitly taught to recognize different text structures, become aware of their distinctive features, practice the application of this awareness through extensive reading of different text types, and receive corrective feedback. As noted in Chapter 1, non-fiction, or expository, texts can be classified into different text types, or genres, and being familiar with these facilitates comprehension for EL2 learners. Types of expository texts in secondary school are expanded to include procedures, such as directions and instruction manuals, reports, essays, and expositions, such as position papers. The way ideas are developed and organized in a text is revealed to the reader when different text structure components are explicitly identified and understood. In addition to the types of reading material already discussed in Chapter 3—descriptive, sequential, compare-and-contrast, cause-and-effect, and problem–solution—secondary school students are presented with the highly demanding task of reading and understanding persuasive essays. Persuasive essays have a distinctive structure: thesis statement, argument, and conclusion.

Adversative connectives, such as 'nonetheless' and 'whereas', are used in persuasive essays to refute an argument (Crosson & Lesaux, 2013b; Geva, 2007). Pointing out the way the writer uses these conjunctions to put forward arguments and counter-arguments would help readers achieve deep comprehension of persuasive essays. Crosson and Lesaux recommend that:

> [i]deally, this work would begin by first analyzing models of persuasive writing, and as part of the analysis, pointing to the connectives that the writer uses to communicate relationships between warrants and claims, counter-warrants, and counter-claims.
>
> (Crosson & Lesaux, 2013b, p. 199)

Moreover, understanding the structure of persuasive essays prepares learners for writing them.

Studies in which EL2 seventh graders (Tang, 1992) and EL2 eighth graders (Sam & Rajan, 2013) were trained in identifying expository text discourse structure have shown that the use of **graphic organizers** can make different discourse structures and idea relationships transparent to readers. These studies demonstrate the positive impact of direct and explicit teaching of different text structures on reading comprehension. Encouraging students to use their knowledge of text structures when they read expository texts is clearly beneficial for both EL1 and EL2 learners.

Explicit teaching of such structures may be especially important for EL2 learners because the rhetorical structures of academic material in students' L1 and L2 may be different (Grabe & Stoller, 2011). It is important to note here Carrell's (1985) caution that 'the mastery of the strategy should not displace reading for meaning' (p. 742). In other words, recognizing text structure should be tied to comprehension of what is read, not only at the micro- or local level—for example, when the EL2 reader realizes that two clauses are related causally—but also at the macro- or general level—for example, when the EL2 reader recognizes that the first paragraph states a position or argument and subsequent paragraphs provide evidence to support that argument. In sum, EL2 reading instruction programs should be comprehensive, engaging students in training in numerous linguistic, cognitive, and metacognitive skills and strategies, and involving teachers from different disciplines.

Metalinguistic Strategies

Metalinguistic strategies involve reflecting on how language is used to convey meaning explicitly or metaphorically. In Chapter 3, we provided examples of metalinguistic strategies, such as phonological awareness, that help young readers to decode words. In this chapter, we examine metalinguistic strategies, such as cognate and morphological awareness, that help readers to figure out the meaning of new words and develop an appreciation of words used to signal cohesion in texts.

Instructional support and explicit teaching of strategies that can facilitate inference about unknown vocabulary can also enhance EL2 learners' reading comprehension (Proctor, Dalton, & Grisham, 2007). Classroom Snapshot 4.2 illustrates morphological analysis, one of the strategies that can aid adolescents in inferring the meaning of unfamiliar words.

Classroom Snapshot 4.2

Moheen, a Somali- and English-speaking eighth grader, came across the word 'necessarily' in an article about the soccer star Lionel Messi. Messi's quote read: 'I don't necessarily want to break the record this season.' When Moheen read it he started to parse the sentence meaning by focusing on the words he didn't know. When asked if he could problem-solve and figure out the meaning of the word 'necessarily' he commented that it was similar to 'necessary':

Interviewer:	So what do you think 'necessarily' could mean?
Moheen:	Maybe, like, you have to do something?
Interviewer:	How did you know that?
Moheen:	It looks kind of the same, 'necessary' and 'necessarily'.
Interviewer:	What's the same?
Moheen:	The root!

(Pacheco & Goodwin, 2013, p. 541)

Table 4.2 on page 113 provides additional examples of metalinguistic strategies and the language skills needed to capitalize on them.

Morphological analysis was one of the strategies successfully implemented in an after-school tutoring program designed to help adolescents who were struggling with literacy (see Lin et al., 2012). EL1 and EL2 students received individual or small-group tutoring once or twice a week, for one hour each time, over a period of six months. Overall, students significantly increased their morphological awareness and vocabulary knowledge, but the gains in morphological awareness were especially remarkable for adolescents who, before the intervention, were alarmingly low on these skills. To teach morphological awareness, the tutor explained how each part—prefix, root, or suffix—of morphologically complex words encountered in reading passages contributed to the meaning of the word. The tutor then created a word web (see Figure 4.1 on page 114) to show meaning relationships of the base word 'drama' with other words sharing the same root, prefix, or suffix.

Metalinguistic Strategies	Linguistic Skills
• What words do I not know? • Are they crucial in understanding this text?	• identify unknown words • identify unknown words that are critical for text comprehension
• Can I figure out the meaning of this new word from the context?	• go back one or two sentences and re-read up to one or two sentences past the sentence where the new word is
• Can I figure out the meaning of this sentence by looking at its internal structure? • Do I see prefixes and suffixes? • Do I know the meaning of the root word? • How do the prefixes or suffixes modify the meaning of this root word?	• apply morphological analysis: identify known roots, affixes, and suffixes • deduce the meaning of the word by integrating the meaning of its morphological parts
• Is there a word in my L1 that sounds or looks like this? • Does the meaning of this word in my L1 make sense in this passage?	• identify cognates • retrieve the meaning of the cognate word and try it in the passage to see if it makes sense
• If I cannot deduce the meaning from context or through morphological or cognate examination, what else can I do?	• check a dictionary or thesaurus (online or offline)
• Why does it say 'However' at the beginning of this paragraph?	• consider that this paragraph might bring counterarguments to what I read before

Table 4.2 Metalinguistic Strategies and the Corresponding Linguistic Skills

The tutor also wrote the root, prefixes, and suffixes of morphologically complex words on separate sticky notes. Once several roots and affixes were collected, the tutor challenged the adolescent to create as many words as possible by combining the sticky notes of root words with prefixes and suffixes in different ways. For example, from the roots *nation* and *culture*, the prefix *inter–*, and the suffixes *–al*, *–ization*, *–ize*, and *–ity*, students could form words such as 'international', 'internationalize', 'internationalization', 'internationality', 'cultural', 'intercultural', and 'interculturality'.

As discussed in Chapters 2 and 3, some languages share cognates, and when these cognates exist, L2 learners can sometimes figure out the meaning of unfamiliar words in the L2. For example, 30 to 40 percent of English words share a cognate with Spanish. This may be especially productive in secondary school where words whose source is Latin or Greek

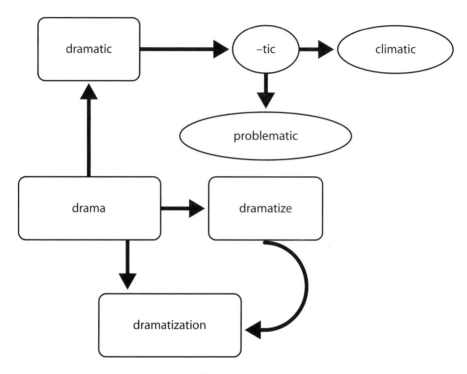

Figure 4.1 Word Web for Morphologically Complex Words

occur in school subjects such as biology, chemistry, geometry, mathematics, and others. Montelongo, Hernández, Herter, and Cuello (2011) suggest teaching EL2 learners how to identify cognates in combination with the contextual clues provided by surrounding words to deduce the meaning of unknown English words. To obtain clues to the meaning of a new word, EL2 learners in Grade 4 were taught to search for a cognate word before, after, or within the sentence in which the unknown word appeared. The cognate would appear in the form of a synonym, an antonym, a definition, an example, or an **appositive**, or signaled by punctuation, as illustrated in Table 4.3 on page 115. The table provides examples used to teach and practice the use of the context-clue-cognate strategy. In each example the Spanish–English cognate is underlined.

In a study with Spanish-speaking EL2 students in Grades 4 and 7, Ramírez et al. (2013) found that students who had better knowledge of cognates were more successful in identifying morphemes in complex words and had better general English vocabulary and reading comprehension than students who were less successful at identifying Spanish–English cognates.

1 Context Clue: Synonyms	
The Indian children **gathered** the olives. They **collected** these small fruits for use in cooking.	From the context, you can tell that 'gathered' means the same as _____ . (collected)
2 Context Clue: Antonyms	
Bandits **raided** farms and ranches for food and money. The farmers and ranchers **defended** themselves with guns and rifles.	From the context, you can tell that 'raided' means the opposite of _____ . (defended)
3 Context Clue: Definition	
A **settlement** is usually **a small community** of people who have recently moved there.	From the context, you can tell that a 'settlement' means the same as _____ . (community)
4 Context Clue: Examples	
Many of the **crops** come from the fields of California. For example, **broccoli**, **spinach**, and **olives** are grown in this state.	From the context, you can tell that 'crops' means the same as _____ . (broccoli, spinach, olives)
5 Context Clue: Appositive Word or Phrase	
Each pueblo had many adobe houses grouped around a **town square**, or **plaza**.	From the context, you can tell that 'town square' means the same as _____ . (plaza)
6 Context Clue: Punctuation	
The writer revealed her **thoughts** (**ideas**) in a diary.	From the context, you can tell that 'thoughts' means the same as _____ . (ideas)

Table 4.3 English–Spanish Cognates in Context Clues Exercises to Scaffold Comprehension (Montelongo, Hernández, Herter, and Cuello, 2011)

The researchers explain that knowledge of the cognate root makes it easier for Spanish-speaking EL2 learners to unpack the meaning of the word through morphological analysis. Not all EL2 learners notice cognates in roots or suffixes (Hancin-Bhatt & Nagy, 1994), but those who do are able to more easily infer the meaning of morphologically complex words and have better reading comprehension (Jiménez, García, & Pearson, 1996).

EL2 learners may not immediately recognize a morphologically complex word as a cognate because sometimes the suffix is a non-cognate. For example, in the word 'partially', 'partial' is a cognate with Spanish, but the suffix –*ly* is not. Moreover, there are slight phonetic and spelling shifts. In Spanish, the base of this word is spelled with a *c*—'parcial'—and the stress falls on the last syllable, –*al*, whereas in English, it is spelled with a *t* and the stress falls on the first syllable, *par*. The non-cognate suffix and slight changes in spelling and pronunciation may obscure the semantic, or meaning, relationship of the word across the two languages. This issue can be easily addressed, however, by teaching EL2 learners how to carry out morphological analyses and to recognize substitutions that occur regularly. For example, the *t* in the English suffixes –*tial* and –*tion* is represented with a *c* in the equivalent Spanish suffixes –*cial* and –*ción*, and the suffix –*ly* in English is equivalent to the Spanish suffix –*mente*. As these examples show, teaching children to become aware of cognates is done more effectively when it is tied to morphological analysis. EL2 learners whose L1 is one of the Latin-derived languages can benefit greatly from teaching that draws their attention to cognates shared with their L1 and to how morphological awareness can help them infer the meaning of words in the L2. In fact, skills involved in analyzing complex words into their morphemes are important to teach, whether the L1 and L2 share cognates or not.

Metalinguistic skills also include the understanding of metaphorical language. Understanding metaphors involves 'understanding and experiencing one kind of thing in terms of another' (Lakoff & Johnson, 2003, p. 5). This language is commonly found in idiomatic expressions, such as 'break a leg' and 'break the ice', that are used in social contexts and in bantering among peers, and in literary materials, such as short stories, poems, and novels, to enhance the language. As explained in Chapter 1, the meaning conveyed by metaphors can be presented in an indirect way, and cannot therefore be interpreted literally. It takes time to learn to understand metaphors. Developmental research has shown that older children understand metaphors better than younger children and that, typically, children who find it easier to understand metaphors in their L1 are relatively better at doing so in their L2 as well (Johnson, 1989). Both EL1 speakers and EL2 learners struggle with understanding metaphors. For EL1 children, the difficulty with understanding metaphorical language has to do mainly with the demands it places on working memory (Johnson, Fabian, & Pascual-Leone, 1989). In addition to the challenges related to cognitive demands on working memory, EL2 learners have difficulties because of insufficient background knowledge of the L2 culture and of idioms that are used in social interaction, such as 'don't pull my leg'. By contrast, EL1 learners grow up hearing such expressions in social contexts that provide cultural familiarity and exposure to the idioms in context-rich situations. Through continuous exposure, they develop an implicit understanding of figurative language—unless they are afflicted with a language impairment. EL2 learners, on the other hand, need explicit instruction on how to interpret idiomatic expressions, whether or not they have a language impairment.

Modified Versus Unmodified Reading Material for EL2 Learners

An intriguing question in the field of L2 teaching is the importance of using authentic reading material. The term 'authentic' relates to material—visual, oral, or written—that has not been produced for the specific purpose of L2 teaching and is presented to the learner in its intact form or just in the way a native speaker of the language would encounter it (Nunan, 1989). Exposing learners to authentic communicative situations is a hallmark of the **communicative approach** to language teaching which, over the years, has evolved to include the use of authentic material in L2 reading instruction, particularly for adolescents and adults.

Reading materials produced for the purpose of teaching L2 are characterized by adaptations that include vocabulary and syntactic simplifications to make the text appropriate for different proficiency levels. This practice began with the conversion of lengthy classic novels into short versions, accompanied by illustrations and scaffolded with definitions of key vocabulary terms to make them accessible to L2 readers with low language proficiency. More recently, these adaptations have extended to content-area materials. Supporters of using authentic materials for L2 teaching argue that they expose L2 learners to the way language is used in real life (Fenner, 2002). In L2 teaching for academic purposes or for members of a specific profession like medicine or business, the use of authentic text is viewed as a motivating tool for learners as it relates directly to the community to which they belong or aspire to belong (Mishan, 2005).

While each of these arguments has merit, teachers of EL2 learners also need to consider the extent to which authentic reading materials written for high school students might be appropriate from the perspective of cognitive processing and emotional maturity. We would argue that in most cases authentic materials are far beyond the language proficiency of the EL2 reader. As we saw in Chapter 3, reading material can be characterized as appropriate for independent or scaffolded reading. The level of difficulty of secondary school content-area texts would place most of them at the 'frustration' level. Moreover, authentic materials do not always provide the best example of language use (Hyland, 2003). A language barrier can put the content beyond the reach of the reader and, rather than motivating, could discourage and frustrate.

As mentioned earlier, EL2 students may have language skills that are considerably below what is needed to learn from grade-appropriate texts (Lin et al., 2012). A key aspect of L2 language proficiency is vocabulary. In the past, it was suggested that L2 learners should be familiar with 90 to 95 percent of the vocabulary in text (Hu & Nation, 2000; Schmitt, Jiang, & Grabe, 2011) in order to be able to infer the meaning of new words from text. However, more recent research has raised the bar further—it has shown that in order to infer the meaning of new words, L2 readers should be familiar with the meaning of 98 to 99 percent of the words in general reading material. In the case of academic content, it is especially important to ensure that only a very small percentage of the words are unknown in order to facilitate comprehension (Schmitt et al., 2011, cited in Webb & Macalister, 2013).

EL2 learners need direct instruction on a wide range of reading-related skills and strategies, and vocabulary instruction. However, teachers must remember that EL2 learners also need to read extensively for their reading proficiency to grow significantly. To achieve this, reading materials need to be age-appropriate, engaging, and linguistically accessible. So where can EL2 teachers find such materials? Some reading researchers argue that texts written for younger L1 children are useful as a means of promoting extensive L2 reading because they are written in fairly simple language, use a great proportion of high-frequency words and illustrations to aid comprehension, are appropriate in length, and present content that can be appealing and motivating for older readers (Gardner, 2004, 2008; Mikulecky, 2009). These claims are supported by studies involving university students (Hitosugi & Day, 2004; Tabata-Sandom & Macalister, 2009). However, the successful use of certain materials to engage EL2 university students and young EL2 learners in extensive reading does not guarantee that the same materials will be effective with EL2 adolescents. Adolescents are in the midst of asserting their identity and eager to leave childhood behind. They do not usually want to engage in activities perceived as childish. They may not embrace children's reading material with the same enthusiasm that adults do. Moreover, the unfamiliar vocabulary load of reading materials written for L1 children can actually be quite large and may be too challenging for L2 adolescent readers.

Spotlight Study 4.2

Webb and Macalister (2013) analyzed the vocabulary size and degree of repetition necessary for the comprehension of texts written for three groups of readers: EL1 children whose age ranged from seven to 11, EL1 adolescents aged 12 years or older, and EL2 learners with different reading abilities. Their objective was to determine whether texts written for children in these three groups were suitable for L2 extensive reading. The texts written for EL2 learners were graded material adjusted for different levels of reading and language proficiency. The researchers compared the recurrence of low-frequency words in narrative and expository texts written for the three audiences listed above.

Especially relevant to the discussion about the kind of texts one should use for extensive reading with EL2 learners was the finding that the lexical demands of authentic texts written for EL1 seven- to 11-year-old children were higher than the lexical demands of authentic texts written for older EL1 learners, as well as of the graded texts written for EL2 learners. The researchers explain this finding in relation to the fact that stories written for EL1 children use many genre- and content-specific words, such as 'dragon', 'pirates', and 'fairy'. In addition, some of the informational readings often presented to children are on topics that lend themselves to the use of rare words—the topic of wildlife, for instance. This leads to a surprisingly high number of low-frequency words in children's reading material. The study suggests that EL2 adolescents may actually find texts written for EL1 children challenging because they contain many unfamiliar words. On the other hand, a unique feature identified in graded reading materials written for EL2 learners is that they are written with a controlled vocabulary and use mostly high-frequency words. Moreover, when low-frequency words are included in texts written for EL2 learners, they appear repeatedly throughout the text. This repetition is likely to facilitate learning of these words.

Webb and Macalister's study suggests that graded reading materials that take into account the learners' linguistic capabilities are an appropriate way to promote L2 extensive reading for learners who have not fully developed their L2 language proficiency. In contrast, when authentic reading materials are used, they require a high level of assistance and scaffolding by the teacher. Graded readers—that is, 'high-interest-low-vocabulary' books—can encourage reading because they appeal to the interests of older readers while at the same time keeping the vocabulary at a lower reading level. EL2 adolescents may be more motivated to read when the books are appropriate in terms of content but accessible in terms of vocabulary. On the internet, one can find a variety of books classified as high-interest-low-vocabulary texts, and examples are provided in Chapter 3.

EL2 teachers often modify authentic material themselves in an effort to make it accessible to students with lower EL2 proficiency. Unfortunately, sometimes this well-intentioned effort results in a text that is shorter and has shorter and less complex sentences, but that is actually harder for the reader to understand. This can happen when, in the process of reducing text complexity, critical cohesive markers such as conjunctions are omitted. Consider the following statements:

1 Because the internet puts an ocean of information at our fingertips, readers need to be more efficient in filtering reliable information.
2 The internet puts an ocean of information at our fingertips. Readers need to be more efficient in filtering reliable information.

As discussed earlier, the causal relationship between the two statements is made explicit by the conjunction 'because' in Example 1. However, because there is no explicit conjunction in Example 2, the reader has to infer the cause and the effect, and this places additional demands on the reader.

Read Classroom Snapshot 4.3 for another example of how conjunctions make visible the logical relationships between ideas in a passage.

Classroom Snapshot 4.3

EL1 children in Grades 5 and 7 were presented with a paragraph followed by comprehension questions. Half of the children were presented with Passage A, and the other half were presented with Passage B.

A Frost

Frost is formed at night in much the same way as dew. Moisture in the night air forms into large drops of water. The earth cools rapidly at night. The temperature drops below zero degrees. The drops of water freeze into the ice crystals that we call frost. Farmers worry on chilly nights. Many growing fruits and vegetables are killed when frost strikes. Wind, even a tiny breeze, can prevent frost. It brings down a lot of the warm air that sometimes floats just above housetops and trees. Wind acts like a spoon in a cup of tea. It stirs things around.

B Frost

Frost is formed at night in much the same way as dew. Moisture in the night air forms into large drops of water **because** the earth cools rapidly at night. The temperature drops below zero degrees **so** the drops of water freeze into the ice crystals that we call frost. Farmers worry on chilly nights **because** many growing fruits and vegetables are killed when frost strikes. Wind, even a tiny breeze, can prevent frost **because** it brings down a lot of the warm air that sometimes floats just above housetops and trees. Wind acts like a spoon in a cup of tea **because** it stirs things around.

The children were then asked to answer the following comprehension questions:

1 Why are farmers worried on cold nights?
   a   because it may be very windy
   b   because they have to stay awake
   c   because plants can be killed
2 When the earth cools at night, moisture forms into large drops of water
   a   but water freezes into the ice crystals that are called frost.
   b   but frost forms when the temperature drops below zero degrees.
   c   but wind keeps ice from becoming frost when it is cold.

(Adapted from Geva & Ryan, 1985)

Versions A and B are identical in terms of content, but in Version B the conjunction 'because' is used to combine ideas into one sentence and has been set in bold type to make it more salient. Geva and Ryan (1985) found that students who read Passage B comprehended the text better than students who read Passage A. The students benefited from the highlighted conjunctions in Passage B, presumably because the highlighting drew their attention to the conjunctions so that they were more likely to process the logical relationships between the statements. In Passage A, it was up to the children to draw the necessary inferences about how the idea units were related to each other. Children who were poor comprehenders were especially affected by the lack of conjunctions in Passage A and were much less likely to be able to infer the relationships than the good comprehenders.

Meeting the Needs of EL2 Adolescents With Interrupted or No L1 Schooling

The strongest predictor of EL2 student achievement is the amount of formal L1 schooling they had before entering an EL2 educational environment. (See Thomas & Collier, 2001, for a large-scale study on minority students' long-term achievement.) Unfortunately, many EL2 learners, for example, refugees, do not have formal schooling in their L1. Consider the case of Farah, a 16-year-old adolescent who recently arrived in England from Gaza. She has spent most of her life in refugee camps, where she rarely had the opportunity to go to school. She is an articulate speaker in her L1, Arabic, but she does not speak English and does not know how to read in any language. Upon her arrival, she was placed in an EL2 class with other recent immigrants from non-English-speaking countries in a school in London, England.

Activity 4.2

Take a moment to consider the following questions:

1 What do you think should be the initial focus of Farah's EL2 instruction?
2 How should she be taught to read?
3 When should she be taught to read?
4 What will be the main challenges of teaching Farah to read?
5 How does reading instruction for this adolescent compare to reading instruction for a seven-year-old EL2 learner?
6 How does reading instruction for this adolescent compare to reading instruction for an EL2 learner of a similar age who attended school in the home country?

The teaching and learning challenges for an adolescent like Farah are tremendous. She needs intensive EL2 instruction, combined with key concepts and skills from the elementary and middle school curriculum, to accelerate her literacy development and build the skills necessary for her transition to high school. It is clear that an EL2 learner like Farah needs a comprehensive EL2 program, and literacy should be a specific area of instruction in such a program. Although there is abundant literature addressing the challenges of developing literacy skills in individuals with interrupted schooling, very little empirical evidence has directly examined effective EL2 reading programs for such adolescents.

A sensible EL2 reading program for an adolescent without L1 literacy skills should be provided in tandem with the development of oral and written language skills. As pointed out in Chapter 2, this should include each of the components of reading that are introduced gradually to children who begin their schooling at an early age. These components include phonemic awareness and phonics skills; decoding; rapid and accurate word recognition; fluency in reading passages; general and academic vocabulary knowledge; and strategic reading for comprehension. Reading texts based on academic content in such a program would serve both as a means to further language development and as an end in themselves.

One of the few programs currently available for students with interrupted schooling is Reading Instructional Goals for Older Readers (RIGOR) (Calderón, 2007a, 2007b). The program is designed for older EL2 learners with low or no literacy skills in their L1 or in English. It promotes the development of literacy skills in both the L1 and the L2. Although the program was originally developed for Spanish-speaking EL2 learners, the principles, methodological recommendations, and many of the resources are appropriate for EL2 learners from different L1 backgrounds. EL2 teachers are encouraged to balance comprehensible input with rich, challenging vocabulary. Dosage and intensity are highlighted in this program: it is recommended that the program should be delivered for at least seven hours each week, and teachers are encouraged to complete one 'skill bag' per week. Each skill bag contains a teacher's guide with daily lessons on how to support the five steps of the program:

1 develop phonemic awareness and phonics skills
2 build vocabulary through seven-step instruction and practice sequences
3 increase reading comprehension, fluency, and content knowledge
4 use writing to expand and reinforce literacy
5 compile assessment data to inform instruction.

Another sound feature of this program is that it embeds the teaching of low-level literacy skills in an age-appropriate and meaningful context. Phonics and basic reading comprehension skills are taught using content from science and social studies. Research on this program suggests that EL2 adolescent learners with interrupted schooling who participate in RIGOR outperform their peers in reading (Calderón, 2007b).

Spotlight Study 4.3

A five-year study was conducted to evaluate the outcomes of a program designed to expedite reading comprehension development for English language learners (Expediting Comprehension for English Language Learners, ExC-ELL). The program integrates 'the teaching of vocabulary, reading comprehension, and writing skills into all math, science, social science, and language arts classes' (Calderón, Slavin, & Sanchez, 2011, p. 118) and has a strong focus on cooperative learning. Teachers structure activities for students to work in small mixed-ability groups, allowing them to help each other through regular opportunities to discuss content. Professional development for literacy coaches, content-area teachers, and principals is a strong component of ExC-ELL. A five-day workshop on how to teach vocabulary, reading comprehension, and writing through the content areas is followed by extensive coaching during teaching implementation throughout one year. After two years of implementation, the EL2 learners in the study, some of whom were students with interrupted formal education, displayed an improvement of 45 percent in their reading scores, and the schools participating in the program, which before implementation were low-performing schools, became high-performing schools. (See Calderón et al., 2011.) ■

On the whole, the same teaching considerations that have been examined throughout this book for younger EL2 learners who may or may not have literacy skills in their L1 appear to be applicable to EL2 adolescents with little or no L1 reading ability. These readers need to progress through the various milestones discussed in Chapter 2. However, they need more intensive support to develop all the other required skills, and the curriculum materials need to be adapted to reflect their age, life experiences, background, and cultural knowledge. Here, too, the use of high-interest-low-vocabulary materials may be appropriate, whether presented through print or through multimedia.

Effective Reading Assessment of EL2 Adolescents

Typically developing EL2 learners should not experience difficulties in developing accurate and fluent decoding skills, especially if they receive systematic reading instruction in EL2, starting in the primary grades (Lesaux & Siegel, 2003; Lesaux & Geva, 2006). Most EL2 learners can make good progress in their word-level decoding, even when their English oral language skills are still developing. If, in spite of consistent high-quality instruction, they have persistent difficulties in developing fluent word reading skills or comprehending what they read, one reason may be that they struggle with decoding skills, which are effortful and dysfluent. Another reason may be difficulties with language comprehension skills (Geva & Herbert, 2012; Sparks et al., 2009).

Assessing Reading Comprehension: One Test Does Not Say It All

One issue that deserves at least some mention in this chapter concerns how reading comprehension is measured and what is measured by different tests (Fletcher, 2006). The general conclusion of recent research on this topic is that reading comprehension tests are not interchangeable and that different reading comprehension tests draw on somewhat different underlying skills. For example, Cutting and Scarborough (2006) examined the contributions of different measures of word decoding and oral language skills to three different reading comprehension tests. These tests varied in terms of the material to be read and also the format used to assess reading comprehension. One of the tests presented short passages of two to three sentences to be read silently, followed by open-ended questions—literal and inferential—related to each passage. Another test involved reading longer passages. For this one, individuals read narrative and expository passages silently and responded to multiple-choice questions that followed each text. A third reading test involved reading aloud passages that were six to seven sentences long. Here, too, the response format involved multiple-choice questions. Two of these reading tests allowed readers to look back at the passage as they responded to the comprehension questions, whereas in the one where the passage was read aloud, looking back was not an option. Cutting and Scarborough found that these tests were not identical in terms of the correlation between reading comprehension, decoding skills, and oral language skills.

In a similar vein, Francis et al. (2006a) reported that two different tests of reading comprehension provided different results about readers' performance. In one of them, participants were asked to read passages of increasing length and to complete sentences by supplying missing words in the text as they read to demonstrate comprehension. The second test required participants to read short passages of three sentences each. The decoding demands of the different passages were controlled, but they were constructed to manipulate the role of memory, inference-making, knowledge access, and the comprehension of linguistic discourse devices. The researchers found that decoding and phonological awareness skills were more strongly related to the test in which readers were asked to read and provide missing words as they read than to the second test, where they simply read the complete sentences.

These studies demonstrate the importance of considering text variability when interpreting performance on reading comprehension tests and, more importantly, when trying to adapt instruction to the needs of EL2 learners. Diagnostic tests of reading comprehension are intended to provide information on the strengths and weaknesses of individuals in their ability to read and to comprehend the materials they read. These assessments are important because they can help to guide the selection and implementation of relevant interventions at the classroom, small-group, or individual level in order to enhance reading comprehension (Fletcher, 2006). However, EL2 teachers need to be aware that one test does not say it all. When educators examine the performance of EL2 learners on reading comprehension tests with the intent of using this information to inform subsequent teaching, it is important to be familiar with the kind of skills that each test assesses and the range of 'stumbling blocks' that may impede reading comprehension. Caution should be exercised in drawing inferences about reading comprehension on the basis of one test, because the material to be comprehended in different tests and the response format used for assessing comprehension of the material may highlight different strengths and weaknesses.

When interpreting the performance of EL2 learners on standardized reading comprehension measures, additional caution is needed, because most of the tests have been standardized on monolingual learners. Research reviewed in Chapter 2 has shown that the typical reading comprehension scores of EL2 learners are lower than those of EL1 students (Farnia & Geva, 2013) and that these differences reflect a gap in L2 vocabulary and other language skills (Farnia & Geva, 2011).

It is important to remember that high-stakes assessments or group tests should be supplemented by complementary methods, including classroom observations, think-alouds, and teacher interviews (Fletcher, 2006; Geva & Wiener, 2015). The use of different procedures, with different materials to be read and different response formats, should provide more comprehensive and nuanced information about EL2 students, enhance precision in understanding the learners, and point to relevant instruction and instructional support. The section on assistive technology (AT) and, in particular, Figure 4.2, demonstrate the possibilities available to teachers for adapting instruction to a student's individual learning needs.

Research on Learning Difficulties in EL2 Learners: Implications for Instruction

EL2 Learners With Decoding Difficulties

Persistent difficulties in decoding skills of students who begin studying in EL2 in the primary grades cannot be attributed simply to lack of proficiency in the target language. This is probably the case with older EL2 learners as well, but at this point there is little research to support this conjecture. When it is first observed that an EL2 student is not making the expected progress in reading when compared to other students of similar background receiving similar instruction, further assessment and intervention are required. It is not necessary to wait until a certain level of EL2 proficiency is achieved, and teachers should resist the belief that EL2 learners should be given at least five years to develop EL2 proficiency before considering other possible reasons for reading difficulties (Geva & Wiener, 2015).

While there is a scarcity of research on the effectiveness of interventions with EL2 learners and, in particular, with adolescents experiencing reading difficulties, findings from the available research indicate that EL2 learners benefit from the same types of instruction as struggling EL1 readers (Geva & Herbert, 2012). The available intervention research with EL2 learners who may be at risk for decoding problems (Cirino et al., 2009; Lovett et al., 2008) suggests that interventions that work for EL1 learners also work for EL2 learners with decoding difficulties. Phonological awareness is necessary for word recognition and spelling. To help EL2 learners with decoding difficulties, it is important to develop their phonological awareness through activities that involve counting, segmenting, and blending syllables; segmenting and blending words; comparing and matching sounds; identifying sounds with letters; and matching sounds. It is also helpful to teach the meaning of the words used in these activities in order to increase learners' EL2 vocabulary (Linan-Thompson & Hickman-Davis, 2002) and to draw attention to phonemes that do not exist in their L1 (Wang & Geva, 2003). EL2 learners with a reading disability will need additional practice with decoding strategies and with recognizing words that have irregular spelling patterns. They will also need additional practice reading words with fluency in order to build orthographic and visual representations of words in memory. Figure 4.2 on page 132 provides some useful and relevant tools involving AT that can support these learning activities.

Morphology instruction is another effective means for teaching EL2 learners who have reading disabilities. Teaching common suffixes and prefixes and using them in speeded drills and word-building exercises are some useful strategies. Word sorts can be used to help students discriminate words based on morphological features—for example, recognizing that *re–* in 'recall' is a prefix but that *re* in 'red' is part of the base word (Goodwin & Ahn, 2010; Lovett et al., 2008).

How a student responds—or not—to the intervention and to the progress made can inform further intervention and support for that learner. EL2 learners with a reading disability need both continued support to develop their English language skills and focused instruction on reading skills— decoding, fluency, etc.—using instructional methods that have been found to be effective for L1 students with reading disabilities. Additional research is needed to investigate persistent word-level reading difficulties of L2 learners who begin to learn the L2 in the upper elementary grades and beyond, and for those who have had interrupted schooling.

EL2 Learners Who Are 'Unexpected' Poor Comprehenders

It is important to note that persistent language comprehension challenges that extend beyond normal EL2 language learning processes may be indicative of a language disorder. Some students have serious difficulties in developing various aspects of oral language, including vocabulary, listening comprehension, semantics, morphosyntax, oral storytelling, inference-making, understanding figurative language, and comprehension-monitoring. These learners tend to have deficits in working memory (Cain, Oakhill, & Bryant, 2004; Catts et al., 2006).

So far, there has been little research on 'unexpected' poor comprehenders among EL2 learners, but we know that they exist. It may be rather complex to identify EL2 learners who are poor comprehenders because they tend to have relatively fluent oral reading and good decoding skills, and their poor EL2 skills are often attributed to their need to learn EL2. Geva and Massey-Garrison (2013) showed that it was possible to identify a small group of EL2 and EL1 readers who, *relative* to their respective reference group of other EL1 or EL2 students, had serious reading comprehension and language comprehension difficulties, even though they had no decoding difficulties. Interestingly, both the EL1 and EL2 'unexpected' poor comprehenders had persistent difficulties in drawing inferences. We can only make tentative conclusions about identifying underlying reading comprehension problems in L2 learners that may indicate language impairment and require specialized interventions. This is because the area has been studied even less than the treatment of persistent decoding problems in L2 learners. However, we would venture to suggest that approaches that work for EL1 learners should also work for EL2 learners.

One effective approach for ongoing assessment, monitoring, and preventative intervention of reading difficulties is Response to Intervention (RTI) (Fuchs & Fuchs, 2006). In this approach, students are provided with intervention as soon as it is evident that support is required, and without the need to wait for a formal assessment. The principles defining RTI are based on high-quality, evidence-based assessment and instructional methods, and the provision of timely intervention that is systematic and sequential. How students respond to the intervention provided in each tier guides future decisions about the need to offer more or less support, and to use different approaches and teaching methods. Table 4.4 provides a synthesis of the Three-Tier Model of RTI.

Tiers	% of students in a class	Instruction	Assessment
Tier I	80%	• whole-class instruction mostly, supplemented with small-group work • core reading curriculum, usually 90 minutes daily	• school outcomes-based assessment three times per year • students not meeting expectations are moved to Tier II
Tier II	15%	• core reading curriculum plus … • 30 minutes of small-group instruction daily • homogeneous grouping • focus on component skills such as phonemic awareness, the alphabetic principle, basic decoding skills, fluency, comprehension • 14-week instruction cycles	• as in Tier I, plus bi-monthly progress monitoring on specific component skills • students not meeting expectations are moved to Tier III
Tier III	5%	• more intensive intervention in language, literacy, or numeracy • core reading curriculum plus … • 60 minutes of small-group (1:3) instruction daily • focus on component skills such as phonemic awareness, the alphabetic principle, basic decoding skills, fluency, comprehension according to results from assessment data	• weekly progress monitoring

Table 4.4 Three-Tier Model Summary

The Use of AT With EL2 Adolescents Who Have LD or Struggle With Reading

Multimedia components involving audio and video can help EL2 readers understand key concepts related to a challenging or new topic. In Chapter 3, we focused on the use of technology to enrich and enhance reading development. In this chapter, we focus on the use of AT as a tool to support learners who are experiencing reading difficulties. AT is any technology that can assist, maintain, or improve the functional capabilities of individuals with disabilities (Wissick & Gardner, 2008). It is beyond the scope of this book to provide an exhaustive review of the available AT or of the research that evaluates its efficacy with different groups of learners, especially because it is an extremely dynamic area. Instead, we discuss some general principles of intelligent use of AT with EL2 adolescents.

One of the challenges educators face today is identifying the right AT for a student. With over 400 AT products to choose from, finding the exact fit between the AT and the student's learning profile is complex. Often, the same AT is recommended to all students within a particular education environment without an explanation of what tools are appropriate, and this means that teachers and students may not be fully aware of why a particular AT has been recommended (Todd Cunningham, personal communication, October 2014). When one examines AT *products* currently available—for example, Kurzweil 3000, Read and Write Gold, or Premier Literacy—it is clear that each of these products has many different AT *tools* built in. Students are not guided to a specific tool within a product and instead are told to use the product in general. To use a related example, Microsoft Word is a word-processing *product*. It includes a number of different functions or *tools*, such as those for text-editing, spell-checking, formatting, reviewing, and others. AT products, such as Kurzweil 3000 and Read and Write Gold, are similar in that they are software products that offer a variety of tools, such as text-to-speech—any software that converts text on a computer screen into spoken words—optical character recognition, word prediction, and study tools. Teachers should become familiar with the specific tools contained in the AT products their students are using so that they can direct the students to the AT tools that are the right fit for them.

The AT Selection Procedure developed by Cunningham (2014, www.learndifferent.org) provides a Decision Map for educators to help make explicit the skill to be supported and developed with the right AT tool. The Decision Map (see Figure 4.2) comprises branches of varying thickness. The thick innermost branches identify the general academic domains: oral language, reading, and writing. The next set of branches elaborate academic skills within each academic domain. The smallest branches on the periphery provide the connection between the academic skills and specific associated AT tools.

In order to use the Decision Map, the educator needs to identify first the specific academic skill that students require help with, and then the AT tool(s) that they can use to enable the skill change. For example, EL2 learners are often challenged in two key academic domains: weaker oral vocabulary and less background knowledge in academic subjects

Activity 4.3

Think of a current or former EL2 student who experienced persistent difficulties with EL2 reading and answer the following questions:

1 What were some general learning characteristics of this student? For example, did the student struggle with reading in L1?
2 Which of the following areas was this student struggling with? Select all that apply:
- ☐ decoding
- ☐ fluency
- ☐ vocabulary knowledge
- ☐ remembering facts
- ☐ making inferences
- ☐ background knowledge
- ☐ oral language
- ☐ synthesizing information

Photocopiable © Oxford University Press

3 Now examine Figure 4.2 on page 132 and use this Decision Map to identify the AT tool(s) that you could use to enable your struggling reader.

(Shany & Geva, 2012). As Figure 4.2 shows, picture dictionaries are a great AT tool for oral vocabulary. By learning more about picture dictionaries, we learn that a Google image search or the Oxford Picture Dictionary app are two useful AT products that can help EL2 learners with unfamiliar vocabulary.

As for background knowledge, an AT tool should be scalable in English. Websites such as Wikipedia have this tool built in. On a Wikipedia page, one can scroll down the left-hand side and find the Simple English link. This represents the current Wiki page using language that is not too detailed and that uses high-frequency words. Accessing a Wiki page associated with the Simple English link should allow EL2 students to access the same main ideas and content knowledge that is accessible to EL1 students in the class.

When reading comprehension is the area of difficulty, it is likely that lack of familiarity with vocabulary is the source of the problem. The AT Decision Map shows that e-dictionaries, picture dictionaries, or translation software can be accessed to aid students in their comprehension. When using e-dictionaries, it is important to ensure the definitions use vocabulary the student can understand. Teachers should be wary of dictionary definitions that are too complex and do not aid the student in figuring out the meaning

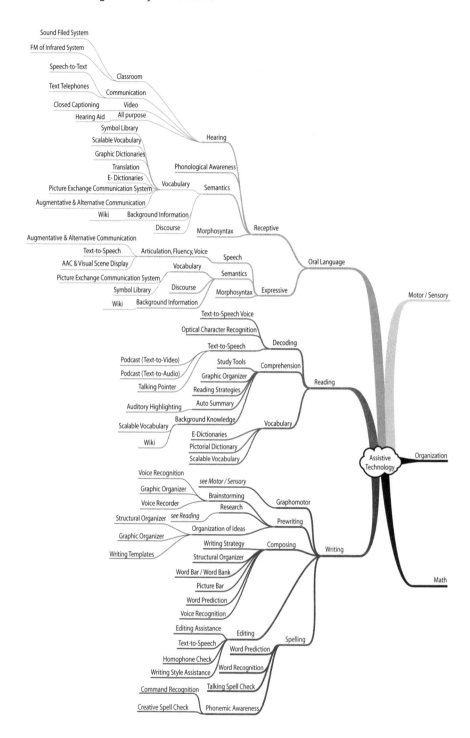

Figure 4.2 Decision Map for the Use of AT (Cunningham, 2014, www.learndifferent.org)

of new words. Picture dictionaries or translation software may be a better means of enabling EL2 students to understand unfamiliar vocabulary.

When faced with an EL2 student who is experiencing difficulty reading, we first have to determine whether the difficulty is due to decoding, word recognition and fluency, or reading comprehension. If the source of the difficulty is in decoding, word recognition, or word reading fluency, then one can see on the AT Decision Map that a suitable AT tool is text-to-speech software. There are many different types of text-to-speech programs on the market. A good one has the following traits (Todd Cunningham, personal communication, October 2014):

1 It is possible to select a high-quality voice, i.e. one that sounds like a human voice.
2 It is possible to control the reading speed.
3 The text-to-speech feature highlights the words on the screen as they are read.
4 It allows one to control the amount of text being presented.

Summary

Students in secondary school face increasing challenges in reading material. There are greater demands for background knowledge and the information density of texts increases. Therefore, this chapter has focused on text-level skills. However, we have also reviewed basic skills, such as decoding and word reading, because these skills continue to be critical aspects of reading instruction for EL2 adolescents with poor or no L1 literacy skills due to interrupted or lack of schooling in their home countries.

Drawing on classroom research, we have examined the skills that EL2 learners with regular and interrupted schooling need in order to become successful readers beyond Grade 6. We have looked at ways effective teachers can help EL2 students develop academic vocabulary, as well as the metacognitive and metalinguistic strategies necessary to understand written academic language. Although these skills and strategies were examined separately in this chapter, we want to emphasize that their implementation before, during, and after reading is recurrent and fluid.

We concluded this chapter by reviewing issues in the assessment of reading of EL2 in secondary school, the identification of reading disabilities in EL2 adolescents, and the way that AT can be used to support these learners.

5

Reading: What We Know Now

Preview

To summarize the theory, research, and teaching practices discussed throughout the book, we will revisit the statements about reading that you responded to in Chapter 1. We will provide a response for each statement based on the research evidence we have examined. Before you read our responses, we invite you to reconsider how you responded to the statements in Activity 1.1.

Activity 5.1: Review your opinions

In Activity 1.1 (page 6), you indicated how strongly you agreed with some statements about EL2 reading. Before you continue reading this chapter, go back and complete the questionnaire again. Compare the responses you gave then to those you would give now. Have your views about EL2 reading development been changed or confirmed by what you have read in the preceding chapters? What are the most surprising shifts in your knowledge and understanding? How might the new information change your ideas about teaching reading skills to EL2 learners?

Reflecting on Ideas About EL2 Reading: Learning From Research

1 Learning to read in L2 is the same as learning to read in L1.

There are both similarities and differences between EL1 and EL2 reading. Whereas EL1 and EL2 readers need the same set of skills to understand what they read, one can expect that the context—ESL, EFL, bilingual, English immersion, etc.—and intensity of English instruction will affect the rate of development and instructional practices. Typically, EL1 learners acquire listening and speaking skills before learning to read (Chall, 1996). In contrast, EL2 learners develop their listening, speaking, and reading skills at the same time (Geva, 2000). Although EL2 children move through the benchmarks of reading development in a similar fashion to their EL1 peers, they start out with less well developed vocabulary, grammar, and listening comprehension in their new language (Farnia & Geva, 2011). Intensity also matters. When EL2 students learn to read and speak English in a context where English is the language usually heard outside the classroom, they become more fluent in English than students who learn it as a foreign language in classes that are taught for only a few hours a week.

Teaching EL2 learners to read is like teaching EL1 students in many ways. Both EL1 and EL2 teachers need to:

- target the development of accurate word recognition skills
- enhance word and text reading fluency
- provide explicit instruction of academic language
- provide opportunities to read and write various age-appropriate materials
- teach cognitive and metacognitive strategies for reading and writing—comprehension, monitoring, etc.
- consider text types—narrative, expository, digital, etc.
- consider text structure—descriptive, sequential, compare-and-contrast, cause-and-effect, problem–solution, etc.
- link prior knowledge to materials read
- have high expectations
- motivate and engage
- remember that 'time on task', i.e. amount of practice, is important
- think developmentally—what is hard for EL1 learners is likely also to be hard for EL2 learners
- consider developmental differences and adapt instruction
- consider individual differences—ability, cognition, opportunities to learn, etc.—and adapt instruction.

On the other hand, there are aspects of reading instruction that are unique to EL2. EL2 teachers need to:

- consider written and oral influences from the L1—positive and negative
- aim to address knowledge gaps for EL2 readers with interrupted schooling
- remember that automatic transfer will occur for some skills, such as phonological awareness, whereas others, like cognate awareness, require explicit teaching
- consider unique characteristics of EL2 readers—for example, that they are developing language and reading skills in tandem

- consider unique demands of certain reading material for EL2 readers—literary texts, pragmatic language, lack of background knowledge, etc.
- remember that reading in two languages is not a liability and not a cause of persistent problems
- remember that timely identification and intervention are essential because persistent reading and language problems do not simply disappear.

2 All L2 learners need to be taught the same set of reading skills regardless of their L1.

Reading is essentially the process of interpreting a writing system according to the conventions of a linguistic community. The skills L2 learners can transfer from their L1 depend, to some extent, on how closely the writing systems of readers' L1 and L2 are related. The more orthographic similarities there are across the two languages, the more skills learners can transfer from one language to the other; the more orthographically distant the languages, the fewer the structural elements that can be transferred. For example, many languages, including Spanish, French, German, English, and Dutch, use the Roman alphabet to represent sounds of speech in print. Although readers of these languages need to learn the specific conventions of letter–sound correspondence in the new language, familiarity with the Roman alphabet may give them an advantage over learners whose L1 has a completely different writing system—Chinese characters, for example. Moreover, the transfer of some reading-related skills—such as phonological awareness or metalinguistic strategies—across learners' languages is less affected by typological differences in the writing systems than by other components, like vocabulary and decoding. For example, extensive research evidence indicates that if EL2 learners have good phonological awareness in their L1, they also have this skill at their disposal in their L2, and they can be expected to have good word reading skills in both languages. This is true regardless of the learners' L1. Therefore, EL2 learners who are already successful readers in their L1 do not need training on phonological awareness when learning to read in EL2. They need to learn the rules of decoding in the L2 but can be expected to develop these skills without serious difficulties.

Facilitation, i.e. transfer, may also occur at higher levels. For example, because English has been greatly influenced by Latin and Greek, readers of English whose native language is a Romance language, such as Spanish, Portuguese, or Italian, will find many cognates that can help them comprehend texts. Likewise, research suggests that metacognitive skills such as comprehension monitoring can 'transfer' across languages—that is, students who are good comprehenders and good strategy-users in their L1 are likely to be good comprehenders, good strategy-users, and fluent readers in their L2 as well.

3 Lack of language comprehension explains the difficulties that EL2 learners may have in comprehending texts.

While lack of reading comprehension strategies can make understanding a passage more challenging, this is not the only cause of reading difficulties. No reading strategy compensates for the absence of decoding skills, fluency, extensive vocabulary knowledge, and understanding of grammar and syntax. As reviewed through the lenses of the extended Simple View of Reading in Chapter 2 and relevant classroom research in Chapters 3 and 4, reading comprehension entails the interaction and coordination of a range of skills, including:

- discrete units such as letter recognition
- letter-to-sound mappings
- automatic, i.e. accurate and fast, word recognition
- understanding the meaning of words—semantics—and figuring out the possible meaning of unknown words
- understanding how words are put together in a given language—phonology, morphology, and orthography
- using the grammar, i.e. syntax
- aiming to get the big picture
- activating comprehension-monitoring strategies
- drawing on prior knowledge to make inferences
- generating abstract representations of texts
- evaluating and critiquing what one has read.

In achieving reading comprehension, both lower-level reading skills and higher-level processes are activated, and they support each other (Stanovich, 1984). At times, processes at the lower level can enhance higher-level comprehension skills; at other times, higher-level comprehension skills can help readers to accurately decode a new unfamiliar word and figure out its meaning.

EL2 teachers of reading need to keep in mind that teaching reading comprehension strategies is important but not sufficient to help readers overcome text comprehension challenges. Similarly, teaching basic reading skills is important but not sufficient to reach high levels of reading comprehension. Fluent word-level reading skills and good knowledge of the language are necessary, but instruction should also focus on developing strategies and metacognitive monitoring. All these aspects are critical for reading comprehension.

4 *L2 learners have difficulties reading in the L2 because they have underdeveloped L2 language proficiency.*

While it is true that EL2 learners are still developing their EL2 language proficiency, this is not a good explanation of persistent reading difficulties when students are receiving excellent teaching. EL2 reading comprehension is complex, and difficulties in comprehension can be related to various factors. Figure 1.1 in Chapter 1 captures this complexity, illustrating the range of factors that contribute to EL2 reading comprehension. Understanding this complexity is helpful in identifying EL2 learners who may have persistent learning difficulties that cannot be understood only as a reflection of lack of proficiency in EL2.

Research has taught us that by the time they reach Grade 3 or 4, EL2 learners should not be expected to have serious difficulties with decoding and developing word reading fluency. If they do, this is a warning sign that the student may have a specific learning disability. The EL2 teacher can make such observations, and provide teaching adaptations and intervention in a timely fashion (Fraser, Adelson, & Geva, 2014; Linan-Thompson, 2014).

In some cases, these difficulties are due to a learning disability. It is critical that EL2 reading teachers understand the difference between reading difficulties that are due to a lack of L2 proficiency and those that are due to a learning disability because, as explained throughout the book, EL2 learners with an LD require special support. As we would expect, EL2 learners typically do not have the same level of EL2 proficiency as their age-matched EL1 classmates. It is more useful to consider individual differences among EL2 learners in *patterns of development over time* of reading and language skills in relation to a reference group of EL2 learners with similar language and educational backgrounds. This approach, which acknowledges EL2 status, avoids biased comparison with EL1 peers and can help to uncover learning disabilities in EL2 students. By comparing typically developing EL2 learners with EL2 children from similar backgrounds who are not typically developing, one can minimize assessments that are not valid and offer relevant interventions (Geva & Wiener, 2015).

5 *To identify L2-reading-related strengths and weaknesses, it is necessary to assess skills in the L1.*

When L2 learners have had sustained exposure to reading in their L1, it may be useful to find out what they can do in their L1 and what kind of skills they may be able to transfer to EL2, for example, decoding or metacognitive reading strategies. If they are good readers in their L1, it is reasonable to expect that they will become good EL2 readers as well. On the other hand, a history of difficulties with reading in the L1 may suggest that difficulties in developing adequate EL2 reading skills are related to an underlying learning disability. However, when exposure to reading in the L1 has been limited, assessing in the L1 may be futile. Furthermore, it is not always practical to assess in the L1. This is the case, for example, when there are no appropriate assessment materials in the L1, when no individuals are available to reliably assess and interpret observations in the L1, and when academic exposure to the L1 has not occurred for a while.

6 *To learn to read in L2, students just need to be exposed to rich literature.*

There is no doubt that exposure to rich literature is important, but research has shown that it is not sufficient. Young EL2 learners will benefit from exposure to various types of text, but they also need to develop their decoding skills. Older L2 learners can benefit from exposure to and implicit learning of new vocabulary and unfamiliar spelling patterns in the interesting and engaging literature they read, but they also benefit from systematic instruction on derivational morphology, multiple meanings of words, and distinguishing between confusing, similar phonemes. Finally, we know that rapid and accurate word recognition skills are essential for reading comprehension. L2 learners may be frustrated if the literature they read presents too much unfamiliar vocabulary and too many words that they cannot decode with ease.

7 *The best strategy for figuring out word meaning is to use context clues.*

Research with older L2 learners has shown that if fewer than five percent of the words are unfamiliar, L2 learners can often work out the meaning of new words. If the proportion of unfamiliar words is higher, the text is deemed to be too difficult and readers are less likely to be able to infer meaning from context. Therefore, while deducing meaning from context is one of the strategies EL2 learners should include in their toolkit, they should not rely on it exclusively, and they should know how to use other metacognitive and metalinguistic strategies to figure out word meanings.

8 *It is easier for younger children to learn to read in L2 than for adolescents.*

The response to this statement is that it depends. It is true in that both EL1 and EL2 learners in the lower grades 'learn to read'—that is, accuracy and fluency in basic word reading skills are established—whereas in the higher grades they are required to 'read in order to learn' (Chall, 1996), and encounter new information and language structures. As noted earlier, some EL2 adolescents actually struggle with decoding skills (see Pasquarella et al., 2012). From this perspective, the statement is probably valid. At the same time, adolescents may have better study strategies and a better understanding of how the L1 and L2 languages work. In other words, they may bring more maturity and sophistication than younger learners, especially if they have had high-quality instruction in their L1. Because we tend to highlight individual differences, we are also mindful of overgeneralizations that do not apply to all L2 learners in a given age group. So, for example, some younger L2 learners may, unlike their peers, struggle with L2 reading, because they have difficulties in remembering new words or reading words fluently. Likewise, some L2 adolescents may do better than their peers due to cognitive skills that help them to excel at learning, greater motivation, more sustained instruction, or perhaps commonalities between English and their L1.

9 *Learning to read and comprehend is more complex in L2 than in L1.*

The same components that are important for comprehending a passage in L1 are critical for comprehending a similar passage in L2. However, learners usually find it harder to understand an L2 passage than a passage with the same content read in their L1 because, by definition, L2 learners are less proficient in their L2 than in their L1. Furthermore, although language proficiency is not the only determining factor, it does play an important role in comprehension. L2 readers need to learn how to read the words on the page fluently in the L2 and, at the same time, figure out the meaning of new words and expressions, novel morphological constructions, and syntactic structures—all while focusing on new information and learning from text. Depending on their L1 skills and the kind of orthography associated with their L1, for example, whether it is Spanish or Chinese, they may be able to draw on resources from their L1. Nevertheless, learning to read and comprehend in L2 is more complex and more demanding than doing so in one's stronger language. One must also remember that it is challenging for L2 students to reach the proficiency of their L1 peers, especially with regard to academic vocabulary, text reading fluency, and reading comprehension. These additional constraints should be taken into account in assessments.

10 Digital reading poses unique reading comprehension demands for L2 readers.

All the skills needed for successful reading of traditional written texts are also important for reading digital text, for example, on a tablet or on the internet. Nevertheless, some characteristics of digital reading, especially online reading, are different from reading print text. Hyperlinked online reading passages are multimodal, interactive, and non-linear, and navigating them demands more flexibility, attention, focus, and quick judgment than reading traditional text, in order to distinguish trustworthy and valuable content from junk. It is also important to remember that digital technology, if used effectively, has the potential to both enhance L2 reading development and support EL2 reading for learners with an learning disability.

11 It is easier for L2 readers to understand narrative texts than expository or non-fiction reading material.

At first glance, it would seem that this statement is true. After all, we know that readers are usually more familiar with the structure of narratives than with that of non-fiction because they are exposed to stories even before they learn to read. Fiction—mostly narrative in style—is the most common material read both in school and for pleasure. Moreover, the elements of narrative texts—characters, setting, plot, etc.—are universal. It has also been argued that written information is less dense in narratives. However, a closer examination of the language typical of narrative passages reveals unique features that pose challenges for EL1 and EL2 readers alike. It is important to note that EL2 readers have difficulties understanding literary devices, like metaphors and idiomatic expressions, that are characteristic of fiction, such as poems or novels. Their meaning cannot be interpreted in a literal way or inferred easily from context. EL2 learners need explicit teaching of these literary devices. Furthermore, subtle allusions to cultural knowledge made in poems and novels are essential for deep comprehension and literary appreciation. In sum, while some elements of narrative texts may be easier to comprehend, other elements may be even more challenging than the more straightforward language of non-fiction texts.

12 It is more beneficial for L2 learners to receive reading instruction in their L1 first.

Research on reading instruction certainly supports teaching reading in the L1 first when possible, for various reasons. The strongest argument concerns the benefits of cultural empowerment and heritage language preservation in societies where the learners' L1 is a minority language. The bulk of research currently available on crosslinguistic transfer of reading skills suggests that when the L1 has a more shallow orthography than the L2, it is particularly beneficial to teach reading in the L1 first (Dressler & Kamil, 2006). However, considerable research evidence has shown that L2 learners can develop L2 reading skills successfully when taught in their L2 first. Moreover various studies, for example, those dealing with French immersion and other bilingual programs, also point to the benefits of learning to read concurrently in both languages. Research shows that whether provided in the L1 or the L2 first, quality of reading instruction is what distinguishes successful and unsuccessful EL2 readers.

13 Cultural background and strategic knowledge are the most important factors in reading comprehension.

We often encounter EL2 teachers who tell us how crucial it is to take into account learners' prior knowledge, including cultural knowledge, when selecting material. Others stress the importance of making sure learners use higher-level metacognitive strategies to ensure reading comprehension. The underlying assumption is that students can learn more when they are given opportunities to connect the text to what they know already. EL2 learners also understand text better when they have cultural knowledge that helps them interpret what they read. Indeed, there is strong and consistent evidence that having background knowledge and familiarity with various reading strategies, as well as actually accessing prior knowledge and a range of comprehension-monitoring strategies, is important for reading comprehension (Grabe, 2009). However, there is also overwhelming evidence that lower-level reading skills—such as mapping spelling patterns to morphemes and meaning, fluent decoding, and reading sight words with automaticity—and higher-level language skills—such as metalinguistic and metacognitive strategies—need to be fostered at developmentally opportune times, for both EL1 and EL2 reading comprehension (Ehri et al., 2001; August & Shanahan, 2006). In addition, rich vocabulary and a good command of language structures—syntax, knowledge of cohesive markers, etc.—are extremely important.

Conclusions

Multiple factors play a role in EL2 reading and need to be considered for effective teaching and assessment of EL2 reading with children and adolescents. The demands on reading instruction change over time and as a function of diverse learners' needs, age, and reading experience. Therefore, a developmental perspective in EL2 reading instruction is critical. Like any learners, EL2 learners are not a blank slate; they bring to school a range of learning experiences and reading skills that vary according to their L1 literacy experience and the orthographic characteristics of their L1. Some skills can be transferred from their L1, but others need to be learned in EL2. Regardless of the numerous challenges that exist in EL2 reading instruction, effective teaching and assessment is ultimately the most influential factor in the development of EL2 learners' reading skills, which is:

> a function of the content coverage, intensity or thoroughness of instruction, methods used to support the special language needs of second-language learners and to build on their strengths, how well learning is monitored, and teacher preparation.
>
> (August & Shanahan, 2006, p. 9)

Coordinated screening and assessment strategies with targeted and evidence-based intervention can be beneficial to any children, including EL2 learners, who are experiencing difficulties with reading. Instruction for struggling EL2 students should be comprehensive, systematic, explicit, and timely. It should include a combination of developmentally appropriate strategies addressing phonological awareness, phonics, fluency, guided oral reading, academic vocabulary and morphological knowledge, cohesive devices, grammatical skills, and reading comprehension strategies. For readers struggling in both EL1 and EL2, instruction should target the specific areas of difficulty. For all EL2 readers, focused instruction in oral language, specifically vocabulary development, is particularly important. Finally, technology can be a useful tool for enhancing EL2 reading development, as well as an assistive tool for EL2 learners with learning difficulties or those struggling with EL2 reading.

Suggestions for Further Reading

Below we suggest readings that will help you deepen your knowledge and understanding of different issues related to the teaching and learning of L2 reading. We have selected readings that provide further information on several key aspects covered in the book and for different age groups. Some of these readings are research reports and others are practical guides that are grounded in research.

August, D., & **Shanahan, T.** (Eds.). (2008). *Developing reading and writing in second-language learners: Lessons from the report of the National Literacy Panel on language-minority children and youth.* New York, NY: Routledge.

This book is a shorter version of the full volume, *Developing literacy in second-language learners*, that reported the findings of the National Literacy Panel on language-minority children and youth (August & Shanahan, 2006). The Panel, consisting of experts in reading, language, bilingualism, research methods, and education, was appointed to identify, assess, and synthesize research published between 1980 and 2003 on the literacy and language development of language-minority children and youth. This shorter version consists of chapters adapted from the original report (August & Shanahan, 2006). The chapters summarize in a concise manner what is known from empirical research about the development of literacy in language-minority children and youth, with a specific focus on the development of various components of literacy, L1 and L2 relationships, the sociocultural context of language and literacy learning, instructional approaches, professional development, and assessment.

Chall, J. S. (1996). *Stages of reading development, second edition.* Fort Worth, TX: Harcourt Brace.

This is a highly valuable resource for teachers of EL1 and EL2 reading alike. It provides educators with a strong foundation for effective reading instruction from childhood to adulthood. The trajectory that typically developing readers move through is captured in the stages that EL2 reading educators can use as benchmarks. It emphasizes the changing nature of the reading process, the different demands of reading at different stages of development, and the skills required.

Cummins, J. (2012). The intersection of cognitive and sociocultural factors in the development of reading comprehension among immigrant students. *Reading and Writing, 25,* 1973–90.

This paper was part of a special issue entitled *Understanding literacy development of language minority students: An integrative approach,* which was co-edited by Xi Chen, Esther Geva, and Mila Schwartz. In his paper, Cummins critiques the conclusions of the National Literacy Panel. He synthesizes the research literature on the educational achievement of immigrant and minority language students and then offers three conclusions: (1) that literacy engagement is important for promoting reading comprehension; (2) that bilingual students' L1 proficiency plays a positive role in L2 academic development, i.e. through transfer; and (3) that societal power relations play a direct role in promoting school failure in low-SES communities. Cummins underscores the importance of training educators to promote literacy engagement, to teach for crosslinguistic transfer, and to affirm students' identities as bilinguals.

Domínguez de Ramírez, R., & **Shapiro, E. S.** (2006). Curriculum-based measurement and the evaluation of reading skills of Spanish-speaking English language learners in bilingual education classrooms. *School Psychology Review, 35,* 356–69.

This study compared the reading skills of 83 students who were enrolled in general education classrooms and 62 Spanish-speaking EL2 learners who were enrolled in bilingual education classrooms. Children were assessed three times annually using curriculum-based measurements. Text reading fluency in Spanish was assessed for Spanish-speaking EL2 learners who attended the bilingual education program. Consistently, across various grade levels, students who attended the bilingual program read English passages less fluently than their peers in the general education programs. In addition, students in general education made more gains over time in reading English than Spanish-speaking students made in reading Spanish passages. This study demonstrates the merits of curriculum-based measurement as a methodology for evaluating the rate of progress of Spanish-speaking EL2 learners—and of other L2 learners who attend bilingual education programs. The authors conclude by pointing out that, in fact, we do not know what gains in reading fluency can be expected in various groups of L2 learners.

Eunice Kennedy Shriver National Institute of Child Health and Human Development, NIH, DHHS. (2001). *Put reading first: The research building blocks for teaching children to read.* Washington, DC: US Government Printing Office.

This is a teacher-friendly version of the much larger report of the National Reading Panel (NRP) published in 2000. The NRP reviewed hundreds of studies to identify key skills for effective reading and instructional approaches from kindergarten through Grade 3. This teacher's guide translates the findings of the panel into specific instructional recommendations organized around five pillars of reading instruction: phonological awareness, phonics, fluency, vocabulary, and text comprehension. Each chapter focuses on one of these pillars and provides a definition, a succinct review of the evidence, implications for classroom instruction, instructional examples, and answers to frequently asked questions.

Francis, D. J., Rivera, M., Lesaux, N., Kieffer, M., & Rivera, H. (2006a). *Practical guidelines for the education of English language learners: Research-based recommendations for instruction and academic interventions.* Texas Institute for Measurement, Evaluation, and Statistics at the University of Houston for the Center on Instruction. Retrieved March 9 2015 from www.centeroninstruction.org

This is the first in a series of books offering practical guidelines, grounded in research evidence, for policy makers, administrators, and teachers on how to teach EL2 learners effectively. It emphasizes the importance of academic language skills for general academic success. One of the chapters offers recommendations specific to reading instruction and interventions for EL2 learners, while another is specific to mathematics, with an examination of the role of language and reading in mathematics proficiency.

Francis, D. J., Rivera, M., Lesaux, N., Kieffer, M., & Rivera, H. (2006b). *Practical guidelines for the education of English language learners: Research-based recommendations for serving adolescent newcomers.* Texas Institute for Measurement, Evaluation, and Statistics at the University of Houston for the Center on Instruction. Retrieved March 9 2015 from www. centeroninstruction.org

This is the second book in the series of practical guidelines on how to teach EL2 learners effectively. It provides evidence-based recommendation for instruction in five areas of need: language and literacy skills that adolescent newcomers need for content-area learning; instruction in academic language—the language they need for text comprehension and school success; direct, explicit instruction to support their comprehension of challenging texts; intensive instruction in writing for academic purposes; and systematic assessment of students' strengths and needs, as well as ongoing monitoring of their progress. It also offers recommendations for program and curriculum organization.

Geva, E. (Ed.). (2014). Learning difficulties in English language learners. *Perspectives on Language and Literacy, Special Issue, 40(4)*.

A publication of the International Reading Association. This special issue consists of five short, reader-friendly papers written by researchers from the United States, Canada, and Hong Kong who carry out research on learning disabilities in L2 learners in various contexts. Four of the articles address research that pertains to language and literacy skills in EL2 contexts, the challenges in identifying learning disabilities among these learners, and implications for practice. The fifth article addresses the challenges of communication with families of culturally and linguistically diverse learners with learning difficulties. The five articles are written in plain language, and provide solid, research-based observations, advice, and suggestions for working with children and adolescents who are L2 learners and who may have a learning disability.

Geva, E., & Farnia, F. (2012b). Assessment of reading difficulties in ESL/ELL learners: Myths, research evidence, and implications for assessment. In *Encyclopedia of language and literacy development* (pp. 1–9). London, ON: Western University. Retrieved March 9 2015 from http://www.academia.edu/6374288/Assessment_of_Reading_Difficulties_in_ESL_ELL_Learners_Myths_Research_Evidence_and_Implications_for_Assessment

In this brief, accessible article, the authors address six common myths related to the assessment of EL2 reading difficulties. Clarification for each myth is provided by drawing on sound research evidence. The authors also provide recommendations for assessment and directions for future research.

Koda, K., & Zehler, A. M. (Eds.). (2007). *Learning to read across languages: Crosslinguistic relationships in first- and second-language literacy development*. London: Routledge.

This book provides an overview of reading processes and development across five typologically different languages which differ in their writing systems. The chapters provide insights into what to expect in reading development for L2 learners who already have literacy skills in their L1. It will help teachers of EL2 reading deepen their understanding of how various aspects of the spoken and written L1 might affect reading in the L2 and what aspects might transfer crosslinguistically.

Melby-Lervåg, M., & Lervåg, A. (2014). Reading comprehension and its underlying components in second language learners: A meta-analysis of studies comparing first and second language learners. *Psychological Bulletin, 140(2)*, 409–33.

This is a systematic review of studies that compared L1 and L2 learners' reading comprehension and its underlying components: language comprehension, decoding, and phonological awareness. The authors reviewed 82 studies and report on the strength of the evidence for factors that affect reading comprehension in L2. Key findings were that compared to L1 learners, L2 learners have a medium-size deficit in reading comprehension, and a large deficit in language comprehension. However, there were only small differences in phonological awareness. A further analysis showed that the type of reading comprehension test can account for some of the differences in reading comprehension between L1 and L2 learners. The authors also report on the role of variables such as socioeconomic status, the extent to which the L1 or L2 is used at home, test characteristics, and the country where studies were conducted, for example, Canada versus the USA. Importantly, the authors conclude that interventions that aim to ameliorate reading comprehension problems among L2 learners should target language comprehension skills.

Shanahan, T., & Lonigan, C. (2010). The National Early Literacy Panel: A summary of the process and the report. *Educational Researcher, 39*, 279–85.

This article summarizes key findings of an extensive review of research —about 300 studies—on early literacy conducted by a panel of experts and published in 2008. The main purpose of the Early Literacy Panel was to identify early precursors of effective literacy development, the instructional approaches that result in substantial literacy growth, the effects of school and home environments, and the factors related to individual child characteristics. The report covered the examination of evidence on the effects of code-based instruction, shared book readings, home/parent interventions, preschool/kindergarten interventions, and early language teaching. This brief article summarizes key findings in each of these areas.

US Department of Education, National Centre for Education Evaluation and Regional Assistance, Institute of Education Sciences. (2014). *Teaching academic content and literacy to English learners in elementary and middle school (NCEE 2014–4012).* Retrieved March 9 2015 from http://ies.ed.gov/ncee/wwc/practiceguide.aspx?sid=19

This document synthesizes evidence from experimental studies on the most effective ways to help EL2 students to learn across the content areas and translates the evidence into an educator's practice guide. Innovative methods to teach academic language and literacy are highlighted, and numerous examples of teaching activities elicited from successful interventions are provided.

Appendix

Phonetic Symbols in American English

/i/	sea	/p/	pen
/ɪ/	bit	/b/	bee
/e/	get	/t/	time
/æ/	hat	/d/	dog
/u/	do	/k/	cat
/ʊ/	wood	/g/	got
/ɔ/	paw	/f/	fun
/ɑ/	dot	/θ/	thank
/ə/	away	/ð/	this
/ʌ/	luck	/s/	say
/ɝ/	girl	/z/	zoo
/aʊ/	now	/n/	nut
/aɪ/	why	/ŋ/	hang
/ɔɪ/	toy	/l/	lip
/eɪ/	play	/r/	rob
/oʊ/	so	/w/	will
		/h/	hen
		/ɹ/	yet
		/ʃ/	shape
		/ʒ/	pleasure
		/tʃ/	cheese
		/dʒ/	joke

Glossary

academic vocabulary: words critical for the understanding of content-area readings. Some are subject-specific and others appear across the curriculum.

acculturation: the process by which members of one cultural group adopt the values, beliefs, and behaviors of another group.

adversative conjunction: a conjunction that expresses contrast between two statements, such as 'but', 'still', 'yet', 'whereas', 'however', and 'nevertheless'.

alphabetic principle: the concept of sound–letter correspondence, which drives the written representation of most words in alphabetic languages.

appositive: a noun or a noun phrase that identifies or renames another noun that precedes it. Sometimes an appositive is introduced by a word or phrase, such as 'namely' or 'that is'. For example: 'Young users today are digital natives, that is, they interact naturally with a wide range of digital technologies.'

assistive technology (AT): an umbrella term referring to different forms of technology that can be used to adapt instruction for students with various learning needs.

authentic reading materials: texts originally created for L1 readers and used with L2 readers without modifying the language or content.

bilingual education: general education provided in two languages. There are different models of bilingual education and the intensity of the instruction provided in the L2 varies from model to model.

cognates: words in different languages that are related by origin through a common ancestral language. Cognates can also be related because of borrowing between languages.

cognitive skills: mental or thinking skills needed to carry out any task. Cognitive skills such as working memory, attention, auditory processing, visual processing, processing speed, and reasoning are critical for successful reading and learning.

cognitive theories: different theories on the study of mental processes. In this book, we use cognitive theories in relation to the examination of cognitive skills critical for reading.

cohesion markers: language devices that connect words and ideas in discourse. In English, the main cohesion markers are conjunctions and pronouns.

communicative approach: an approach to L2 development that highlights language as a communicative system and emphasizes the use of real-life situations. It is often juxtaposed with approaches that emphasize direct instruction of language skills.

compound word: a word formed by putting two or more morphemes together, for example, 'campfire'. Compounding as a way of making words varies between languages.

comprehension-monitoring: checking 'online' whether one comprehends and whether the text makes sense. It is a metacognitive strategy that effective readers use.

consonant cluster: a group of consonants that are not separated by vowels. For example, the second syllable in the word 'contexts' has a cluster of four consonants: /ksts/.

coordinating conjunction: a conjunction such as 'and', 'but', 'or', 'nor', 'for', 'yet', and 'so', used to join two nouns or independent clauses that are grammatically equal or similar. For example: 'My sister likes to dance *and* she plays the banjo.'

crosslinguistic transfer: the transfer of language and reading-related skills developed in L1 to L2, or vice versa.

decode: read words or pseudowords by applying letter–sound correspondence rules.

deep (opaque) orthography: a writing system that does not have regular letter-to-sound correspondences, such as English or French. In such languages the spelling of many words is inconsistent. In contrast, see 'transparent (shallow) orthography'.

derivational morphology: a process of word formation that involves adding prefixes and suffixes to a root (stem or base) to create a new word, for example, the formation of 'implication' from 'imply' or 'picturesque' from 'picture'.

developmental benchmarks: points of reference for skills that are needed and acquired by typically developing readers at a given point. Teachers can use these to gauge whether their students are making good progress in their reading development.

developmental theories: theories that examine development across the life span. In this book, they are used to examine L2 reading development from childhood to adolescence.

EL1: a term used in this book to refer to learners with English as a first language.

EL2: a term used in this book to refer to learners for whom English is not the first language.

EL2 proficiency: the level of ability in listening, speaking, reading, and writing possessed by a learner of English as a second language.

executive function: an umbrella term referring to neurologically based skills that are responsible for planning, mental control, and self-regulation.

expository text: non-fiction reading material with an internal structure that is different from a narrative and that provides facts.

expressive vocabulary: the words that speakers can use when speaking and writing. In contrast, see 'receptive vocabulary'.

extensive reading: using abundant reading as the main vehicle for L2 learning.

factual comprehension question: a question that refers to information the reader can find directly in the text.

first language (L1): the first language learned by an individual. Also referred to as 'native language', 'home language', or 'mother tongue'.

fluency: at the word level, the ability to read words quickly and accurately; at the text level, reading that is not 'choppy' and includes intonation patterns that reflect the text.

foreign language: a term commonly used to refer to an L2 being learned in a country where it is not the societal language, for example, English being learned in China.

graded (modified) reading material: reading material whose vocabulary, grammar, or content density is modified to make it more accessible to L2 readers.

grapheme: a letter or combination of letters that represents a phoneme (an individual sound).

graphic organizer: a pictorial representation of concepts and ideas. It shows visually how the ideas and concepts are organized, interconnected, and related to each other.

high-frequency words: words that appear frequently in written materials, such as 'the', 'where', 'to', and 'two', and that readers should recognize automatically. See also 'sight words'.

higher-level language skills: language skills that go beyond basic vocabulary and grammar. They include aspects of language such as advanced vocabulary and grammar, understanding metaphors, and using language to express and understand complex ideas—determining cause and effect, making inferences, etc.

higher-order reading skills: reading skills that go beyond basic skills such as decoding and fluency. They include the use of metacognitive strategies, such as comprehension-monitoring, activating prior knowledge, noting cause–effect relations, considering text structure, and articulating points of view.

immersion: a method of teaching L2 where the L2 is a vehicle of instruction across the curriculum.

inferential comprehension question: a comprehension question requiring readers to draw meaningful conclusions that follow from the text but are not stated explicitly in the text structure.

interactive vocabulary: vocabulary presented through the use of multimedia to aid learning.

intonation: raising or lowering the pitch (i.e. the melody) in grammatically appropriate spots in connected speech or while reading aloud.

L1: see 'first language'.

L2: see 'second language' and 'foreign language'.

language impairment: a language disorder characterized by persistent language learning difficulties, despite normal hearing. It affects learning to read in both EL1 and EL2.

language proficiency: the level of a learner's skills in listening, speaking, reading, and writing in a given language.

learning disability (LD): a disorder that makes it difficult to learn across one or more domains. Dyslexia, a learning disability characterized by persistent difficulties in decoding and spelling isolated words, is associated with poor phonological skills.

'learning to read': a stage of reading development (typically K–3) characterized mainly by the learning of word-level reading skills. It is often juxtaposed with 'reading to learn'.

letter–sound recognition: a pre-literacy skill that involves being able to identify the sound that each letter makes.

metacognitive strategies: self-assessment and self-correcting strategies applied actively during reading in order to comprehend text.

metalinguistic strategies: strategies that involve actively thinking about the language and how it works. Such strategies, for example, syntactic awareness, can help learners deduce the meaning of new words and understand nuances in meaning encoded in word order.

minority language: a language spoken by a small group of people in a society.

morpheme: the smallest linguistic unit that carries meaning.

morphological awareness: the awareness that words consist of smaller units (morphemes) that carry meaning. This can help in deducing the meaning of morphologically complex words.

morphologically complex word: a word with more than one morpheme. It can be a base plus an inflection (for example, *work* + *–s* = 'works'), a base with a prefix, a suffix, or both (for example, 'antigovernment'), or a base with a modifier (for example, *book* + *shelf* = 'bookshelf').

morphology: the study or characteristics of word formation.

negative transfer: when aspects of an L1 interfere with the development of related skills in the L2 because the structures are not the same in the two languages.

onset-rime: 'onset' refers to the initial consonant or consonant cluster in a syllable; 'rime' refers to the vowel(s) and consonants that follow it within a syllable. In the word 'sight', /s/ is the onset and /aɪt/ is the rime. Separating the onset from the rime to identify rhyming words is an important aspect of phonological awareness and learning to read.

over-identification: disproportionately high rates of learning disability or intellectual disability diagnoses among certain linguistic and ethnic minority groups. Often related to biased diagnostic procedures that do not consider L2 proficiency, opportunities to learn, or cultural factors.

persistent difficulties: difficulties with reading or writing that remain despite high-quality teaching, program adaptations, and various interventions. Persistent difficulties may suggest that the individual has a learning disability.

phoneme: each individual sound heard in a word. For example, the word 'love' has three phonemes.

phoneme segmentation: the ability to parse words into their individual sounds (phonemes).

phonemic awareness: the metalinguistic ability to identify, distinguish, and manipulate individual sounds (phonemes) in words. Phonemic awareness is a component of phonological awareness.

phonics: a method to systematically and explicitly teach the sound–letter relationships of alphabetic languages. Phonics is important for the development of good decoding skills.

phonological awareness: a broad set of related skills that are essential for learning to decode. They involve the awareness that word parts, such as phonemes, onsets and rimes, and syllables, can be manipulated in various ways. Tasks may require identifying and generating rhymes, clapping out the number of syllables in a word, or recognizing words with the same initial sounds, for example, 'boy' and 'bear'. Phonemic awareness is a component of phonological awareness.

phonological memory: the ability to hold phonemes in memory for a few seconds. It is often assessed by asking individuals to repeat pseudowords of varying lengths.

phonology: the study of the sound structures in a language.

positive transfer: when aspects of an L1 facilitate the learning of related aspects of an L2.

procedural knowledge: the knowledge required to perform a task. Sometimes learners have declarative knowledge (the ability to describe or explain a skill) but lack procedural knowledge (facility in using the skill), and vice versa.

processing speed: the speed of taking in, using, or pulling out information. It is often assessed with tasks requiring rapid naming of highly familiar items, such as colors, digits, or letters.

psycholinguistic theories: theories that explain language learning in relation to various cognitive processes—memory, strategies, etc. Also referred to as the psychology of language.

read-aloud: a teaching activity used by teachers of young children to share books with them and to expose them to rich language. Teachers read aloud to the class and ask questions before, during, and after reading.

reading accuracy: an aspect of word reading fluency that refers to the ability to read words with precision and without mistakes.

reading disability: a persistent difficulty in acquiring new knowledge. Dyslexia, a difficulty with decoding and spelling, is a learning difficulty that affects reading performance.

'reading to learn': a phase of reading development, typically starting in Grade 4, characterized by the use of reading as a vehicle for learning. It is often juxtaposed with the preceding 'learning to read' phase.

receptive vocabulary: words that speakers can recognize and understand when they listen or read. In contrast, see 'expressive vocabulary'.

rhyme awareness: the ability to identify words that rhyme and distinguish them from those that do not rhyme. This is one aspect of phonemic awareness.

rhyming word family: a term used in initial reading instruction to refer to a group of words that share similar rime patterns, for example, 'thick', 'sick', and 'stick'. To help children remember the spelling of such words, they are presented in groups, thus the term 'word family'. In upper elementary grades, 'word family' can refer to a group of words that are semantically related, that is, share the same root, for example, 'electric', 'electrification', 'electrify', etc.

scaffolded reading: a teaching approach that helps learners with reading by giving them the supports (scaffolding) they require. Typically, the scaffolding is gradually removed as learners make progress.

second language (L2): a second or subsequent languages learned by an individual.

sight word: a high-frequency word that cannot be read by relying on letter–sound decoding skills because of inconsistent letter–sound relationships, for example, 'would', 'the', and 'know'. Practice is recommended to enhance automatic recognition of these words.

sight word reading: using a visual memory strategy to read automatically words that appear frequently in written text and cannot be decoded letter by letter because of their irregular spelling. You can find the Dolch Word Lists of the 220 most frequently used sight words on the internet.

Socioeconomic Status (SES): the economic and social position of individuals or groups in relation to others in a society. SES indices are based on income, education, and occupation.

sound blending: combining phonemes to form a word, for example, /s/ + /æ/ + /t/ = 'sat'.

sound deletion: removing a phoneme from a word and saying the resulting word. For example: 'Say "snail". Now say it without the /s/.' Sound deletion tasks are often used to evaluate phonemic awareness.

sound segmentation: see 'phoneme segmentation'.

sound substitution: replacing one sound with another in a word. For example, replacing the initial sound in 'pat' with the /m/ sound results in the word 'mat'.

story grammar: story components that are characteristic of narratives. They include settings, characters, plot, beginning, middle, and end.

strategic knowledge: knowledge of a variety of reading strategies that can be used 'online' (i.e. while reading) to achieve reading comprehension.

stress: see 'word stress'.

Structured English Immersion (SEI): a form of second language instruction in which children are taught mainly or exclusively in an L2, with limited exposure to the L1. The content and the curriculum focus on teaching the language. Grammar and other language components are also taught explicitly and complement the language learning acquired through the content areas.

subordinate clause: a clause that 'depends on' or modifies a main (independent) clause. Also referred to as a dependent clause. Consider the sentence: 'When you find your cellphone [subordinate clause], don't forget to text me [main clause].' The subordinate clause cannot stand alone as a sentence, while the independent clause can.

subordinating conjunction: a conjunction that joins a main (independent) clause to a subordinate (dependent) clause. Examples of subordinate conjunctions are 'although', 'because', 'once', 'when', and 'whether'. Subordinating conjunctions come right before the subordinate clause.

syllable: a word segment that contains at least one vowel sound. Syllables are the parts into which a word can be intuitively divided when it is pronounced. For example, the word 'conjunction' consists of the syllables *con + junc + tion*. A vowel on its own can be a syllable, but a consonant needs a vowel to become a syllable.

syllabic complexity: refers to the structure of a syllable, where the 'C' stands for 'consonant' and the 'V' for 'vowel'. Some syllables are complex and others are simple. A CVC syllable, such as *con* in the word 'conjunction', is considered a simple syllable. However, the CVCC syllable *junc* is a complex syllable because there are two syllables strung together.

syntactic structures: the different ways of structuring sentences in a language that are acceptable to native speakers of the language. Syntactic structures vary in terms of their complexity.

syntax: the principles by which sentences are constructed in a language; the rules that govern word order and sentence structure in a language.

teaching adaptations: any instructional or curricular modification aimed at facilitating learning for students who are struggling.

text-level reading skills: see 'higher-order reading skills'.

transparent (shallow) orthography: a language that represents sounds in the writing system in a regular and consistent manner, for example, Spanish or Finnish. In such languages, there is a one-to-one correspondence between letters and the sounds they make. In contrast, see 'deep (opaque) orthography'.

under-identification: the tendency to delay diagnosing reading difficulties in L2 learners by waiting until adequate L2 proficiency is developed.

vocabulary breadth: the number of words known.

vocabulary depth: thorough knowledge of the meaning of a word. It includes knowing the word's multiple meanings, being familiar with its antonyms, synonyms, homophones, and homonyms, and understanding how to use it across multiple contexts.

word-level reading skills: decoding skills, sight word recognition, and the ability to read words accurately and fluently.

word recognition: involves various phonological and orthographic processes, the ability to recognize word parts accurately and efficiently, and the use of context clues to quickly access the meaning of a word as it is being read.

word stress: the emphasis placed on a syllable in a multisyllabic word. For example, in 'emphasis', the stress is on the first syllable: /em/.

Word Wall: a strategy used by teachers in primary grades, mainly to help children develop automatic word recognition skills. Teachers rehearse the reading of sight words daily and post them in an area of the classroom referred to as the Word Wall.

working memory: a cognitive skill that involves holding information in memory for very brief intervals and, at the same time, processing incoming information. Working memory plays a major role in complex tasks such as L1 and L2 reading comprehension and writing.

References

Afflerbach, P., Pearson, P. D., & Paris, S. G. (2008). Clarifying differences between reading skills and reading strategies. *The Reading Teacher, 61*, 364–73.

Akamatsu, N. (2002). A similarity in word-recognition procedures among second language readers with different first language backgrounds. *Applied Psycholinguistics, 23*, 117–33.

American Psychiatric Association. (2013). *Diagnostic and statistical manual of mental disorders, fifth edition.* Washington, DC: American Psychiatric Association.

Anglin, J. M. (1993). Vocabulary development: A morphological analysis. *Monograph for the Society for Research in Child Development, 58*, 1–186.

Aram, D., Fine, Y., & Ziv, M. (2013). Enhancing parent–child shared book reading interactions: Promoting references to the book's plot and socio-cognitive themes. *Early Childhood Research Quarterly, 28*, 111–22.

Atay. D, & Kurt, G. (2006). Elementary school EFL learners' vocabulary learning: The effects of post-reading activities. *Canadian Modern Language Review, 63*, 255–73.

August, D., Branum-Martin, L., Cardenas-Hagan, E., & Francis, D. J. (2009). The impact of an instructional intervention on the science and language learning of middle grade English language learners. *Journal of Research on Educational Effectiveness, 2*, 345–76.

August, D., & Shanahan, T. (2006). Introduction and methodology. In D. August & T. Shanahan (Eds.), *Developing literacy in second-language learners: Report of the National Literacy Panel on language-minority children and youth* (pp. 175–184). Mahwah, NJ: Lawrence Erlbaum Associates.

August, D., & Shanahan, T. (Eds.). (2008). *Developing reading and writing in second-language learners: Lessons from the report of the National Literacy Panel on language-minority children and youth.* New York, NY: Routledge.

Baker, L., & Beall, L. C. (2009). Metacognitive processes and reading comprehension. In S. E. Israel & G. G. Duffy (Eds.), *Handbook of research on reading comprehension* (pp. 373–88). New York, NY: Routledge.

Baker, S., Lesaux, N., Jayanthi, M., Dimino, J., Proctor, C. P., Morris, J., Gersten, R., Haymond, K., Kieffer, M. J., Linan-Thompson, S., & Newman-Gonchar, R. (2014). *Teaching academic content and literacy to English learners in elementary and middle school (NCEE 2014–4012).* Washington, DC: National Center for Education Evaluation and Regional Assistance (NCEE), Institute of Education Sciences, US Department of Education. Retrieved May 1 2015 from http://ies.ed.gov/ncee/wwc/PracticeGuide.aspx?sid=19

Beck, I. L., & McKeown, M. G. (1991). Social studies texts are hard to understand: Mediating some of the difficulties. *Language Arts, 68*, 482–90.

Beck, B., McKeown, M., & Kucan, L. (2013). *Bringing words to life: Robust vocabulary instruction, second edition.* New York, NY: The Guilford Press.

Beck, I. L., McKeown, M. G., & Worthy, J. (1995). Giving a text voice can improve students' understanding. *Reading Research Quarterly, 30,* 220–38.

Berko, J. (1958). The child's learning of English morphology. *Word, 14,* 150–77.

Berninger, V. W., Abbott, R. D., Nagy, W., & Carlisle, J. (2010). Growth in phonological, orthographic, and morphological awareness in grades 1–6. *Journal of Psycholinguistic Research, 39,* 141–63.

Bialystok, E., Luk, G., & Kwan, E. (2005). Bilingualism, biliteracy, and learning to read: Interactions among languages and writing systems. *Scientific Studies of Reading, 9,* 43–61.

Biemiller, A., & Boote, C. (2006). An effective method for building meaning vocabulary in primary grades. *Journal of Educational Psychology, 98,* 44–62.

Biemiller, A., & Slonim, A. (2001). Estimating root word vocabulary growth in normative and advantaged populations: Evidence for a common sequence of vocabulary acquisition. *Journal of Educational Psychology, 93,* 498–520.

Biro, M., Smederevac, S., & Tovilović, S. (2009). Socioeconomic and cultural factors of low scholastic achievement of Roma children. *Psichologija, 42,* 273–88.

Blachowicz, C., & Ogle, D. (2001). *Reading comprehension.* New York, NY: The Guilford Press.

Bollman, K. A., Silberglitt, B., & Gibbons, K. A. (2007). The St. Croix River education district model: Incorporating systems-level organization and a multi-tiered problem-solving process for intervention delivery. In S. R. Jimerson, M. K. Burns, & A. M. VanDerHeyden (Eds.), *Handbook of response to intervention: The science and practice of assessment and intervention* (pp. 319–30). New York, NY: Springer.

Cain, K. (2009). Making sense of text: skills that support text comprehension and its development. *Perspectives on Language and Literacy, Special Issue, 35(2),* 11–14.

Cain, K., Oakhill, J., & Bryant, P. E. (2004). Children's reading comprehension ability: Concurrent prediction by working memory, verbal ability, and component skills. *Journal of Educational Psychology, 96,* 31–42.

Calderón, M. E. (2007a). *Teaching reading to English language learners, grades 6–12: A framework for improving achievement in the content areas.* Thousand Oaks, CA: Corwin Press.

Calderón, M. E. (2007b). *RIGOR! Reading instruction goals for older readers: Reading program for 6th–12th students with interrupted formal education in English and Spanish.* New York, NY: Benchmark Education Co.

Calderón, M., Slavin, R., & Sánchez, M. (2011). Effective instruction for English learners. *Immigrant Children, 21(1),* 103–27.

Carlisle, J. (2000). Awareness of the structure and meaning of morphologically complex words: Impact on reading. *Reading and Writing, 12,* 169–90.

Carrell, P. L. (1985). Facilitating ESL reading by teaching text structure. *TESOL Quarterly, 19,* 727–57.

Catts, H., Adlof, S. M., & Weismer, S. E. (2006). Language deficits in poor comprehenders: A case for the simple view of reading. *Journal of Speech, Language and Hearing Research, 49,* 278–93.

Center for Applied Linguistics. (2012). Directory of two-way bilingual immersion programs in the US. Retrieved March 9 2015 from http://www.cal.org/twi/directory

Chall, J. S. (1989). Learning to read: The great debate twenty years later. A response to 'Debunking the great phonics myth'.' *Phi Delta Kappan, 71,* 521–38.

Chall, J. S. (1996). *Stages of reading development, second edition.* Fort Worth, TX: Harcourt Brace.

Cho, J. R., & McBride-Chang, C. (2005). Correlates of Korean Hangul acquisition among kindergartners and second graders. *Scientific Studies of Reading, 9,* 3–16.

Cirino, P. T., Vaughn, S., Linan-Thompson, S., Cardenas-Hagan, E., Fletcher, J. M., & Francis, D. J. (2009). One-year follow-up outcomes of Spanish and English interventions for English language learners at-risk for reading problems. *American Educational Research Journal, 46,* 744–81.

Clark, E. (1982). The young word maker: A case study of innovation in the child's lexicon. In E. Wanner & L. Gleitman (Eds.), *Language acquisition: The state of the art* (pp. 391–425). Cambridge: Cambridge University Press.

Clay, M. M. (1993). *An observation survey of early literacy achievement.* Portsmouth, NH: Heinemann Education.

Cleave, P., Girolametto, L., Chen, X., & Johnson, C. (2010). Narrative abilities in monolingual and dual language learning children with specific language impairment. *Journal of Communication Disorders, 43,* 511–22.

Coiro, J., & Dobler, E. (2007). Exploring the online comprehension strategies used by sixth-grade skilled readers to search for and locate information on the Internet. *Reading Research Quarterly, 42,* 214–57.

Collier, V. P. (1987). Age and rate of acquisition of second language for academic purposes. *TESOL Quarterly, 21,* 617–41.

Collins, M. F. (2005). ESL preschoolers' English vocabulary acquisition from storybook reading. *Reading Research Quarterly, 40(4),* 406–08.

Corder, S. P. (1967). The significance of learners' errors. *International Review of Applied Linguistics in Language Teaching, 5,* 161–70.

Cranny, M. (2012). *British Columbia Social Studies, Pathways: Civilizations through time.* Toronto: Pearson.

Crosson, A. C., & Lesaux, N. K. (2010). Revisiting assumptions about the relationship of fluent reading to comprehension: Spanish-speakers' text-reading fluency in English. *Reading and Writing, An Interdisciplinary Journal, 23,* 475–94.

Crosson, A. C., & Lesaux, N. K. (2013a). Does knowledge of connectives play a unique role in the reading comprehension of English language learners and English-only students? *Journal of Research in Reading, 36,* 241–60.

Crosson, A. C., & Lesaux, N. K. (2013b). Connectives: Fitting another piece of the vocabulary instruction puzzle. *The Reading Teacher, 67,* 193–200.

Cumming, A., & Geva, E. (2012). Summary and recommendations. In A. Cumming (Ed.), *Adolescent literacies in a multicultural context* (pp. 133–148). New York, NY: Routledge.

Cummins, J. (1981). *Schooling and language minority students: A theoretical framework.* Los Angeles, CA: National Dissemination and Assessment Center.

Cummins, J. (1983). *Heritage language education: A literature review.* Toronto: Ontario Ministry of Education.

Cummins, J. (1984). *Bilingualism and special education: Issues in assessment and pedagogy*. Clevedon: Multilingual Matters.

Cummins, J. (2000). *Language, power and pedagogy: Bilingual children in the crossfire*. Clevedon: Multilingual Matters.

Cummins, J. (2012). The intersection of cognitive and sociocultural factors in the development of reading comprehension among immigrant students. *Reading and Writing, 25*, 1973–90.

Cunningham, A. E., & Stanovich, K. E. (1991). Tracking the unique effects of print exposure in children: Associations with vocabulary, general knowledge, and spelling. *Journal of Educational Psychology, 83*, 264–74.

Cunningham, A. E., & Stanovich, K. E. (2003). Reading matters: How reading engagement influences cognition. In J. Flood, D. Lapp, J. Squire, & J. Jensen (Eds.), *Handbook of research on teaching the English language arts, second edition* (pp. 666–75). Mahwah, NJ: Lawrence Erlbaum Associates.

Cutting, L. E., & Scarborough, H. S. (2006). Prediction of reading comprehension: Relative contributions of word recognition, language proficiency, and other cognitive skills can depend on how comprehension is measured. *Scientific Studies of Reading, 10(3)*, 277–99.

Dalton, B., Proctor, P., Uccelli, P., Mo, E., Snow, C. E. (2011). Designing for diversity: The role of reading strategies and interactive vocabulary in a digital reading environment for fifth-grade monolingual English and bilingual students. *Journal of Literacy Research, 43(1)*, 68–100.

de Oliveira, L. C. (2007). Academic language development in the content areas: Challenges for English language learners. *INTESOL Journal, 4(1)*, 22–33.

Derwing, B. L., & Baker, W. J. (1986). On assessing morphological development. In P. J. Fletcher & M. Gannan (Eds.), *Language acquisition: Studies in first language development* (pp. 326–28). Cambridge: Cambridge University Press.

Dixon, L. Q., Zhao, J., Shin, J. Y., Wu, S., Su, J. H., Burgess-Brigham, R., Gezer, M. U., & Snow, C. (2012). What we know about second language acquisition: A synthesis from four perspectives. *Review of Educational Research, 82*, 5–60.

Dole, J. A., Duffy, G., Roehler, L. R., & Pearson, D. P. (1991). Moving from the Old to the New: Research on reading comprehension instruction. *Review of Educational Review, 61*, 239–64.

Domínguez de Ramírez, R., & Shapiro, E. S. (2006). Curriculum-based measurement and the evaluation of reading skills of Spanish-speaking English language learners in bilingual education classrooms. *School Psychology Review, 35*, 356–69.

Dressler, C., & Kamil, M. (2006). First- and second-language literacy. In D. August & T. Shanahan (Eds.), *Developing literacy in second-language learners: Report of the National panel of language-minority children and youth* (pp. 197–246). Mahwah, NJ: Lawrence Erlbaum Associates.

Droop, M., & Verhoeven, L. (1998). Background knowledge, linguistic complexity, and second-language reading comprehension. *Journal of Literacy Research, 30*, 253–71.

Durgunoğlu, A. Y., Nagy, W. E., & Hancin-Bhatt, B. J. (1993). Cross-language transfer of phonological awareness. *Journal of Educational Psychology, 85(3)*, 453–65.

Duursma, E., Romero-Contreras, S., Szuber, A., Proctor, P., Snow, C., August, D., & Calderón, M. (2007). The role of home literacy and language environment on bilinguals' English and Spanish vocabulary development. *Applied Psycholinguistics, 28,* 171–90.

Dymock, S., & Nicholson, T. (2007). *Teaching text structures: A key to nonfiction reading success.* New York, NY: Scholastic.

Dymock, S., & Nicholson, T. (2010). 'High 5!' Strategies to enhance comprehension of expository text. *The Reading Teacher, 64(3),* 166–78.

Edmonds, M. S., Vaughn, S., Wexler, J., Reutebuch, C., Cable, A., Tackett, K. K., & Schnakenberg, J. W. (2009). A synthesis of reading interventions and effects on reading comprehension outcomes on older struggling readers. *Review of Educational Research, 79(1),* 262–87.

Ehri, L. C. (1992). Reconceptualizing the development of sight word reading in relation to its relationship to reading. In P. Gough & R. Treiman (Eds.), *Reading acquisition* (pp. 105–42). Hillsdale, NJ: Erlbaum Associates.

Ehri, L. C. (2014). Phonemic awareness and letter knowledge. Paper presented at the International Reading Association (IRA) Research Institute of the IRA 59th Annual Conference, New Orleans, USA.

Ehri, L. C., Nunes, C. R., Wollows, D. A., Schuster, B. V., Yaghoub-Zadeh, Z., & Shanahan, T. (2001). Phonemic awareness instruction helps children learn to read: Evidence from the National Reading Panel's meta-analysis. *Reading Research Quarterly, 36,* 250–87.

Elkonin, D. (1971). Development of Speech. In A.V. Zaporozhets and D. B. Elkonin (Eds.). *The psychology of preschool children.* (pp. 111–82). Cambridge, MA: MIT Press.

Eunice Kennedy Shriver National Institute of Child Health and Human Development, NIH, DHHS. (2000). *Report of the National Reading Panel: Teaching children to read (00-4769).* Washington, DC: US Government Printing Office.

Eunice Kennedy Shriver National Institute of Child Health and Human Development, NIH, DHHS. (2001). *Put reading first: The research building blocks for teaching children to read.* Washington, DC: US Government Printing Office.

Farnia, F., & Geva, E. (2011). Cognitive correlates of vocabulary growth in English language learners. *Applied Psycholinguistics, 32,* 711–38.

Farnia, F., & Geva, E. (2013). Growth and predictors of change in English language learners' reading comprehension. *Journal of Research in Reading, 36,* 389–421.

Fenner, A. (2002). *Cultural awareness and language awareness based on dialogic interaction with texts in foreign language learning.* Strasbourg: Council of Europe.

Fielding, L. G., Wilson, P. T., & Anderson, R. C. (1986). A new focus on free readings: The role of trade books in reading instruction. In T. Raphael (Ed.), *The context of school-based literacy* (pp. 149–70). New York, NY: Random House.

Fletcher, J. M. (2006). Measuring reading comprehension. *Scientific Studies of Reading, 10(3),* 323–30.

Florit, E., & Cain, K. (2011). The Simple View of Reading: Is it valid for different types of alphabetic orthographies? *Educational Psychology Review, 23,* 553–76.

Fountas, I. C., & Pinnell G. S. (1996). *Guiding reading: Good first teaching for all children.* Portsmouth, NH: Heinemann.

Francis, D. J., Rivera, M., Lesaux, N., Kieffer, M., & Rivera, H. (2006a). *Practical guidelines for the education of English language learners: Research-based recommendations for instruction and academic interventions.* US Department of Education. Retrieved March 9 2015 from www.centeroninstruction.org

Francis, D. J., Rivera, M., Lesaux, N., Kieffer, M., & Rivera, H. (2006b). *Practical guidelines for the education of English language learners: Research-based recommendations for serving adolescent newcomers.* Texas Institute for Measurement, Evaluation, and Statistics at the University of Houston for the Center on Instruction. Retrieved March 9 2015 from www.centeroninstruction.org

Fraser, C., Adelson, V., & Geva, E. (2014). Recognizing English language learners with reading disabilities: Minimizing bias, accurate identification, and timely intervention. *Perspectives on Language and Literacy, 40(4),* 11–17.

Frost, R., Siegelman, N., Narkiss, A., & Afek, L. (2013). What predicts successful literacy acquisition in a second language? *Psychological Science,* 1–10. Retrieved March 9 2015 from http://pss.sagepub.com/content/early/2013/05/20/0956797612472207

Fuchs, D., & Fuchs, L. S. (2006). Introduction to response to intervention: What, why, and how valid it is? *Reading Research Quarterly, 41(1),* 93–9.

Fuchs, D., & Vaughn, S. (2012). Responsiveness-to-intervention: A decade later. *Journal of Learning Disabilities, 45(3),* 195–203.

Gagné, E. D., Weidemann, C., Bell, M. S., & Anders, T. D. (1984). Training thirteen-year-olds to elaborate while studying text. *Human Learning: Journal of Practical Research & Applications, 3,* 281–94.

Ganschow, L., Sparks, R. L., & Javorsky, J. (1998). Foreign language learning difficulties: An historical perspective. *Journal of Learning Disabilities, 31,* 248–58.

García, G. E. (1998). Mexican-American bilingual students' metacognitive reading strategies: What's transferred, unique, problematic? *National Reading Conference Yearbook, 47,* 253–63.

García, G. E., & Nagy, W. E. (1993). Latino students' concept of cognates. In D. J. Leu & C. K. Kinzer (Eds.), *Examining central issues in literacy research, theory, and practice* (pp. 361–73). Chicago, IL: National Reading Conference.

Gardner, D. (2004). Vocabulary input through extensive reading: A comparison of words found in children's narrative and expository reading materials. *Applied Linguistics, 25,* 1–37.

Gardner, D. (2008). Vocabulary recycling in children's authentic reading materials: A corpus-based investigation of narrow reading. *Reading in a Foreign Language, 20,* 92–122.

Garnett, B. (2010). Toward understanding the academic trajectories of ESL youth. *Canadian Modern Language Review, 66,* 677–710.

Ge, F., & Xuehong, T. (2002). Temporal reasoning on daily events in primary school pupils. *Acta Psychologica Sinica, 34,* 604–10.

Genesee, F., Geva, E., Dressler, C., & Kamil, M. (2006). Synthesis: Cross-linguistic relationships in working memory, phonological processes, and oral language. In D. August, & T. Shanahan, (Eds.), *Developing literacy in second-language learners: A report of the national literacy panel on language-minority children and youth* (pp. 153–74). Mahwah, NJ: Lawrence Erlbaum Associates.

Genesee, F., & Jared, D. (2008). Literacy development in early French immersion programs. *Canadian Psychology, 49,* 140–47.

Genesee, F., & Lindholm-Leary, K. (2010). *Alternative educational programs for English learners. Improving education for English learners: Research-based approaches.* California Department of Education.

Gersten, R., Baker, S. K., Shanahan, T., Linan-Thompson, S., Collins, P., & Scarcella, R. (2007). *Effective literacy and English language instruction for English learners in the elementary grades: A practice guide (NCEE 2007-4011).* Washington, DC: National Center for Education Evaluation and Regional Assistance, Institute of Education Sciences, US Department of Education. Retrieved March 9 2015 from http://ies.ed.gov/ncee/wwc/pdf/practice_guides/20074011.pdf

Geva, E. (1992). The role of conjunctions in L2 text comprehension. *TESOL Quarterly, 26(4),* 731–47.

Geva, E. (2000). Issues in the assessment of reading disabilities in L2 children: Beliefs and research evidence. *Dyslexia, 6,* 13–28.

Geva, E. (2006). Second-language oral proficiency and second-language literacy. In D. August & T. Shanahan (Eds.), *Developing literacy in second-language learners: A report of the National Literacy Panel on language-minority children and youth* (pp. 123–39). Mahwah, NJ: Lawrence Erlbaum Associates.

Geva, E. (2007). Conjunction use in school children's oral language and reading. In R. Horowitz (Ed.), *The evolution of talk about text: Knowing the world through instructional discourse* (pp. 271–94). Hillsdale, NJ: Erlbaum Associates.

Geva, E. (Ed.). (2014). Learning difficulties in English language learners. *Perspectives on Language and Literacy, Special Issue, 40(4).*

Geva, E., & Farnia, F. (2012a). Developmental changes in the nature of language proficiency and reading fluency paint a more complex view of reading comprehension in ELL and EL1. *Reading and Writing: An Interdisciplinary Journal, 25,* 1819–45.

Geva, E., & Farnia, F. (2012b). Assessment of reading difficulties in ESL/ELL learners: Myths, research evidence, and implications for assessment. In Encyclopedia of language and literacy development (pp. 1–9). London, ON: Western University. Retrieved March 9 2015 from http://www.academia.edu/6374288/Assessment_of_Reading_Difficulties_in_ESL_ELL_Learners_Myths_Research_Evidence_and_Implications_for_Assessment

Geva, E., & Herbert, K. (2012). Assessment and interventions in English language learners with LD. In B. Wong and D. Butler (Eds.), *Learning about learning disabilities* (pp. 271–98). Waltham, MA: Academic Press.

Geva, E., & Massey-Garrison, A. (2013). A comparison of the language skills of ELLs and monolinguals who are poor decoders, poor comprehenders or normal readers. *Journal of Learning Disabilities, 46,* 387–401.

Geva, E., & Ryan, E. B. (1985). Use of conjunctions in expository texts by skilled and less-skilled readers. *Journal of Reading Behaviour, 17(4),* 331–46.

Geva, E., & Ryan, E. B. (1993). Linguistic and cognitive correlates of academic skills in first and second language. *Language Learning, 43,* 5–42.

Geva, E., & Siegel, S. L. (2000). Orthographic and cognitive factors in the concurrent development of basic reading skills in two languages. *Journal of Reading and Writing, 12,* 1–30.

Geva, E., Wade-Woolley, L., & Shany, M. (1997). The development of reading efficiency in first and second language. *Scientific Studies of Reading, 1,* 119–44.

Geva, E., & Wiener, J. (2015). *Psychological assessment of culturally and linguistically diverse children.* New York, NY: Springer.

Geva, E., & Yaghoub-Zadeh, Z. (2006). Reading efficiency in native English-speaking and English-as-a-second-language children: The role of oral proficiency and underlying cognitive-linguistic processes. *Scientific Studies of Reading, 10,* 31–58.

Geva, E., Yaghoub-Zadeh, Z., & Schuster, B. (2000). Understanding individual differences in word recognition skills of ESL children. *Annals of Dyslexia, 50,* 123–54.

Gholamain, M., & Geva, E. (1999). Orthographic and cognitive factors in the concurrent development of basic reading skills in English and Persian. *Language Learning, 49,* 183–217.

Goldenberg, C. (2008). Teaching English language learners: What the research does—and does not—say. *American Educator, Summer,* 8–44.

Goldenberg, C., Rueda, R., & August, D. (2006). Sociocultural influences on the literacy attainment of language-minority children and youth. In August, D. & Shanahan, T. (Eds.). *Developing literacy in second-language learners: Report of the National Literacy Panel on language-minority children and youth* (pp. 269–347). Mahwah, NJ: Lawrence Erlbaum Associates.

Good, R. H., & Kaminski, R. A. (2002). *Dynamic indicators of basic early literacy skills: Administration and scoring guide.* Eugene, OR: University of Oregon.

Goodwin, A. P., & Ahn, S. (2010). A meta-analysis of morphological interventions: Effects on literacy achievement of children with literacy difficulties. *Annals of Dyslexia, 60,* 183–208.

Goswami, U., & Bryant, P. (1990). *Phonological skills and learning to read.* Hove: Psychology Press.

Gottardo, A., Collins, P., Baciu, I., & Gebotys, R. (2008). Predictors of Grade 2 word reading, listening comprehension and reading comprehension from Grade 1 variables in Spanish-speaking children: Similarities and differences. *Learning Disabilities: Research and Practice, 23,* 11–24.

Gottardo, A., & Mueller, J. (2009). Are first and second language factors related in predicting school language reading comprehension? A study of Spanish-speaking children acquiring English as a second language from first to second grade. *Journal of Educational Psychology, 101,* 330–44.

Gough, P. B., & Tunmer, W. E. (1986). Decoding, reading, and reading ability. *Remedial & Special Education, 7,* 6–10.

Grabe, W. (2009). *Reading in a second language: Moving from theory to practice.* New York, NY: Cambridge University Press.

Grabe, W., & Stoller, F. L. (2011). *Teaching and researching reading, second edition.* Harlow: Pearson Education.

Grade 7: Cluster 2: Particle Theory of Matter. (n.d.) Manitoba Education and Advanced Learning. Retrieved March 9 2015 from http://www.edu.gov.mb.ca/k12/cur/science/found/5to8/7c2.pdf

Griffin, S. A., Case, R., & Siegler, R. S. (1995). Rightstart: Providing the central conceptual prerequisites for first formal learning of arithmetic to students at risk for school failure. In K. McGilly (Ed.), *Classroom lessons: Integrating cognitive theory* (pp. 25–50). Cambridge MA: MIT Press.

Gutiérrez-Clellen, V. (2012). Narrative development and disorders in bilingual children. In B. Goldstein (Ed.), *Bilingual language development and disorders in Spanish-English speakers* (pp. 233–50). Baltimore, MD: Brookes Publishing.

Halliday, M. A., & Hasan, R. (1976): *Cohesion in English.* London: Longman.

Hancin-Bhatt, B., & Nagy, W. (1994). Lexical transfer and second language morphological development. *Applied Psycholinguistics, 15,* 289–310.

Hitosugi, C. I., & Day, R. R. (2004). Extensive reading in Japanese. *Reading in a Foreign Language, 16(1).* Retrieved March 9 2015 from http://nflrc.hawaii.edu/rfl/April2004/hitosugi/hitosugi.html

Hoffman, L., & Sable, J. (2006). Public Elementary and Secondary Students, Staff, Schools, and School Districts: School Year 2003–04, NCES 2006-307. US Department of Education. Washington, DC: National Center for Education Statistics. Retrieved March 9 2015 from http://nces.ed.gov/pubs2006/2006307.pdf

Hoover, W. A., & Tunmer, W. E. (1993). The components of reading. In G. B. Thompson, W. E. Tunmer, & T. Nicholson (Eds.), *Reading acquisition processes* (pp. 1–19). Philadelphia, PA: Multilingual Matters.

Howard, E. R., Sugarman, J., & Christian, D. (2003). *Trends in two-way immersion education: A review of the research, Report No. 63.* Baltimore, MD: Center for Research on the Education of Students Placed At-risk. Retrieved March 9 2015 from http://www.csos.jhu.edu/crespar/techreports/report63.pdf

Hu, M., & Nation, I. S. P.(2000). Vocabulary density and reading comprehension. *Reading in a Foreign Language, 13,* 403–30.

Hulme, C., Hatcher, P. J., Nation, K., Brown, A., Adams, J., & Stuart, G. (2002). Phoneme awareness is a better predictor of early reading skill than onset-rime awareness. *Journal of Experimental Child Psychology, Special Issue: Reflections, 82,* 2–28.

Hyland, K. (2003). *Second language writing.* Cambridge: Cambridge University Press.

International Society for Technology in Education (2007). *National educational technology standards for students.* Washington, DC. International Society for Technology in Education. Retrieved May 1 2015 from www.iste.org/standards/ISTE-standards/standards-for-teachers

Jared, D., Cormier, P., Levy, B., & Wade-Woolley, L. (2011). Early predictors of biliteracy development in children in French immersion: A 4-year longitudinal study. *Journal of Educational Psychology, 103,* 119–39.

Jiménez, R.T., García, G.E., & Pearson, P. D. (1996). The reading strategies of bilingual Latina/o students who are successful English readers: Opportunities and obstacles. *Reading Research Quarterly, 31,* 90–112.

Johnson, J. (1989). Factors related to cross-language transfer and metaphor interpretation in bilingual children. *Applied Psycholinguistics, 10,* 157–77.

Johnson, J., Fabian, V., Pascual-Leone, J. (1989). Quantitative hardware stages that constrain language development, *Human Development, 32,* 245–71.

Joshi, R. M., & Aaron, P. G. (2000). The component model of reading: Simple View of Reading made a little more complex. *Reading Psychology, 21,* 85–97.

Joshi, R. M., Tao, S., Aaron, P. G., & Quiroz, B. (2012). Cognitive component of componential model of reading applied to different orthographies. *Journal of Learning Disabilities, 45,* 480–86.

Justice, L. M., Meier, J., & Walpole, S. (2005). Learning new words from storybooks: An efficacy study with at-risk kindergarteners. *Language, Speech, and Hearing Services in Schools, 36,* 17–32.

Kahn-Horwitz, J., Sparks, R. L., & Goldstein, Z. (2012). Relevance of the linguistic coding difference hypothesis to English as an additional language literacy in Israel. In M. Leikin, M. Schwartz, & Y. Tobin (Eds.), *Current issues in bilingualism* (pp. 21–42). New York, NY: Springer.

Kame'enui, E. J., Simmons, D. C., Good, R. H., & Harn, B. A. (2001). The use of fluency-based measures in early identification and evaluation of intervention efficacy in schools. In M. Wolf (Ed.), *Time, fluency, and dyslexia* (pp. 307–33). New York, NY: York Press.

Katz, L., & Frost, R. (1992). The reading process is different for different orthographies: The orthographic depth hypothesis. In R. Frost, & L. Katz (Eds.) *Orthography, phonology, morphology, and meaning* (pp. 67–84). Amsterdam: Elsevier.

Kieffer, M. J., & Lesaux, N. K. (2008). The role of derivational morphological awareness in the reading comprehension of Spanish-speaking English language learners. *Reading and Writing: An Interdisciplinary Journal, 21,* 783–804.

Kieffer, M. J., & Lesaux, N. K. (2012). Knowledge of words, knowledge about words: Dimensions of vocabulary in first and second language learners in sixth grade. *Reading and Writing: An Interdisciplinary Journal, 25,* 347–373.

Koda, K. (2005). *Insights into second language reading: A cross-linguistic approach.* New York, NY: Cambridge University Press.

Koda, K. (Ed.). (2007). *Reading and language learning.* Malden, MA: Blackwell.

Koda, K., & Zehler, A. M. (Eds.). (2007). *Learning to read across languages: Crosslinguistic relationships in first- and second-language literacy development.* London: Routledge.

König, E., & Gast, V. (2008). Reciprocals and reflexives – typology, description and theory. In E. König & V. Gast (Eds.), *Reciprocals and reflexives: Cross-linguistic and theoretical explorations,* (pp. 1–32). Berlin: Mouton.

Lado, R. (1957). *Linguistics across cultures. Applied linguistics for language teachers.* Ann Arbor, MI: University of Michigan Press.

Lan, Y., Sung, Y., & Chang, K. (2009). Let us read together: Development and evaluation of a computer-assisted reciprocal early English reading system. *Computers and Education, 53,* 1188–98.

Lakoff, G., & Johnson, M. (2003). *Metaphors we live by.* Chicago, IL: The University of Chicago Press.

Lawrence, J. F., Capotosto, L., Branum-Martin, L, White, C., & Snow, C. E. (2011). Language proficiency, home-language status, and English vocabulary development: A longitudinal follow-up of the Word Generation program. *Bilingualism, Language, and Cognition*, 1–15.

Leafstedt, J. M., Richards, C., & Gerber, M. (2004). Effectiveness of explicit phonological awareness instruction for at-risk English learners. *Learning Disabilities Research and Practice, 19(4)*, 252–61.

Lee, J. S., & Oxelson, E. (2006). 'It's not my job': K-12 teacher attitude toward students' heritage language maintenance. *Bilingual Research Journal, 30*, 453–77.

Lesaux, N., & Geva, E. (2006). Synthesis: Development of literacy in language-minority students. In D. August & T. Shanahan (Eds.), *Developing literacy in second-language learners: Report of the National Literacy Panel on language-minority children and youth* (pp. 53–74). Mahwah, NJ: Lawrence Erlbaum Associates.

Lesaux, N. K., & Siegel, L. S. (2003). The development of reading in children who speak English as a second language. Developmental Psychology, 39, 1005–19.

Leung, C. (2008). Preschoolers' acquisition of scientific vocabulary through repeated read-aloud events, retellings, and hands-on science activities. *Reading Psychology, 29(2)*, 165–93.

Lightbown, P. M. (2014). *Focus on content-based language teaching.* Oxford: Oxford University Press.

Limbos, M., & Geva, E. (2001). Accuracy of teacher assessments of second-language students at-risk for reading disability. *Journal of Learning Disabilities, 34*, 136–51.

Lin, D. M., Ramírez, G., Shade Wilson, J., & Geva, E. (2012). Bridging lexical knowledge and literacy. In A. Cumming (Ed.), *Adolescent literacies in a multicultural context* (pp.102–117). New York, NY: Routledge.

Linan-Thompson, S. (2014). Understanding the needs of English language learners with dyslexia issues in assessment and instruction. *Perspectives on Language and Literacy, Fall 2014*, 19–22.

Linan-Thompson, S., & Hickman-Davis, P. (2002). Supplemental reading instruction for students at-risk for reading disabilities: Improve reading thirty minutes at a time. *Learning Disabilities Research and Practice, 17*, 241–50.

Lindholm-Leary, K. J. (2011). Student outcomes in Chinese two-way immersion programs: Language proficiency, academic achievement and student attitudes. In D. J. Tedick, D. Christian, & T. W. Fortune (Eds.), *Immersion education: Practices, policies, possibilities* (pp. 81–103). Bristol: Multilingual Matters.

Lindholm-Leary, K. J. (2012). Success and challenges in dual language education. *Theory into Practice, Special Issue: Rethinking language teaching and learning in multilingual classrooms, 51(4)*, 256–62.

Lindholm-Leary, K., & Block, N. (2010). Achievement in predominantly low SES/Hispanic dual language schools. *International Journal of Bilingual Education and Bilingualism, 13(1)*, 43–60.

Lindholm-Leary, K., & Howard, E. R. (2008). Language development and academic achievement in two-way immersion programs. In T. W. Fortune & D. J. Tedick (Eds.), *Pathways to multilingualism: Evolving perspectives on immersion education* (pp. 177–200). Oxford: Blackwell.

Linebarger, D. L., Kosanic, A. Z., Greenwood, C. R., & Doku, N. S. (2004). Effects of viewing the television program *Between the Lions* on the emergent literacy skills of young children. *Journal of Educational Psychology, 96,* 297–308.

Lovett, W. M., De Palma, M., Frijters, J., Steinbach, K., Temple, M., Benson, N., & Lacerenz, L. (2008). Interventions for reading difficulties a comparison of response to intervention by ELL and EFL struggling readers. *Journal of Learning Disabilities, 41,* 333–52.

Mancilla-Martinez, J., & Lesaux, N. K. (2010). Predictors of reading comprehension for struggling readers: The case of Spanish-speaking language minority learners. *Journal of Educational Psychology, 102,* 701–11.

Marinova-Todd, S. H. (2012). 'Corplum is a core from a plum': The advantage of bilingual children in the analysis of word meaning from verbal context. *Bilingualism: Language and Cognition, 15(1),* 117–27.

Marinova-Todd, S. H., Zhao, J., & Bernhardt, M. (2010). Phonological awareness skills in the two languages of Mandarin-English bilingual children. *Clinical Linguistics and Phonetics, 24,* 387–400.

McColgan, K., & McCormack, T. (2008). Searching and planning: Young children's reasoning about past and future event sequences. *Child Development, 5,* 1477–97.

Melby-Lervåg, M., & Lervåg, A. (2014). Reading comprehension and its underlying components in second language learners: A meta-analysis of studies comparing first and second language learners. *Psychological Bulletin, 140(2),* 409–33.

Metsala, J. L., & Walley, A. C. (1998). Spoken vocabulary growth and the segmental restructuring of lexical representations: Precursors to phonemic awareness and early reading ability. In J. L. Metsala and L. C. Ehri (Eds.), *Word recognition in beginning literacy* (pp. 89–120). Mahwah, NJ: Lawrence Erlbaum Associates.

Mikulecky, L. J. (2009). Using internet-based children's and young adult literature for extensive reading in EFL instruction. In A. Cirocki (Ed.), *Extensive reading in English language teaching* (pp. 333–47). Munich: Lincom.

Mishan, F. (2005). *Designing authenticity into language learning materials.* Bristol: Intellect.

Montelongo, J. A., Hernández, A. C., Herter, R. J., & Cuello, J. (2011). Using cognates to scaffold context clue strategies for Latino ELs. *The Reading Teacher, 64,* 429–34.

Nagy, W., Berninger, V., Abbott, R., Vaughan, K., & Vermeulen, K. (2003). Relationship of morphology and other language skills to literacy skills in at-risk second-grade readers and at-risk fourth-grade writers. *Journal of Educational Psychology, 95(4),* 730–42.

Nagy, W., Herman, P., & Anderson, R. (1985). Learning words from context. *Reading Research Quarterly, 17,* 233–55.

Nakamoto, J., Lindsey, K. A., & Manis, F. R. (2007). A longitudinal analysis of English language learners' word decoding and reading comprehension. *Reading and Writing: An Interdisciplinary Journal, 20,* 691–719.

Nassaji, H., & Geva, E. (1999). The contribution of phonological and orthographic processing skills to adult ESL reading: Evidence from native speakers of Farsi. *Applied Psycholinguistics, 20,* 241–67.

Nation, K., & Snowling, M. J. (2004). Beyond phonological skills: Broader language skills contribute to the development of reading. *Journal of Research in Reading, 27,* 342–56.

National Early Literacy Panel. (2008). *Developing Early Literacy: Report of the National Early Literacy Panel.* Washington, DC: National Institute for Literacy. Retrieved May 1 2015 from http://lincs.ed.gov/publications/pdf/NELPReport09.pdf

National Institute of Child Health and Human Development. (2000). *Report of the National Reading Panel: Teaching children to read: An evidence-based assessment of the scientific research literature on reading and its implications for reading instruction (NIH Publication No. 00-4769).* Washington, DC: US Government Printing Office.

National Reading Panel (2000). *Report of the national reading panel: Teaching children to read.* Retrieved March 9 2015 from http://www.nichd.nih.gov/publications/pubs/nrp/documents/report.pdf

Nelson, K., & Grundel, J. (1986). Children's scripts. In K. Nelson (Ed.), *Event knowledge: Structure and function in development* (pp. 231–47). Hillsdale, NJ: Erlbaum Associates.

Nunan, D. (1989). *Designing tasks for the communicative classroom.* Cambridge: Cambridge University Press.

Oakhill, J., & Cain, K. (2012). The precursors of reading ability in young readers: Evidence from a four-year longitudinal study. *Scientific Studies of Reading, 16,* 91–121.

Obadia, A. A. (1996). La formation du professeur d'immersion française: Une perspective historique. (The development of the French immersion teacher: An historical perspective.) *Canadian Modern Language Review, 52,* 271–84.

O'Connor, R. E., Bocian, K., Beebe-Frankenberger, M., & Linklater, D. L. (2010). Responsiveness of students with language difficulties to early intervention in reading. *Journal of Special Education, 43(4),* 220–35.

Oller, D. K., & Jarmulowicz, L. (2007). Language and literacy in bilingual children in the early school years. In E. Hoff and M. Shatz (Eds.), *Blackwell handbook of language development* (pp. 368–86). Malden, MA: Wiley-Blackwell.

Orçan, M. (2013). Investigation of communication abilities of Roma and non-Roma mothers and school readiness levels of their children. *International Journal of Social Sciences & Education, 3,* 612–18.

Ornstein, M. (2000). Ethno-racial inequality in the city of Toronto: An analysis of the 1996 census. Retrieved March 9 2015 from http://www1.toronto.ca/static_files/equity_diversity_and_human_rights_office/pdf/ornstein_fullreport.pdf

Pacheco, M. B., & Goodwin, A. P. (2013). Putting two and two together: middle school students' morphological problem-solving strategies for unknown words. *Journal of Adolescent & Adult Literacy, 56,* 541–53.

Paradis, J., Genesee, F., & Crago, M. (2011). *Dual language development & disorders: A handbook on bilingualism & second language learning.* Baltimore, MD: Brookes Publishing Co.

Paradis, J., and Kirova, A. (2014). English second-language learners in preschool: Profile effects in their English abilities and the role of home language environment. *International Journal of Behavioral Development, 38,* 342–9.

Pasquarella, A., Gottardo, A., & Grant, A. (2012). Comparing factors related to reading comprehension in adolescents who speak English as a first (L1) or second (L2) language, *Scientific Studies of Reading, 16*, 475–503.

Pelletier, J. (2011). Supporting early language and literacy. Retrieved May 3 2015 from www.edu.gov.on.ca/eng/literacynumeracy/inspire/ research/ww_early_language.pdf

Piasta, S. B., & Wagner, R. K. (2010). Developing early literacy skills: A meta-analysis of alphabet learning and instruction. *Reading Research Quarterly, 45*, 8–38.

Pikulski, J. J., & Chard, D. J. (2005). Fluency: Bridge between decoding and reading comprehension. *The Reading Teacher, 58*, 510–19.

Porter, R. P. (1990). *Forked tongue: The politics of bilingual education.* New York, NY: Basic Books.

Prensky, M. (2001). Digital natives, digital immigrants: Part 1. *On the Horizon, 9*(5), 1–6.

Prior, A., Goldina, A., Shany, M., Geva, E., & Katzir, T. (2014). Lexical inference in L2: Predictive roles of vocabulary knowledge and reading skill beyond reading comprehension. *Reading and Writing, 27*, 1467–84.

Proctor, C. P., August, D., Carlo, M., & Barr, C. (2010). Language maintenance versus language of instruction: Spanish reading development among Latino and Latina bilingual learners. *Journal of Social Issues, 66*, 79–94.

Proctor, C. P., Dalton, B., & Grisham, D. L. (2007). Scaffolding English language learners and struggling readers in a universal literacy environment with embedded strategy instruction and vocabulary support. *Journal of Literacy Research, 39*(1), 71–93.

Proctor, C. P., Dalton, D., Uccelli, P., Biancarosa, G., Mo, E., Snow, C. E., & Neugebauer, S. (2011). Improving comprehension online (ICON): Effects of deep vocabulary instruction with bilingual and monolingual fifth graders. *Reading and Writing: An interdisciplinary journal, 24*(5), 517–44.

Puranik, C., Petscher, Y., Al Otaiba, S., Catts, H., & Lonigan, C. (2008). Development of oral reading fluency in children with speech or language impairments: A growth curve analysis. *Journal of Learning Disabilities, 41*(6), 545–60.

Quiroga, T., Lemos-Britton, Z., Mostafapour, E., Abbott, R. D., & Berninger, V. W. (2002). Phonological awareness and beginning reading in Spanish-speaking ESL first graders: Research into practice. *Journal of School Psychology, 40*, 85–111.

Ramírez, G., Chen, X., Geva, E., & Luo, Y. (2011). Morphological awareness and word reading in English language learners: Evidence from Spanish- and Chinese-speaking children. *Applied Psycholinguistics, 32*, 601–18.

Ramírez, G., Chen-Bumgardner, X., & Pasquarella, A. (2013). Cross-linguistic transfer of morphological awareness in Spanish-speaking ELLs: The facilitating effect of cognate knowledge. *Topics in Language Disorders, 33*(1), 73–92.

Ramírez, J. D., Pasta, D. J., Yuen, S., Billings, D. K., & Ramey, D. R. (1991). *Final report: Longitudinal study of structural immersion strategy, early-exit, and late-exit transitional bilingual education programs for language-minority children.* San Mateo, CA: Aguirre International.

Ramírez, G., Walton, P., & Roberts, W. (2014). Morphological awareness, vocabulary, and reading among kindergarteners with different ability levels. *Journal of Learning Disabilities, 47,* 54–64.

RAND Reading Study Group (2002). *Reading for understanding: Toward an R&D program in reading comprehension.* Retrieved March 9 2015 from http://www.rand. org/pubs/monograph_reports/MR1465.html

Reaching for the Sky: A History of Great Buildings. (2013). ReadWorks, Inc. Retrieved May 4 2015 from http://www.readworks.org/sites/default/files/ passages/990_reaching_for_the_sky_a_history_of_great_buildings_0.pdf

Riordan, R. (2005). *The lightning thief.* Toronto: Scholastic.

Rossell, C. H., & Baker, K. (1996). The educational effectiveness of bilingual education. *Research in the Teaching of English, 30(1),* 7–74.

Sam, D. P., & Rajan, P. (2013). Using graphic organizers to improve reading comprehension skills for the middle school ESL students. *English Language Teaching, 6(2),* 155–70.

Savage, R. S., & Wolforth, J. (2007). An additive simple view of reading describes the performance of good and poor readers in higher education. *Exceptionality Education Canada, 17(1),* 243–68.

Scarborough, H. S. (2005). Developmental relationships between language and reading: Reconciling a beautiful hypothesis with some ugly facts. In H. W. Catts & A. G. Kamhi (Eds.), *The connections between language and reading disabilities* (pp. 3–24). Mahwah, NJ: Lawrence Erlbaum Associates.

Scarcella, R. (2003). *Academic English: A conceptual framework.* The University of California Linguistic Minority Research Institute, Technical Report 2003-1.

Schmitt, N., Jiang, X., & Grabe, W. (2011). The percentage of words known in a text and reading comprehension. *Modern Language Journal, 95,* 26–43.

Schoonen, R., Hulstijn, J., & Bossers, B. (1998). Metacognitive and language-specific knowledge in native and foreign language reading comprehension: An empirical study among Dutch students in grades 6, 8 and 10. *Language Learning, 48,* 71–106.

Schwartz, M., & Shaul, Y. (2013). Narrative development among language minority children: The role of bilingual versus monolingual preschool education. *Language, Culture and Curriculum, 26(1),* 36–51.

Sénéchal, M., & LeFevre, J. A. (2001). Storybook reading and parent teaching: Links to language and literacy development. In P. R. Britto & J. Brooks-Gunn (Eds.), *The role of family literacy environments in promoting young children's emerging literacy skills* (pp. 39–52). San Francisco, CA: Jossey-Bass.

Seymour, P., Aro, M., & Erskine, J. (2003). Foundation literacy acquisition in European orthographies. *British Journal of Psychology, 94,* 143–74.

Shanahan, T., & Lonigan, C. (2010). The National Early Literacy Panel: A summary of the process and the report. *Educational Researcher, 39,* 279–85.

Shany, M., & Geva, E. (2012). Cognitive, language and literacy development in socio-culturally vulnerable school children: The case of Ethiopian Israeli children. In M. Leikin, M. Schwartz, & Y. Tobin (Eds.), *Current issues in bilingualism* (pp. 77–117). New York, NY: Springer.

Shany, M., Geva, E., & Melech-Feder, L. (2010). Emergent literacy in children of immigrants coming from a primarily oral literacy culture. *Written Language & Literacy, 13,* 24–60.

Share, D. L. (2008). On the Anglo centricities of current reading research and practice: The perils of over-reliance on an 'outlier' orthography. *Psychological Bulletin, 134,* 584–616.

Shu, H., Peng, H., & McBride-Chang, C. (2008). Phonological awareness in young Chinese children. *Developmental Sciences, 11(1),* 171–81.

Silverman, R., & Hines, S. (2009). The effects of multimedia-enhanced instruction on the vocabulary of English-language learners and non-English-language learners in pre-kindergarten through second grade. *Journal of Educational Psychology, 101(2),* 305–14.

Slavin, E. R., Madden, N., Calderón, M., Chamberlain, A., & Hennessy, M. (2011). Reading and language outcomes of transitional bilingual education. *Educational Evaluation and Policy Analysis, 3(1),* 47–58.

Snow, C. E., & Dickinson, R. D. (1990). Social sources of narrative skills at home and at school. *First Language, 10,* 87–103.

Snow, C. E., Porche, M. V., Tabors, P. O., & Harris, S. R. (2007). *Is literacy enough?* Baltimore, MD: Brookes Publishing Co.

Sparks, R. L., & Ganschow, L. (1993). Searching for the cognitive locus of foreign language learning difficulties: Linking native and foreign language learning. *Modern Language Journal, 77,* 289–302.

Sparks, R., Patton, J., Ganschow, L., & Humbach, N. (2009). Long-term crosslinguistic transfer of skills from L1 to L2, *Language Learning, 59,* 203–43.

Stahl, K. D. (2014). Phonics. Paper presented at the International Reading Association (IRA) Research Institute of the IRA 59th Annual Conference, New Orleans.

Stanovich, K. E. (1984). The interactive-compensatory model of reading: A confluence of developmental, experimental, and educational psychology. *Remedial and Special Education, 5,* 11–19.

Stanovich, K. E., & Siegel, L. S. (1994). The phenotypic performance profile of children with reading disabilities: A regression based test of the phonological core variable difference model. *Journal of Educational Psychology, 86,* 24–53.

Storch, S. A., & Whitehurst, G. J. (2002). Oral language and code-related precursors to reading. Evidence from a longitudinal structural model. *Developmental Psychology, 38,* 934–47.

Swanson, H. L., Harris, K., & Graham, S. (2013). *Handbook of learning disabilities, second edition.* New York, NY: The Guilford Press.

Tabata-Sandom, M., & Macalister, J. (2009). That 'Eureka feeling': A case study of extensive reading in Japanese. *New Zealand Studies in Applied Linguistics, 15(2),* 41–60.

Tang, G. M. (1992). The effect of graphic representation of knowledge structures on ESL reading comprehension. *Studies in Second Language Acqusition, 14,* 177–95.

The Ice Returns ... The Hunt Begins. (2005). Athropolis Productions Limited. Retrieved March 9 from http://www.athropolis.com/arctic-facts/fact-sealhunt-inuit.htm

Thomas, W., & Collier, V. (2001). *A national study of effectiveness for language minority students' long-term achievement.* Berkeley, CA: Centre for Research in Education, Diversity and Excellence (CREDE). Retrieved March 9 2015 from http://www.usc.edu/dept/education/CMMR/CollierThomasExReport.pdf

Turnbull, M., Hart, D., & Lapkin, S. (2003). Grade 6 French Immersion students' performance on large-scale reading, writing, and mathematics tests: Building explanations. *The Alberta Journal of Educational Research, 49,* 6–23.

Uchikoshi, Y. (2006). English vocabulary development in bilingual kindergarteners: What are the best predictors? *Bilingualism: Language and Cognition, 9,* 33–49.

US Department of Education, National Centre for Education Evaluation and Regional Assistance, Institute of Education Sciences. (2014). *Teaching academic content and literacy to English learners in elementary and middle school (NCEE 2014–4012).* Retrieved March 9 2015 from http://ies.ed.gov/ncee/wwc/practiceguide.aspx?sid=19

Valdés, G. (1997). Dual language immersion programs: A cautionary note concerning the education of language minority students. *Harvard Educational Review, 67(3),* 391–429.

Vaughn, S., Cirino, P. T., Linan-Thompson, S., Mathes, P. G., Carlson, C. D., Cardenas-Hagan, E., … Francis, D. J. (2006). Effectiveness of a Spanish intervention and an English intervention for English-language learners at-risk for reading problems. *American Educational Research Journal, 43(3),* 449–87.

Vaughn, S., Martinez, L. R., Linan-Thompson, S., Reutebuch, C. K., Carlson, C. D., & Francis, D. J. (2009). Enhancing social studies vocabulary and comprehension for seventh-grade English language learners: Findings from two experimental studies. *Journal of Research on Educational Effectiveness, 2(4),* 297–324.

Verhoeven. L., & van Leeuwe, J. (2012). The simple view of second language reading throughout the primary grades. *Reading and Writing, 25(8),* 1805–18.

Wade-Woolley, L., & Geva, E. (2000). Processing novel phonemic contrasts in the acquisition of L2 word reading. *Scientific Studies of Reading, 4(4),* 295–311.

Walter, C. (2004). Transfer of reading comprehension skills to L2 is linked to mental representations of text and to L2 working memory. *Applied Linguistics, 25,* 315–39.

Walton, P., & Ramírez, G. (2012). Reading acquisition in young Aboriginal children. Retrieved May 3 2015 from http://www.researchgate.net/publication/236154074_Reading_Acquisition_in_Young_Aboriginal_Children

Wang, M., & Geva, E. (2003). Spelling acquisition of novel English phonemes in Chinese children. *Reading and Writing: An Interdisciplinary Journal, 16,* 325–48.

Wang, M., & Koda, K. (2005). Commonalities and differences in word identification skills among English second language learners. *Language Learning, 55(1),* 73–100.

Webb, S., & Macalister, J. (2013). Is text written for children appropriate for L2 extensive reading? *TESOL Quarterly, 47(2),* 300–22.

Wissick, C. A., & Gardner, J. E. (2008). Conducting assessment in technology needs: From assessment to implementation. *Assessment for Effective Intervention, 33,* 78–93.

Witherell, N. L., & McMackin, M. C. (2009). *Teaching reading: Differentiated instruction with leveled graphic organizers (Grades 1–3).* New York, NY: Scholastic.

WordWorksKingston. (2011, May 17). *Investigating graphemes in Grade 1* [video file]. Retrieved March 9 2015 from https://www.youtube.com/watch?v=UeNnLwNzlkU

Yopp, H. K. (1992). Developing phonemic awareness in young children. *The Reading Teacher, 45,* 696–703.

Young, C., & Rasinski, T. (2009). Implementing Readers Theatre as an approach to classroom fluency instruction. *The Reading Teacher, 63,* 4–13.

Ziegler, J. C., & Goswami, U. (2005). Reading acquisition, developmental dyslexia, and skill reading across languages: A psycholinguistic grain size theory. *Psychological Bulleting, 131(1),* 3–29.

Ziegler, J. C., & Goswami, U. (2006). Becoming literate in different languages: Similar problems, different solutions. *Developmental Science, 9(5),* 429–53.

Index

Page numbers annotated with 'g' refer to glossary entries.